The Dilemma of Contemporary Political Theory

Toward a Postbehavioral Science of Politics

Thomas A. Spragens, Jr.

Foreword by Morton A. Kaplan

UNIVERSITY PRESS OF CAMBRIDGE, MASS. 1639

DUNELLEN
New York

International Standard Book Number 0-8424-0059-1.

Library of Congress Catalogue Card Number 72-86222.

Printed in the United States of America.

Contents

Foreword

When I received my Ph.D. in 1951, the Cold War was on, liberals supported the government against conservative isolationists, logical positivism in the social sciences was "in," values were thought to be subjective preferences about which science had nothing to say, and political philosophy was being relegated to the mothballs along with our battleships. My dissertation had been written on Morris R. Cohen, a longtime foe of the logical positivists. Cohen believed in science—and so did I—but our tradition was rooted in an American pragmatism, more related to Peirce than to James, that was neo-Aristotelian in character and influenced by Hegel and Marx. However, despite my views, when *System and Process* was published, I was called a logical positivist by those "scientists" who welcomed me to the tribe and by those traditionalists who were fighting a holy war against them. It was perhaps a good thing for my career that no one except Marion Levy had read, or at least had understood, the appendices to *System and Process*.

In the last few years, younger political scientists have been waging a strident and at least partly successful attack upon the influence of logical positivism in political science. They have been attempting to resurrect the world of values, to remind us that the great political philosophers dealt with issues that are relevant today, and that the methods of science must be adapted to one's subject matter. If not all the heat generated by this younger group of political scientists has produced illumination, they have revealed some of the shadowed crevasses lying before us.

Those who were too ready to dismiss the great classics of political philosophy should perhaps have reflected upon the fact that the great theoretical physicists—such as Einstein, Bohr, Schrodinger, and Born—were all natural philosophers. Or perhaps they should have reflected upon the fate of psychology after its divorce from philosophy in the post-Jamesian period—a fate from which it is just slowly beginning to recover. Fortunately, the reaction is occurring far more quickly in political science than it did in psychology.

Among the most intellectually vigorous of the new breed of political theorists is Thomas A. Spragens, Jr., the author of this important volume. Professor Spragens' attack upon the failures of positivism in political science is surpassed only by the skill with which he resurrects the relevance and meaningful quality of values in political life. He demonstrates that it is an improper understanding of scientific method that leads to the disavowal of the realm of values.

Professor Spragens' approach is related to the philosophy of personal knowledge that has been developed by the noted natural philosopher and chemist Michael Polanyi. This is not a school of thought with which I am very sympathetic, although I appreciate the role of intuition both in discovery and in recognition. Surely someone may "know" how to ride a bicycle without being able to communicate this knowledge to another person. One can recognize someone as his wife without necessarily being able to describe her to a stranger. On the other hand, public communication is essential to the enterprize of science. Moreover, I do not believe that the major part of Professor Spragens' book is dependent upon Polanyi's position and would argue that his reliance upon Polanyi in his last chapter introduces some inconsistencies in his thesis. No matter! Few of us are in entire agreement. I read Professor Spragens' book with profit. He has something of importance to say. Even where his readers disagree with him, the disagreements should produce a better understanding of the great issues of political philosophy and of political science.

Morton A. Kaplan

Preface

An essay of the following type is subject to virtually infinite expansion, simply because it is an attempt to tie together into a coherent pattern a whole panoply of complex problems. Since the essay was originally written, more and more possibilities for expansion have come to my attention, both in the course of my own reading and through the suggestions of knowledgeable readers. Moreover, new articles and books continue to appear which have a bearing on one part or another of this book's argument. For example, the March 1971 issue of the *American Political Science Review* contained articles by Karl Deutsch and Duncan Macrae and a book review by Alan Wertheimer that have clear relevance to the problems considered here.

Nothing I have encountered, however, would lead me to recast or to revise my basic argument, although much I have encountered would lend helpful substantiation, provide further examples, or be appropriately discussable at certain stages of the argument. Only some of this material has been incorporated into the manuscript. Once the overall paradigm is clearly delineated, its various components can bear, indeed will require, elaboration. Before the context of the encompassing paradigm is established, however, such elaboration would be premature, for its significance would not have been established. The reader, therefore, is encouraged to "plug in" his own area of special concern and expertise where it is relevant, whether this be a knowledge of recent analytic philosophy, a concern with Theodore Lowi's account of the growth of "interest-group liberalism" out of descriptive pluralism, an interest in the latest conceptual refinements in the study of political development, or whatever. Such applications and connections are intended to be very real possibilities; but had this essay attempted to follow each of them out, whatever coherence it has would have been dissipated.

In order to forestall possible misunderstanding, moreover, two caveats should be entered at the outset. First, the treatment of figures such as Hobbes, Skinner, and Ayer is not intended to be balanced or comprehensive. These figures, and others like them, are cited quite selectively for one specific purpose: to demonstrate the persistence of key components of the objectivist paradigm through several centuries. If these accounts are taken for what they are not, they will undoubtedly seem overly schematic; if they are understood in context, their significance should be clear.

Second, it will probably be maintained by some that the argument which follows attacks a straw man, on the grounds that rather few political scientists would explicitly affirm, or even be aware of, the Cartesian and Laplacean tenets which are alleged to be at the bottom of the problems discussed. While the grounds for this criticism are accurate, the criticism itself is not, for the following reason. The argument of this essay is that the seventeenth century produced a cosmological and epistemological paradigm which both logically and historically gave rise to a set of corollary assumptions about the nature of scientific theory. If these corollary assumptions are still operative in the work of a discipline, and I try to show that they are, then it is not necessary for that discipline to be explicitly aware of and committed to the parent paradigm in order to justify the claim that the paradigm is still influential. The basic paradigm, in other words, continues to govern us through the hold which its intellectual progeny have upon us, even if that paradigm is itself utterly unconscious, considered metaphysical and hence irrelevant, or even disavowed.

The professing atheist who genuflects at every cross, may after all be giving a sincere account of his conscious beliefs, but he is not providing an accurate statement of the principles which in fact govern his actions. Similarly, until political scientists recognize that political theory cannot be neatly bifurcated into "normative" and "empirical," that no description is wholly "neutral" or unstructured by interpretative canons of order, and that norms perform descriptive functions, they are governed by the operational assumptions of the objectivist paradigm, whatever their explicit epistemological beliefs or lack thereof.

The debts which I have accumulated in the process of writing this essay are many and profound. Dr. John H. Hallowell has lent his time and encouragement throughout. Dr. William H. Poteat has also given his advice and insight, especially with regard to the import of Michael Polanyi's ideas. Dr. William Connolly and Dr. Ruel Tyson both read the entire manuscript and made many helpful comments and suggestions and lent encouragement to the completion of the project. And Dr. Morton Kaplan has provided a memorable example to me of a noted scholar who is willing to give unselfishly of his own store of wisdom and of his precious time to help a novice. His assistance has been invaluable in many ways. Needless to say, none of these may be held responsible for any of the views which are expressed in this essay or for any shortcomings in its style or content.

I would also like to thank Mr. Samuel M. Hines, Jr., for his helpful research assistance and the Duke University Research Council for its financial contribution toward the preparation and publication of this manuscript.

1   Introduction

It is both a thesis and a presupposition of this extended essay that the conceptual structure of contemporary political theory is shaky and confused. At best, the fundamental concepts that order our thought and research are unsatisfactory; at worst, the situation could be called a crisis. The principal manifestation of this intellectual difficulty at the level of the practicing political scientist is the barrenness of theorizing that relentlessly and rigidly tries to maintain the alleged hiatus between empirical and normative theory. The use of the distinction between "empirical" and "normative," with the explicit or implied generic difference between them, has barely become entrenched in our professional terminology and self-understanding; but already the most penetrating minds of the discipline are beginning to suggest that the divorce was too hasty and that some sort of reconciliation may be possible if not necessary. I share the feeling that if empirical theory and normative theory have nothing to say to each other, ultimately they will have nothing to say. The following inquiry, therefore, is intended to be a contribution toward the needed reintegration of our theoretical enterprise.

This reintegration cannot proceed satisfactorily, however, unless the real depth of the problem is appreciated and confronted. The fundamental assumptions that have caused us difficulty have both a long historical legacy and a pervasive and deep philosophical background. No superficial reunion of the two halves of the theoretical enterprise, based upon sheer necessity rather than upon genuine understanding, will ultimately prove viable or durable. Political science did not manufacture the assumptions about epistemology and permissible scientific concepts out of whole cloth but rather adopted them from the more general intellectual climate of the time, specifically from philosophy and philosophy of science. As a consequence, unraveling our present dilemmas calls for consideration of the relevant inquiry in these areas. Having been helped into some of its difficulties, political science can legitimately expect some help in extricating itself from them.

Fortunately, contemporary developments in philosophy and the philosophy of science do offer some helpful leads for our reconsideration of the nature of political theory. The view of science which led to the attempt to scourge norms from the scientific study of politics has been subjected to some penetrating criticism from several quarters in recent years, and it should soon be largely superceded by a more sophisticated understanding of the dynamics and cognitive status of scientific inquiry. The view prevalent at the time political scientists began to formulate the structure of an empirical theory of political reality will then be seen as the expression of a dying mode of philosophy which was inadequate to the task of explaining and justifying the actual practice of working scientists. And the emerging understanding of science should enable political theory to retain its scientific credentials without imposing upon itself the mutilating conceptual asceticism required by the earlier view. In part, to be sure, the basis of this development will be the relinquishing by science in general of the claims to total explicitness and detachment which characterized its positivist self-understanding.

Some of the suggestions advanced here may seem radical. Extenuating circumstances, however, are present. Principal among these is necessity; a radical and pervasive problem ("radical" in the sense of striking at the very foundations) requires radical steps, so a measure of presumption is simply inescapable. Certainly no one individual will begin to succeed in cutting the Gordian knot with a single stroke, but a bold effort is necessary even to begin to unravel it. Undoubtedly the prescription suggested here will be indigestible to many, but simply gaining appreciation of the depth and scope of the problem will constitute a real success.

The body of this essay ventures into more areas than it could possibly cover with any real justice. However, any substantial delimitation of the scope of our concern would defeat one of the principal purposes of our inquiry: namely, to suggest the existence of common problems and themes across a broad range of theoretical divisions, both within the discipline of political science and between political science and other disciplines. Establishing the elements of commonality and complementarity is essential to our thesis, and it therefore must precede, rather than follow, a fully satisfactory elaboration of all the various component parts of the argument. In fact, only after the general contours and interrelationships of the problem are discernible, can what is worth elaborating be determined with any degree of accuracy. At some points in the argument, of course, considerable elaboration can be found in the sources cited.

While some issues in our argument bear a resemblance to the old intradisciplinary battle over the behavioral movement, there is no intention to return to that battleground here. That quarrel managed to generate considerably more heat than light. The heat of this controversy testified to its importance, and the bitterness of much of it testified to its depth. The lack of illumination which it brought, however, reflected the unavailability of some of the necessary analytical concepts in the field of philosophy of science and the "unripeness" of the controversy in its relation to actual empirical research and theorizing. The use of the judicial criterion of ripeness is peculiarly appropriate here, for an unripe issue is one which has insufficient grounding in experience and hence would have to be adjudicated in an a priori and abstract fashion. The hypothetical and conjectural nature of any ruling in such unripe situations has led our courts to avoid them, and the original quarrel over behavioralism was unsatisfactory, unclear, and inconclusive for largely similar reasons. Both of these situational problems have largely been remedied today. Philosophers of science have been active in refining and revising some of the more simpleminded notions about science which have become highly problematic not so much because of difficulties in the social sciences as because of problems in the natural sciences. By now the movement toward empirical theory in political science has advanced to a level of genuine theoretical relevance. Thus, it can itself now be analyzed empirically rather than treated as a mere prospectus.

To forestall any possible misunderstanding, it might be well to note at the outset that the claim that norms perform an irreducible function in scientific inquiry in no way implies the derogation of the sophisticated and potent tools and methods of empirical research that have been developed in the past two decades. To draw this unwarranted implication would entail the sort of either-or presumption which needs so badly to be transcended. It should be taken as granted that the new modes of empirical inquiry have already made significant contributions to our knowledge of politics and that they should continue to do so at an increasing pace. Any assertion to the contrary at this point in our disciplinary development would rightly be considered antediluvian.

At the same time, it is—or should be—becoming equally clear that the new modes of inquiry are no panacea at the level of theory. Based in part upon the relatively naive view of science that was widely popularized in the social sciences as recently as a decade ago, some practitioners of the behavioral approach apparently expected a new theoretical edifice to arise whole from the welter of data provided by well-trained cadres of researchers. This expectation has by now been dampened considerably except among the truest of the true believers. We have been almost swamped with a proliferation of partial, "middle-range" theories whose relationship and even compatability with each other is far from clear. The bulk return of the new empirical studies has been great, but the theoretical landscape has become more confused rather than more clarified.

It is misleading and evasive to claim that the trouble is merely a passing difficulty encountered because political science is still an infant science. Wittgenstein's remarks about another human science, psychology, apply equally to political science. He observes:

> The confusion and barrenness of psychology is not to be explained by calling it a "young science;" its state is not comparable with that of physics for instance in its beginnings. . . . For in psychology there are experimental methods and *conceptual confusion.*
>
> The existence of experimental methods makes us think we have the means of solving the problems which trouble us; though problem and methods pass one another by.[1]

An analogous view of political science lies behind this inquiry. We also have "experimental methods and conceptual confusion" and our concepts and data often "pass one another by." Our present intent, then, is to examine the nature and implication of this conceptual confusion, to analyze some instances of it, and perhaps to contribute to its amelioration. To suggest that our problems can be fully resolved would probably be to indulge in a new form of intellectual millenarianism, but it is perhaps not too much to hope that we can attain a clearer view of what our problems really are.

Substantively, the principal contentions of this essay can be broadly summarized in the following propositions:

1. The central conceptual distortions in contemporary political theory result from the attempt to divide the discipline into empirical and normative halves. This dichotomy is based on a faulty

epistemology, and it therefore cannot be maintained without generating theoretical inconsistencies, incapacities, or evasions.

2. The ultimate source of the insistence upon dichotomizing political theory is the legacy of the Western philosophical tradition that originated in the seventeenth-century "scientific revolution." Other disciplines, therefore, exhibit problems similar to those in political science.

3. The incapacities and confusions of dichotomized theory have clearly manifested themselves in some of the most important recent theoretical efforts of the discipline, such as the attempts to conceptualize political development, democracy, and the nature of politics itself.

4. These problems can be systematically remedied only by a postbehavioral political science that takes its bearings from contemporary achievements in the philosophy of science—achievements which are radically revising the traditional concept of scientific knowledge.

Such, in very sketchy outline, are the presuppositions, intentions, and substance of this essay. Some of these bear further introductory elaboration. To begin with, the claim that the fundamental conceptual basis of political science is in a state of crisis is made in a technical sense and not as a sensationalistic cliché. Specifically, I have lifted the word "crisis" with its meaning rather directly from Thomas Kuhn's important inquiry into the structure of scientific revolutions.[2] In Kuhn's incisive and well-documented view, a particular area of scientific inquiry acquires the coherence to be considered a science and to pursue research effectively only with the general acceptance of a paradigm. This paradigm, which undergirds the research and hypothetical formulations of the practitioners of the science, is a kind of conceptual and perceptual model which provides the accepted framework for what is to be seen as "real" and what as problematic. The paradigm provides, or implies, accepted basic assumptions about certain questions: What are the fundamental entities with which we, as members of the discipline deal? How are they related to each other? What questions may be legitimately asked about them and what methods legitimately employed? As Kuhn observes, a scientific discipline "scarcely begins" effective research until "the scientific community thinks it has acquired firm answers" to questions like these.[3] A paradigm may also be more limited in scope and depth, but in any case it provides the accepted contours of what constitutes relevant scientific inquiry within the field it informs.

Scientific inquiry which proceeds fruitfully on the basis of an accepted paradigm Kuhn refers to as normal science. That is, the basic framework of the science is not considered problematic for the moment at least, since it has been successful in incorporating within its boundaries the key problems of the discipline. Scientific research in this setting, conceptually speaking, is a kind of "mopping-up operation."[4] This form of inquiry, which can be extremely challenging and exciting despite the somewhat mundane term Kuhn uses to characterize it, consists basically of refining, filling in, and elaborating the accepted paradigm. Various types of specific endeavors are significant in this situation. For example, the practitioner of normal science may be engaged in trying to increase the accuracy and scope with which facts indicated as significant by the paradigm are known.[5] Or such research may be directed to determination of intrinsically insignificant facts whose importance is their degree of comparability to predictions derived from the paradigm. Such normal scientific research may also consist in the resolution of residual ambiguities in the paradigm, the refinement of the paradigm, or the extension of it to phenomena to which it has not been applied. All of these tasks are important and meaningful scientific endeavors, but all have in common that they proceed on the basis of an accepted paradigm and so far from seeking to challenge its validity actually derive their self-interpretation from its presumed validity.

The value of an accepted paradigm to a field of scientific inquiry is obviously very great. It provides both the matrix for accepted research and a principle of limitation without which the field would dissipate into a mélange of unrelated inquiries. Accordingly, various defense mechanisms are employed in behalf of an accepted paradigm. Most of these are intrinsic to the functioning of a paradigm and require no external purpose or intent to make them operative. For example, since the paradigm provides the fundamental categories for what shall be deemed a real phenomenon, it is quite difficult for an irreconcilable conception to gain the necessary basis for even becoming perceived. Part of science, in fact, consists in a deliberate lack of concern with superficially anomalous phenomena, largely because the successful functioning of the accepted paradigm gives the scientist reasonable ground to assume that the anomaly is superficial or illusory. The consequence is that "science may deny, or at least cast aside as of no scientific interest, whole ranges of experience which to the unscientific mind appear both massive and vital."[6] This deliberate refusal to entertain seriously such apparently anomalous data is well founded in general, but it does result in a peculiar sort of intellectual conservatism for what is vulgarly presumed to be a wholly noncommittal form of knowledge. This conservatism is particularly marked when it is

6

enforced by the scientific community quite consciously rather than by an individual scientist or by the natural exclusivism of the functioning of a paradigm.[7]

Besides simply ignoring an apparent anomaly or denying it a perceptual basis, the adherents of a fruitful paradigm may attempt to deal with an apparent anomaly by refining or expanding the paradigm. The classic case of such a procedure, of course, was the attempt to save the Ptolemaic geocentric astronomical paradigm and its account of planetary orbits as perfectly circular by the addition of epicycles. Such paradigm expansion, if it may be so termed, is nothing unusual, however. Any elaborate, formal, allegedly comprehensive conceptual system possesses the capacity to expand into epicyclical refinements when pressed, just as it is capable of adjusting perceptions to fit its postulates.[8]

Despite the best efforts of these defenses, however, from time to time the anomalies within a previously accepted paradigm become so deep, so persistent, and so important that the intellectual situation could be labeled a crisis. The essence of the crisis is the incapacity of the scientific discipline to solve what are recognized as genuine problems or to account for what are recognized as genuine realities on the basis of the previously accepted paradigm. The onset of the crisis is marked by confusion and by what Kuhn calls a blurring of the paradigm, and one consequence is often perplexity and insecurity among the members of the particular scientific community.[9] The paradigm is not immediately rejected, however, until and unless a new paradigm is perceived which can resolve both the new anomalies and the old problems out of which the original paradigm developed.

The application of this scheme to contemporary political science involves an act of judgment, of course. It might be held with considerable justification that political science is at the pre-paradigm stage—that it has as yet no overarching model which is generally accepted as providing the basic guidelines of the discipline's problems, realities, and research. And some might further contend that the study of politics can never reach the status of a paradigm science since its subject matter is so complex, diffuse, and far-ranging as to be unamenable to any single paradigm. In any case, it is probably true that paradigms in political science will always be somewhat looser and more numerous than in the simpler and more precise sciences. Another application of the term "paradigm" to political science was made by Gabriel Almond, who argued that the idea of the political system had emerged as the paradigm that was giving coherence and stability to the practice of political science.[10] This contention also has a great deal of validity. Certainly the concept of the political system has performed many of the functions of a genuine paradigm for political scientists. There is no need to consider such an appreciation of systems analysis incompatible with the view stated here.

The use of the term "crisis" in the present context refers to what is perhaps the root paradigm in the contemporary understanding of political theorizing: namely, that there are two distinct kinds of political theory, one of which is empirical and the other normative. This very fundamental ordering principle provides basic categories by relation to which practicing political scientists understand their own mode of inquiry, its methods, scope, standards, and theoretical boundaries. The pursuit of empirical theory, however, has already become involved in important anomalies—realities and problems which are not manageable under the ground rules set by the paradigm. Some of these anomalies will be explored in succeeding chapters. Difficulties in the theory of political development provide one excellent example of these anomalies, but they may also be found in some areas of democratic theory and systems analysis. Another facet of occurrences which are anomalous in the context of the prevailing paradigm is the heated political squabbles which have broken out over particular formulations of empirical theory. Theoretically, the value-neutral and objective nature of the latter should render it politically neutral, but such does not appear to be the case. In these instances, then, there must be either misunderstanding on the part of those who object to facets of the empirical study or some misconceptions inherent in the self-understanding of the practitioners. In most cases, both are present.

Perception of some of these anomalies has generated awareness in some quarters that normative and empirical theory are not disparate and separable forms of inquiry but instead have intrinsic relevance to each other which cannot be denied without resultant confusion. "The principal challenge to political theory at the present time," Gabriel Almond has recently written, "is to pull ourselves out of this conceptual confusion."[11] And he goes on to predict that at the end of this process of clarification "we shall soon be moving on a substantial scale across the now forbidden boundary between so-called empirical and normative theory."[12] Confronted with some of the conceptual confusion that contributed to the ruckus over the ill-fated Project Camelot, another observer reaches a somewhat similar conclusion:

> As social science begins to emerge from the morass of inconsequentiality in which so much of it has for so long been embedded, its obligation to develop more sophisticated methods for

normative analysis become urgent. It can no longer afford to relegate this subject to the obscurity of philosophy texts or to the sporadic emotional outbursts of its practitioners.[13]

These admonitions imply the need to move away from the notion of some kind of unbridgeable dichotomy between two logically distinct types of theory toward another understanding of the relationship between empirical and normative theory. Indeed, as the situation stands, any relationship between the two kinds of theory would have to be purely fortuitous, since they take place in different logical contexts altogether. Ultimately, the model of two separate categories of theory will have to be superceded by something like Abraham Kaplan's suggested model of the empirical-theoretical continuum. That is to say, while more delimited studies dealing with relatively unambiguous data have a higher ratio of fact to theory than more extended descriptive appraisals of political order, the former cannot dispense with norms and the latter cannot dispense with empirical data. In Kaplan's words, "The basic point is that no observation is purely empirical—that is, free of any ideational elements—as no theory (in science at any rate) is purely ideational."[14] It will be necessary on this model to understand that norms are operative throughout theory and that so-called normative theory is the upper end of the continuum, where the impact of the norms is more extensive and the criteria which underlie them require more judgment.

Considerable clarification is necessary, however, before any new model can become operable. At the moment, we are rather like the fly in Wittgenstein's famous simile that cannot find its way out of the fly-bottle. We are bound on all sides by deep-seated linguistic conventions which assume the conclusions which we are trying to escape and therefore keep forcing us back into our original predicament. To note only one tiny example of this systematized entrapment, consider how Gabriel Almond, even while advocating interaction between empirical data and normative appraisal in the study of political systems, finds himself speaking in terms of crossing a "boundary" between two types of theory. Ultimately, the sort of interaction which he advocates will be possible and meaningful only when we can shake ourselves free of the necessity to think in terms of boundaries at all. The interaction he seeks must be adjudged to be literally nonsense so long as the existing ground rules about the limits of sensible discourse hold sway; so, if we are persuaded by his basic recommendation, we must examine and finally change the existing ground rules. To accomplish this sort of examination and change, it will be necessary to think closely and critically about the actual usage of what we call facts, norms, observations, and so on and then to determine whether this actual usage is best accounted for by the more abstract signification attributed to the terms. Only by this critical process of "looking at the use," to follow Wittgenstein's admonition, can the enchantment of our deep-seated images and their terminological progeny be dispelled.

The roots of our terminological and conceptual entrapment run very deep in the tacit assumptions underlying our linguistic conventions. Part of the progress to more satisfactory conventions of discourse, then, needs to come from an appreciation of the location and nature of these intellectual roots. Ultimately, a full examination of this kind, which is beyond the scope of this essay, would take us back at the very least to the Aristotelianism which set the basic framework for the Western intellectual tradition which followed. Somewhat more proximately, we need to reexamine the basic assumptions behind the scientific revolution of the seventeenth century, for it is these assumptions which still operate to structure our expectations about what can count as factual, what is real, what it means to observe, and so on. In the present context, it is the seventeenth century that provided the philosophical foundation for the concept of empirical reality which persists into our vocabulary to designate a kind of political theory. Whitehead emphasized this persistence of "the characteristic scientific philosophy which closed the seventeenth century" as follows: "It is still reigning. Every university in the world organizes itself in accordance with it. No alternative system of organizing the pursuit of scientific truth has been suggested. It is not only reigning, but it is without a rival."[15]

Whitehead did not, of course, intend to claim here that this "characteristic scientific philosophy" is consciously understood and affirmed by those who order their inquiries and actions in accordance with its implications. Indeed, the contrary is true: the impact of this world view comes through a largely tacit adherence to its premises. This impact is none the less potent; in fact it may be all the more powerful because of its essentially tacit functioning.

Similarly, contemporary political scientists are largely unaware of the philosophical and epistemological theories of figures such as Descartes, LaPlace, and Bacon. However, the canons of scientific procedure and substance to which they ascribe are ultimately a product of this regnant philosophical tradition. Keynes once said that the premises behind many political speeches are distillations from the ideas of some defunct economist. It is correspondingly true that conventional wisdom about scientific procedures and theories is the distillation of the ideas of ostensibly defunct philosophers.

For several reasons, the time is now ripe for a reconsideration of the cognitive status and foundations of political theory. We are witnessing today the confluence of various intellectual and political developments which together both challenge the present conventional wisdom about the nature of political theorizing and provide the bases for formulating a more satisfactory model. Among the many motivating and structuring forces which led to the definition of the enterprise of empirical theory in this country—and this enterprise is to an astonishing extent American in origin and composition—two were highly important. First, the discipline of political science decided that it was time to become truly scientific at a time when the prevailing view of scientific theory and scientific method was considerably less sophisticated and more narrowly positivistic than the prevailing outlook today. Second, there was at this time so deep and widespread a consensus about the proper structure and ends of politics that it was not unreasonable to speak of an "end of ideology."

Today, both of these important structuring forces have been altered significantly. One significant transformation was actually occurring almost simultaneously with the growth of political behaviorism—namely, the shift from logical positivism to linguistic analysis in the field of philosophy. In a sense, many political scientists were boarding an intellectual vehicle just as its creators were disembarking through another exit. This shift in philosophy carries with it some significantly transformed assumptions and implications which have import for political theory. For example, implied in this development is a denial of the possibility of any ideal language, pruned of distortion by human purposes and perspectives. The important implications of this abandonment of belief in a purely objective language for political theory have hardly begun to be absorbed. A related but distinct transformation has been the recently altered understanding of scientific knowledge and inquiry reflected in the works of such philosophers of science as Thomas Kuhn, Michael Polanyi, Norwood Hanson, Stephen Toulmin, and Abraham Kaplan.[16] These authors destroy completely any illusions about the unambiguity of scientific data and leave little doubt that the Baconian model of scientific method is, in Donald Price's words, a "vulgar view of science."[17] As for the second structuring force, the political setting, it too has undergone obvious transformation. The significant ideological battles that mark the contemporary academic and political scene make it fairly clear that the forecast of any imminent demise of ideology was premature at best.[18]

The convergence of these two significant transformations, one theoretical and one political, serves to undermine some of the foundations of the recently prevailing view of political theory, especially of empirical theory. We are beginning to witness the

11

breaking down of the earlier, partially prospective theoretical comfort which was made possible by consensus-induced myopia plus a neo-Cartesian faith in the possibility of certain, impersonal, and unequivocal knowledge. The loss of this theoretical comfort comes from the impact of the reemergence of ideological conflict within the nation and the intellectual community itself, from the erosion of its philosophical basis, and from the manifestation of conceptual problems within burgeoning theories which had been conceived in terms of this view. The first of these factors need not be demonstrated, but the latter two are not self-evident and will therefore be elaborated in the chapters to follow.

It is important that criticism of the paradigm (which, while unable to resolve some emerging anomalies, still shapes the prevailing view of the cognitive status and foundations of political theory) not be negative only. As Kuhn observes, any assault on a prevailing paradigm is destined for failure unless the outlines of a more satisfactory paradigm are discernible. So, even considered simply from the standpoint of tactical advisability, such negativism is inappropriate. Beyond purely tactical considerations, moreover, it is only fair that a critic be expected to indicate the nature of a more satisfactory substitute for the intellectual construct he is asking his fellows to discard. Therefore, it will be part of the purpose of this essay to sketch the basic configuration and rationale behind a more appropriate paradigm for our understanding of the nature and status of political theory.

This constructive attempt can only be in outline form, of course, for ultimately what is being suggested is the overturning of the basic epistemological paradigm which has prevailed in the West since the seventeenth century. Obviously such an ambitious restructuring cannot be elaborated in detail here, but the basic contours of such a transformation and its relevance for our understanding of political theory can be indicated. Kuhn himself clearly perceives in passing that his own historical inquiry into the nature of scientific growth reveals patterns which are scarcely compatible with the seventeenth-century epistemological paradigm. That "philosophical paradigm initiated by Descartes and developed at the same time as Newtonian dynamics," Kuhn says:

> has served both science and philosophy well. Its exploitation, like that of dynamics itself, has been fruitful of a fundamental understanding that perhaps could not have been achieved in another way. But as the example of Newtonian dynamics also indicates, even the most striking past success provides no guarantee that crisis can be indefinitely postponed. Today research in parts of philosophy, psychology,

linguistics, and even art history, all converge to suggest that the traditional paradigm is somehow askew. That failure to fit is also made increasingly apparent by the historical study of science. . . . None of these crisis-promoting subjects has yet produced a viable alternate to the traditional epistemological paradigm, but they do begin to suggest what some of that paradigm's characteristics will be.[19]

If the contemporary quest for empirical theory in political science is to be fruitful, the limitations and inadequacies of philosophical empiricism which have resulted in widespread confusion and distortion must be recognized and transcended. To recall Wittgenstein's injunction, it is not our increasingly powerful and sophisticated experimental methods that have led to such problems as ethnocentrism, theoretical triviality, and overproliferation of unrelatable models; it is our conceptual confusion which is at fault. And just as experimental methods are not the source of our difficulties, they are also not the cure. Technical virtuosity can overcome many problems, but it is as intrinsically incapable of resolving conceptual confusion into conceptual clarity as the medieval alchemist was incapable of transforming lead into gold. The only cure for a conceptual problem is conceptual analysis, and in our present circumstances the requisite analysis must be far-ranging and profound. The present essay is offered as one contribution to this analytical task in the hope that our ultimate destination will be the reintegration of political theory in a postbehavioral political science.

Notes

1. Ludwig Wittgenstein, *The Philosophical Investigations*, G.E.M. Anscombe, trans. (Oxford: Blackwell's, 1953), p. 232 (emphasis in original).

2. Thomas Kuhn, *The Structure of Scientific Revolutions* (Chicago: Phoenix Books, 1962).

3. Ibid., pp. 4-5.

4. Ibid., p. 24. "Mopping-up operations are what engage most scientists throughout their careers."

5. Ibid., p. 26. "From Tycho Brahe to E.O. Lawrence, some scientists have acquired great reputations, not from any novelty of their discoveries, but from the precision, reliability, and scope of the methods they developed for the redetermination of a previously known sort of fact."

6. Michael Polanyi, *Personal Knowledge* (New York: Harper and Row, 1964), p. 292.

7. Cf. Bernard Barber, "Resistance by Scientists to Scientific Discovery," *Science*, CXXXIV (1961), 596-602.

8. Cf. Polanyi, pp. 286-294.

9. For example, consider the complaint of the physicist Wolfgang Pauli

just prior to the time that Heisenberg led the way to a new quantum mechanics: "At the moment physics is again terribly confused. In any case, it is too difficult for me, and I wish I had been a movie comedian or something of the sort and had never heard of physics." Quoted by Kuhn, p. 84.

10. Gabriel Almond, "Political Theory and Political Science," *American Political Science Review,* LX (1966), 689-879.

11. Almond, "Political Development," *Comparative Political Studies,* I (1969), p. 448.

12. Ibid., p. 466.

13. Robert Boguslaw, "Ethics and the Social Scientist," *The Rise and Fall of Project Camelot,* Irving Horowitz, ed. (Cambridge, Mass.: M.I.T. Press, 1967), p. 126.

14. Abraham Kaplan, *The Conduct of Inquiry* (San Francisco: Chandler Publishing Co., 1964). p. 58.

15. Alfred North Whitehead, *Science and the Modern World,* (New York: Mentor Books, 1948), p. 55. "And yet," he goes on to observe, "it is quite unbelievable." And Ernest Nagel has written: "The scientific foundations of what is, in the main, still the educated man's outlook on the universe and on his fellow human beings were laid in the seventeenth century." Quoted by Gerald Holton, *Science and the Modern Mind* (Boston: Beacon Press, 1958), p. viii.

16. Each of these men have published rather extensively, but a fairly good understanding of the change of view indicated can be obtained by referring to Kuhn, op. cit.; Kaplan, op. cit.; Polanyi, op. cit.; Hanson, *Patterns of Discovery* (Cambridge: Cambridge University Press, 1958); and Toulmin, *Foresight and Understanding* (Bloomington: University of Indiana Press, 1961).

17. Don K. Price, *The Scientific Estate* (New York: Oxford University Press, 1968), p. 173.

18. For some suggestive commentary and analysis, cf. Joseph La Palombara, "Decline of Ideology: A Dissent and an Interpretation," *American Political Science Review,* LX (1966), 5-16, and William Connolly, *Political Science and Ideology* (New York: Atherton Press, 1967).

19. Kuhn, p. 120.

2 Origins and Ambiguities of the Empirical Tradition

It is a commonplace that the discipline of political science has undergone some significant transformations in the past two or three decades. It is considerably less commonplace to find any clear understanding of the meaning and nature of the transformation. Even those who find themselves in basic agreement about the worth and validity of the new trends may not characterize the essential features of these trends in the same way. Any univocal interpretation of the theoretical ferment in political science will predictably meet with more disapproval than acceptance, since few would feel that it does justice to that particular aspect of inquiry and that particular methodological bent with which they themselves are most involved.

Several reasons lie behind this difficulty in attaining any consensus in disciplinary self-characterization. The first reason is that the transformation of the field in the past few decades has not been singular but plural. Political science has undergone not one transformation, but numerous transformations which happened to coincide. Some of these various changes are directly and logically related, others are only indirectly related, and still others are related only by temporal juxtaposition and not by any logical nexus at all. Most discussion of the nature of recent trends in political science runs into initial confusion through a failure to discriminate these various strands analytically. In the context of this essay, it is important to make this kind of analytical discrimination in order to identify clearly the essay's own focus.

The recent developments in political science and political theorizing originated as a response to several felt deficiencies in prewar political science. Widespread consensus was reached that political science was first of all excessively parochial. The range of disciplinary concern extended only sporadically beyond Western Europe, and the events of the war years made this limitation seem an obvious inadequacy. Second, it was widely felt that analysis in political science had been too exclusively focused on the formal and institutional manifestations of political life. The rich welter of more informal political phenomena and their relationship to in-stitutionalized political operations was all too often systematically ignored by researchers, and this aspect of previously accepted research methodology seemed inadequate. Perhaps the notable collapse of such theoretically sound formal structures as the Weimar Constitution helped to inspire discontent in this respect. Third, the conceptual format of much of the discipline's output was deemed too narrowly descriptive and narrative. Greater conceptual sophistication, it was felt, would make the discoveries and for-mulations of political inquiry more generalizable and comparative. The feelings of dissatisfaction in this regard, as well as in the previous respect, were undoubtedly influenced by the relative sophistication of some of the sister social sciences in their conceptual formulations. And, finally, the technical possibilities opened by the rapid development of computer science and by the rapidly ex-panding numbers of political scientists, it was felt, were not being realized.[1]

At the minimum, then, the resultant revolutions have been at least twofold. The first revolution is technical and methodological, the second, conceptual and theoretical. The convergence of the two revolutions is more chronological than logical, although there has been some overlap and mutual interaction. Therefore, it is im-portant to distinguish them analytically for the sake of un-derstanding, as David Easton has done in the following way:

> [Political science] has been undergoing two revolutions simultaneously. Political Science has come to scientific method at about the same time as the social sciences as a whole have been shifting their emphasis from the methods of research alone to theory as well. . . . Political science is in the process of absorbing the basic assumptions of scientific method at the same time as it proceeds to the equally trying task of giving meaning to the behavior studied by relating it to some empirical theoretical context.[4]

It is probably worth amending this twofold division by noting that the conceptual part of the revolution is itself further divisible into "subrevolutions," for not only has there been a quest for a substantively different conceptual model for theorizing about political reality but also a revolutionary alteration in the conceptual focus and the conceptual scope of the discipline. The shift in focus has been the widening from formal governmental institutions to the full panoply of political transactions in a society, and the shift in scope has been the widening net of comparison to non-Western and developing nations. These changes in scope and focus have had ramifications for the changes in the "empirical theoretical context," as Easton calls it, but they do not account exhaustively for developments in the latter.

Even those political scientists who take care to differentiate the dual or multiple nature of the recent transformations of the discipline are not in full agreement about the relative importance of the different strands. David Truman, for example, in his judicious appraisal for the Brookings Institution in 1955 wrote that the technical transformation was more profound than were the conceptual changes.[3] David Easton, on the other hand, is quite explicit in stating that the key feature of the "behavioral revolution" is not simply methodological allegiance to "what is virtuous in research or for scientific method" but rather involves a "crucial contribution of a substantive kind."[4]

Whatever the final assessment of the relative significance of the methodological and conceptual aspects of the movement toward empirical theory, our concern here will be exclusively with the latter, conceptual part. It can be taken for granted, I think, despite the imprecations of occasional methodological Luddites, that more powerful and refined techniques of factual research and data processing will be a blessing if they are set in a productive theoretical context. There is, of course, the danger that sheer technical virtuosity and mathematical subtlety may become ends in themselves, as though brilliance of technique could atone for conceptual poverty or trivial subject matter. But this is an imperfection of practice, not of principle. The expansion of both scope and focus in the conceptual developments of the discipline are also to be welcomed. The danger here is, of course, that political scientists will simply be overwhelmed by the sheer magnitude of their appointed task; but this has always been the danger of a discipline which—perhaps pretentiously, but with justification—styles itself the master science. Mention of that Aristotelian designation is appropriate in this context, moreover, for the revolutionary expansion of scope and focus contributes to one important part of the salutary movement to reintegrate our theoretical enterprise, specifically to the reestablishment of the juncture between comparative politics and political theory.[5]

The broadened scope and focus of contemporary political science and the infinitely more powerful and sophisticated technical tools which it has begun to utilize, then, are relatively unambiguous and constructive contributions to the study of politics. What is considerably more ambiguous and considerably less constructive is the network of presuppositions which has resulted in the bifurcation of theory into the allegedly distinct enterprises of empirical and normative theory. The nature of this alleged disjunction is rarely examined at anything more than a superficial level; the philosophical origins which have served as its basis have remained largely obscure and undiscussed; and the outcome has been a considerable amount of confusion.

These ambiguities are reflected in the ambiguities of the principal substantively delimiting adjectives used most often to describe the new face of political science in its empirical mode. Either singly or in combination, the terms "scientific," "behavioral," and "empirical" are those constantly present in the attempt to characterize the distinctiveness of the new political science. Yet the meanings of these very words which are offered for the sake of clarification are themselves highly evanescent at best. Each of the terms stands for a rather vague and diffuse consensus which contains broad areas of disagreement and uncertainty. The consensus behind the use of "behavioral," for example, is that political science should focus on the full informal process of political interaction and not merely on legal and constitutional forms. Within this significant but extremely limited consensus, some have contended that "behavioralism" implies a conceptual focus upon the individual, but others have disputed this characterization.[6] In some instances, those who employ the term connote some of the meanings of psychological behaviorism, intimating that political action is basically arational and self-interested or conditioned. Other practitioners do not make these implications.

The symbol "scientific" also represents disagreements within consensus. The consensus is basically that political science should emulate the logical and methodological rigor of the natural sciences, utilizing mathematical tools where possible. Furthermore, it is generally held that the goal of political science is comparable to that of the natural sciences in abstract terms—that is, the goal of a relatively coherent body of theoretically integrated hypotheses. Within this area of general agreement considerable contention remains as to the extent to which the rigor of the natural sciences is productive and possible in political studies. Moreover, there is a range of notions about the extent of formal and linguistic similarity which can and should exist between the theoretical formulations of natural and social sciences. And finally, some real ambiguities arise because of the increasing awareness of the complexity and ambiguity of the natural sciences themselves, both in substance and in method. Not only is the extent of applicability of the model of scientific procedure and discourse debatable, then, but the nature of the model itself is in considerable doubt.

The term "empirical" is perhaps the most general and pervasive adjective of them all, capable of incorporating the notions of "behavioralism" and "scientific" within its penumbra.[7] Of all the recent terms used by political scientists in discussing their form of inquiry in recent years, none has been so widely used as "empirical." Partly because of the near universality of its appropriation, however, its meaning is extraordinarily difficult to determine. The meaning of a word, contemporary philosophies of language are saying, is its use; and this admonition serves to highlight more than to solve the problem of definition here. For no word has been more widely and variously used, both contemporaneously and historically.

At one extreme, the use of "empirical" is almost more of a benediction than a denotation. To be "empirical" is to be virtuous in procedure and realistic in outlook, and not to be empirical is to stray from the narrow and true path. "To be empirical" in this sense is often conjugated: "I am empirical, you are empirical if you agree with me, my opponent is not empirical." Historically, however, the connotations of virtue have not always been present when using "empirical" or its counterpart. An etymological dictionary will reveal that one synonym for "empiricist" has been "quack," meaning one who proceeds wholly by trial and error and without the guidance of theory. (The Greek root is *peira*, meaning "trial.") Fashions apparently change.

More denotatively, the term "empirical" is often used in a methodological context, as a modifier to the noun "procedure." "Empirical" method or procedure tends to be roughly equivalent in signification to "scientific" method or procedure, sharing the same basic meaning and the same ambiguities. Being empirical methodologically then involves following certain accepted canons of procedure whose formulation often tends to be surprisingly vague— such as "Look for all relevant facts," "Be logical," and so on. To some, empirical procedure involves a Baconian inductive model of inquiry, but other avowed empiricists make it clear that they eschew mere fact accumulation or what they call "barefoot empiricism."[8] On this view, the realm of empirical theory would be constituted not by any distinctive substantive limitation so much as by the procedural basis of its formulation.

"Empirical" does signify a kind of substantive limitation as well, however. Put simply, an empirical theory must be one that confines itself to the realm of factuality. Perhaps the best way to formulate the substantive test of empirical status is linguistic. Empirical theory is seen as the realm of synthetic a posteriori statements. In the first place, statements about obligation are excluded. Popularly, the basis for distinction here is the classic Humean claim about the dichotomy of "is" and "ought." Empirical theory is concerned only with the former. Purely analytic statements are also excluded, and for this reason a recent typology of theory adds the category "analytic" to those of "normative" and "empirical."[9] Empirical theory, therefore, becomes description whereas normative theory is prescription and analytic theory is analysis in the technical sense.

One other often cited criterion for delimiting what is "empirical" is partly procedural and partly substantive. Specifically, the scope of empirical theory is conceived by some as comprising the realm of testable, or verifiable, propositions. This test is procedural in that amenability to a particular procedure is set as the standard, but it is also substantive in that only a certain range of propositions is seen as capable of being subjected to the requisite procedure. This understanding of the range of empirical theory reflects the influence of philosophical positivism and its "verifiability theory of meaning." As the vicissitudes of the verifiability theory of meaning have demonstrated, however, this criterion is far from unambiguous. This problem will be discussed later.

Leaving aside for the moment the methodological definition of "empirical theory," the term stands substantively for a theoretical description of reality. Such a description stands in contrast to a prescription or an analysis. It deals with factuality, not with recommendation, preference, or tautology. To be satisfied with this formulation as an answer, however, is to take for a solution what is really only another problem. It is not a satisfactory disposition of the problem to say that empirical data is provided by "observations of real events."[10] Observation, to begin with, is hardly unproblematic, as we shall see later; and the nature and limits of reality are surely what is at issue. Bryce called in 1888 for "facts, facts, facts," but he is not commonly considered an example of an empirical theorist in the modern sense. And Aristotle, that relentless data collector, does not fit within the confines of empirical theory, however empirical his procedure methodologically.[11]

Part of the background of empirical theory, then, is not simply an insistence that it must deal with fact but also an interpretation of what shall count as a fact. Involved is not only the rigorous determination to deal with reality but also certain ideas about the nature and limits of what can be conceived as reality. These notions about the nature and limits of facts and of reality are sometimes made explicit but are more often simply left implicit, since they are derived from the conventional wisdom of the Western scientific tradition since the seventeenth century. This interpretation is principally a substantive one, although it has implications for methodology as well. Therefore, we shall focus upon the substantive aspects of these partly latent notions about what may legitimately be accorded the status of reality, although method will be a subsidiary concern throughout.[1][2]

Briefly put, the thesis is that the weaknesses and confusions of empirical theory are a consequence of a set of presuppositions deriving from the empiricist tradition in philosophy. Furthermore, it will be contended that these weaknesses will be overcome only by transcending the limitations of these presuppositions and that this process will involve a reintegration of empirical and normative theory into a spectrum. In order to explain and substantiate this basic thesis, it will be necessary to consider first of all the nature and origin of these assumptions. Then it should be demonstrated that they are operative, how they are operative, and why their operation is a hindrance to valid theorizing. And finally, the basic outlines of alternative assumptions and their derivative operations should be sketched.

In order even to begin this analysis, it is imperative to disentangle some distinct concepts which have been conflated semantically. Several meanings have become wrapped into the single stem "empiric," and their common linguistic location constitutes a sort of implicit assertion of their relationship in reality. In one of its significations, "empirical" has almost become a synonym for "real." An empirical statement means a statement about the "real world out there" as distinguished from a tautology or an announcement of individual subjective preference: an empirical study refers to a factual research operation, and empirical theory means, similarly, a description of reality. These meanings of "real" and "description" are then tied to the same stem used to characterize a particular set of philosophical assumptions, however. These distinct meanings need to be distinguished, for it is precisely the propriety of their relationship which is in question.

For analytical purposes, therefore, let us distinguish empirical research, empirical theory, and empiricism. An "empirical study" shall be taken to refer to any replicable research into the real world.

Such a study may or may not be consciously and productively tied to any theoretical context. It may be of greater or lesser worth by virtue of the presence or absence of such a relationship, but the factual information and correlations discovered may be deemed of relatively autonomous value. "Empirical theory" shall be taken simply to refer to theory about the real world, although the verbal simplicity belies the practical ambiguities inherent in such a task. Empirical theory is the conceptually integrative tissue of our knowledge of politics as it is. It may be, and should be, connected with empirical studies, but it has not been invariably so connected. "Empiricism" shall be taken as referring to a broad school of the Western philosophical tradition which had its origins in the seventeenth century but which has undergone numerous incarnations, from Hobbes's *De corpore* and Locke's *Essay on Human Understanding* through Russell's logical atomism to more recent neopositivism. A connection between this form of philosophy and the contemporary theory of political reality seems to be implied by the common appropriation of the stem "empiric"; and the allegedly proper limits of empirical theory have at times been determined by postulates derived from the philosophical outlook. In fact, however, the philosophical outlook of empiricism is a quite inadequate basis for a theory of political reality.

Because the term "empiricism" has been so widely applied and appropriated, it might be helpful to specify the family of ideas long associated with empiricism that is most significant in the context of constructing a theory or theories of politics. The first of these ideas is a radical philosophical nominalism. The second is the belief in the radical separability of facts from norms. The third element is the image of true knowledge as utterly objective, in the sense of fully specifiable, unambiguous, and wholly unstructured by the agent of the knowledge. There are several corollaries of these basic tenets and various degrees and versions of each of them, but together they form the critical group of assumptions operative in the context of theory formation which are derived from empiricism. They are, furthermore, ideas that are related both logically and historically, sharing a common basis in the same general ontology and sharing a common origin.[13]

Another term which has been used to designate this cluster of ideas and their common basis is "objectivism."[14] In the remainder of this essay, this term will be employed rather than "empiricism" for two reasons. First, the general use of "empiricism" is somewhat too broad for our concerns. In the context of research methodology, for example, "empiricism" has come to have a signification only partly and peripherally related to the postulates designated above.

These methodological precepts are not directly in dispute here, and therefore the use of the alternative concept "objectivism" helps to delimit our focus more clearly. Second, in another sense, the term "empiricism" is too narrow for our purposes, for fundamentally the empiricist tradition in philosophy since the seventeenth century has actually shared several important presuppositions with what is commonly termed philosophical rationalism. Using the term "empiricism," therefore, might misleadingly suggest contrasts which are not intended or present. In fact, rationalism and empiricism are in large part philosophical alter egos, struggling together over insoluble dilemmas which are the function of mutually shared beliefs. To be precise, then, our concern is with the impact upon empirical theory of those elements of empiricism which grow out of the objectivist tradition—namely, radical nominalism, the dichotomizing of facts and norms, the objectivist ideal of knowledge—and the fundamentally spatial ontology which provided the metaphysical grounding for them.

The objectivist tradition was originated in what Whitehead called the "century of genius." Bacon, Descartes, Hobbes, Locke, Newton, Galileo, and Harvey were all part of that remarkable seventeenth-century intellectual revolution which shaped the contours of our reigning philosophical-scientific tradition. These intellectual giants accomplished the destruction of the desiccated and increasingly sterile Aristotelian world view of scholasticism and simultaneously replaced it with their bright new world, translucent to the mathematicizing mind. Their achievements were monumental; however, they contained weaknesses that became evident only later, overshadowed as they were by the early brilliant successes of the tradition. Ironically, the seventeenth-century developments both provided the impetus and tools for the unparalleled achievements of modern natural science and in the process began, again in Whitehead's words, the "ruin" of modern philosophy.[15] Since this intellectual transformation produced the cluster of linguistic nominalism, ethical subjectivism, and epistemological objectivism, its progress and principal implications warrant a brief review.[16]

The Aristotelian cosmology, baptized and adopted by medieval scholasticism, saw the world as a finite aggregate of immutable "substances." The notion of substance was essentially Aristotle's solution to the problems of order and change in the universe. Order and change were both accounted for and reconciled by the concept of substance. The lines of the various substances provided limits and coherence to the flux of phenomena and accounted for the purposefulness which Aristotle saw in movement. Change, or movement, occurred in the context of stable and unmoved substantive boundaries[17] and was therefore itself finite, possessing a distinct end. "Every change," Aristotle said, "is from something to something, as the word itself [*metabole*] indicates."[18] The movements of nature, therefore, were seen in the famous formulation as the actualizing of potentiality. "The fulfillment of what exists potentially, in so far as it exists potentially, is motion."[19]

The functions of this fundamental model of movement—structured, ordered, and limited by substance—were manifold. It helped to explain the relationship of a seed to the mature tree which grew out of it. It helped to explain desires and instincts through the correlative concept of natural tendencies. It served as an explanation of cosmic order and as a rationale for political hierarchy. However, it was also utilized as an explanation of simple physical locomotion, and this presumption, for which it was ill equipped, proved to be the hubris that led in appropriate Greek tragic fashion to its destruction.

In the Aristotelian cosmos, all movement was finite; all moving things would come to a natural end unless some extraneous force intervened. In the context of physical motion, this outlook contained no principle of inertia. Or, to put it more exactly, inertia was equated with rest, and rest was seen as the contrary of motion.[20] It was always movement and not the cessation of movement that required explanation, for movement was expected to terminate itself naturally by actualizing the potentiality of that which was moved, thereby eliminating the final cause which was the essential force causing the movement. An absence of outside force was deemed to result in a return to rest, not in a constant continuation of motion in a straight line. Similarly, a constant force was held to result in constant motion rather than in constant acceleration, as any moderately diligent high-school physics student knows today.

This equation of inertia with rest not only fit into the symmetry of the Aristotelian model of nature but also accorded with many of the common experiences with motion. Several rather clearly weak points in the theory, to be sure, led to persistent dissatisfaction in many quarters from as early as the fourteenth century, particularly with the cumbersome Aristotelian account of the behavior of projectiles and falling bodies.[21] Despite this recurrent dissatisfaction, however, no new model had been developed that was itself adequate enough to commend widespread acceptance as a substitute. Since, to borrow Kuhn's words, "the decision to reject one paradigm is always simultaneously the decision to accept another,"[22] the situation remained unresolved.

It was Galileo who finally produced the conceptual breakthrough by producing a new paradigm by which to understand physical motion. His stunning achievement rapidly won virtually universal acclaim among the intellectual luminaries of his day and gained for him such encomiums as Hobbes's designation of him as "the first that opened to us the gate of natural philosophy universal."[23] Almost overnight, the new illumination provided by Galileo's explanations relegated the classic potential-actual model of Aristotle with its profound ramifications to the status of obscurantist nonsense. Reflecting this transformation, Descartes says of the scholastics:

> They define motion, a fact with which everyone is quite familiar, as the "actualization of what exists in potentiality, insofar as it is potential." Now who understands these words? And who at the same time does not know what motion is? Will not everyone admit that those philosophers have been trying to find a knot in a bulrush?[24]

Galileo performed his great intellectual feat by abstracting from the sense-manifestations of motion to its mathematically manipulatable components. This geometricization of movement, with its remarkable success, had the most far-reaching and profound consequences for Western philosophy, both in its procedural and in its substantive implications.[25] Cosmologically this conceptual transformation resulted, quite literally, in draining the world of its substance, for the whole notion of substance in the Aristotelian and scholastic world view was inextricably connected with the understanding of motion as finite change to a specified end, completion, rest. A particular substance was seen as composed of the defining boundaries of a particular motion. With the infinitizing[26] of motion on the Galilean model, therefore, the function of substances disappeared and the modern world "had no need of that hypothesis."

Having dissolved the configurations of substance, the infinite, mathematicized view of motion served as the indicator of the proper replacement for the whatnesses, quiddities, and entities that had composed the premodern cosmos. Infinite, mathematicized, and abstract motions clearly belonged in an infinite, mathematicized, and abstract world. Although a radical reversal in content, formally this inference from the nature of motion to the nature of the world directly paralleled the reasoning within the supplanted world view. Hobbes's derivation of the outlines of the new nature from the new view of motion is reflected in his contention that "the gate of natural philosophy universal. . . is the knowledge of the nature of

25

motion."[27] His contention clearly echoes Aristotle's own view that "we must . . . understand the principle of motion, for if it were unknown, the meaning of nature too would be unknown."[28]

The various seventeenth-century intellectual luminaries who set about developing the cosmological implications of the infinitizing of motion were not in agreement on all counts. For example, some thinkers felt that space and matter were actually identical, whereas others felt that space was the vessel of matter and hence distinguishable from it. Descartes took the former view and Locke, the latter. Some, preeminently Descartes, saw a radical dualism between thinking and extended substance, mind and body. Others, like Hobbes, followed a consistently monistic path, seeking to integrate the workings of mind into the material motions which they saw as exhausting the furniture of the cosmos.

These differences, however, while significant in some contexts, were essentially secondary disagreements within a more important consensus about the nature of the objective world. On this latter question, it quickly became taken as a virtual presupposition that objective reality is composed of mathematically comprehensible entities. This conviction served as the basis for the optimistic faith in the limitless possibilities of the mathematical mind to comprehend the world, a faith reflected undimmed in the much later writing of Laplace and Condorcet. It also followed from this view that the stuff from which the universe is composed is quite homogeneous, both in its composition and in its operations. There was no longer a vast but definite number of heterogeneous entities in the world but really only a single uniform substance (or, as in the case of Descartes, two substances, one of which has no detectable location, or, as in the case of Spinoza, two virtually coterminous substances which are really the same thing viewed under different aspects). Everything is composed of simple natures which can be clearly and distinctly conceived, and anything more complex than these simple natures possesses only a secondary kind of reality.

This uniform, empty spatial homogeneity characterized the Cartesian notion of *res extensa*, the Hobbesian notion of body, and Locke's concept of primary qualities. The concept of substance retained its meaning—that is, function—in referring to that permanent fundamental reality which remains constant through change; but the meaning—that is, referent—of the concept had changed radically, almost to the point of reversal.[29] The universe, in Hobbes's words, is "the aggregate of all bodies, for there is no real part thereof that is not also body . . . substance and body signify the same thing. . . ."[30] And body means simply that homogeneous something which fills mathematically conceived homogeneous space. As Locke saw, this body—or pure substance, as he termed it—was really an unknowable something that served as an empty vehicle for qualities.[31]

The objectivist cluster of interrelated ideas about the nature of language and concepts, the excisability of norms from the world of facts, and the impersonal absolute clarity of genuine knowledge grows inferentially out of this world view which originated in the seventeenth century. To begin with, the radical shift in cosmology implies a considerably altered idea of the status and significance of language. The medieval Aristotelian world was a verbal world, a noun-oriented world to be more precise, as contrasted with a mathematical world. Only the heterogeneity of words could do justice to the heterogeneity of reality. Given this integral relationship of words to reality, the process of definition had ontological significance. The word "de-finition" itself indicates that relationship between the process of structuring words and the finitude of reality in the Aristotelian mind. An accurate definition for Aristotle constituted a revelation of the essence of the reality represented by that word.[32]

Definition was also important in the context of creation—or to be more precise, imitative generation—for Aristotelian thought. "Each substance," Aristotle held, "comes into being out of something that shares its name."[33] This view of creation lay behind the Greek inability to entertain the notion of evolution as we understand it today. And, finally, definitions served explanatory functions in the Aristotelian schema, since it was felt that "the 'why' is reducible finally to the definition."[34] The logic behind attributing explanatory functions to definitions rested upon the belief in the efficacy of final causality; definition and cause were united in the *telos*. This tendency to look to final causes, and hence definitions, for explanation is not utterly foolish, of course. It does make sense to explain that Fred is attracted to Sally because of his masculinity and her femininity and because such attraction is in the nature of these substances. But such an explanation is at best a short-circuiting of a full account of the operative causes, and in some cases is quite useless.[35]

There were few tears shed, therefore, by Descartes, Hobbes, and their followers when the new cosmology eliminated the scholastic notion of substance. By consigning this model to the scrap heap, all sorts of vain squabbling over quiddities and whatnesses could be avoided, an advantage that was itself one strong argument in the new cosmology's favor. Freed from excessive concern with the subtleties of definition, however, seventeenth-century thinkers opened the way for an excessive casualness in matters of definition.

27

The assignation of names was no longer the discovery of a structural aspect of reality but instead an arbitrary designation of the intellect. "How can any man imagine that the names of things were imposed from their natures?" asked Hobbes.[36] Names are instead marks "taken at pleasure [to] raise in our mind a thought like to some thought we had before."[37] They are "signs of our conceptions" and manifestly "not signs of the things themselves."[38]

This transformation, with its studied casualness about the designation of names and the relationship of such designation to reality, was a logical outgrowth of the new spatial cosmology, for such a cosmos is essentially numerical rather than verbal, and geometry, the language of *res extensa* and body. The names of primary qualities are numbers, not words. The homogeneity of statistics is wholly appropriate to a universe that is substantially homogeneous. Verbal distinctions may be significant for the understanding, but they are not really significant ontologically. Words represent complex wholes, and complex wholes are only concatenations of mathematically expressible real and simple natures. Mathematics, in fact, as the quest for a single ideal, wholly specifiable, and precise language which began at this time demonstrates, became the model for language to emulate.

The linguistic aspect of the seventeenth-century revolution, then, left an ambivalent legacy. It did accomplish the necessary task of freeing language from the structural rigidities predicated upon a structurally rigid cosmology. This achievement and its worth should not be minimized. However, the replacement of the structurally rigid cosmos of substances by a substantively empty homogeneous spatial cosmos brought its own inadequacies in the understanding of language. The critical process of definition was delivered from the confines of a static world to the arbitrariness of a verbally empty world. The seventeenth century freed words from being distorted into inappropriate functions but left them lacking a distinctive function, incompetent aspirants to the perfection of numbers. Part of the legacy of the scientific revolution to social theory, then, has been a laxity in political language growing from a failure to recognize that definitions involve a significant a posteriori component. The jettisoned tradition had at least recognized the propositional functions of generalizing names even though this recognition was ultimately vitiated by a faulty, static view of the nature of reality's limits on linguistic propriety.

The assumptions made as a part of the seventeenth-century conceptual revolution also lie behind the ideal of total severance of facts and norms. Once again, while not endorsing the Aristotelian position, a look at the view which was superceded helps to bring the new outlook into clearer focus. Viewing the world as a complex of movements that were finite transitions from potentiality to actuality, Aristotelians perceived an element of tension in all existence. Since what existed did so in the context of an origin and an end which defined it, it was possible to talk meaningfully about existence only contextually. One could not describe what is without talking about its fulfillment, and the nature of this fulfillment therefore functioned descriptively as a defining norm. To describe an acorn without reference to an oak tree was seen as a descriptive failure. The norm or standard of actuality, or essence, served an irreducible descriptive role, then, in speaking of anything in existence, for existence was a form of becoming. Norms were a part of the objective world, both verbally and causally.

The geometricization of the cosmos in the seventeenth century transformed the view of what was objective, eliminating the tension of existence in favor of a static view of existence. When the furniture of the world moved, it now simply changed its place rather than approached its fulfillment. The world of existence was no longer a realm of growth, of becoming, but a world in which one spatial configuration was just as fulfilled or unfulfilled as any other spatial configuration. Developmental concepts therefore had no objective grounding. For this reason, as Whitehead observes, such a cosmology could not justifiably speak of evolution.[39]

In this view of the world, an objective description of something need not be contextual at all. Strictly speaking, the context is quite irrelevant to the nature of the thing, in contrast to the earlier view that the context was literally definitive of anything's nature. Especially notable was the loss of temporal contextuality in the new world view. Time, in a world of pure spatiality, exists only as an abstraction; it became, in Hobbes's illuminating term, a "phantasm." Real relationships were now seen as merely spatial, and the relationship through time of the oak and acorn had no role in the description of either. The notions of function and intent, as forms of teleology, which was now illicit, lost their ontological integrity unless conceived in mechanical terms.

The only norms appropriate to description of the objective world, then, were the norms of spatial location. No other norms, such as those relating to substantive identity or to fulfillment, retained any ontological grounding and hence no legitimate descriptive function. Any intrusions of such concepts had henceforth to be construed as illicit intrusions into the homogeneous clarity of reality which would not be tolerated by a true science. Anyone who persisted in speaking about reality with norms, therefore, was seen as misleading and/or misled. Since such assertions are an uneliminatable feature of human discourse and could therefore not be simply expunged from a world which made them senseless, they had to be reinterpreted as phenomena rather than as propositions. Specifically, such normative statements were interpreted as deceptively structured announcements of the speaker's own likes and dislikes. What else could they be, if they could be admitted no objective—that is, real-referent?

The new ontology of the seventeenth century also undergirded the prevalent ideal of genuine knowledge as rigorously impersonal and unambiguously precise. This model of knowledge is clearly appropriate to a world which itself is both impersonal and precise. Neither ambiguity nor personality intrude to obscure the clarity of pure *res extensa*, which is the proper object of knowledge. Accordingly, Descartes made the clarity and distinctness of a conception the ultimate test of its validity. As he reported, he "came to the conclusion that I might assume, as a general rule, that the things which we conceive very clearly and distinctly are all true."[40]

As a corollary, the structure of all knowing was seen as homogeneous. "We must not fancy," Descartes admonished his readers, "that one kind of knowledge is more obscure than another, since all knowledge is of the same nature throughout."[41] Since knowledge was of the same nature throughout, it also followed that the procedure of knowing was properly to be conceived homogeneously. This common method, Descartes prescribed, was to divest any problem of every "superfluous conception" and then to reduce it "to a form in which we no longer deem that we are treating of this or that special matter, but are dealing only in a general way with certain magnitudes which have to be fitted together."[42]

Knowledge, like the reality it was to know, was in this view, then, seen as homogeneous, clear, and distinct. The problem which remained unsolved in this conception, and which has plagued Western philosophy ever since, was that the location of the knower and his relationship with the known were quite unaccountable. The knowing subject was left to become, in effect, a passive mathematicizing spectator, viewing the fully transparent world of *res extensa* from an unspecified Archimedean point. This model of absolutely objective knowledge then set up a peculiar oscillation epistemologically between a Laplacean pride in the possibilities suggested by the model and a despair sometimes engendered by the patent failure of man to effectuate his presumed standard.

The new world view thus implied a whole series of dichotomies which were soon to become entrenched in the most basic presuppositions of Western thought habits. First was the standard split between subjective and objective. Second was a bifurcation of reason and emotion, for since reason took its structure from the reality it was its task to know and since this reality as seen by the new cosmology had no legitimate objects of emotion (*hormé* or "natural tendency" in the earlier view), then the realm of emotion was obviously distinct from the proper object of reason. Emotions were by definition, then, irrational, as the language used to describe them from Spinoza to Freud clearly indicated. And finally there evolved the alleged dichotomy of facts and values, with only the former having reference to the real world and hence a valid place in science.

The parallelism of these three dichotomies is not merely formal, for they are substantively intertwined as well. The concepts of objective, reason, and fact all are expressive of the reality depicted by the seventeenth-century cosmology. Their opposites—subjective, emotional, and values—in each case represent the receptacles for those leftover phenomena which could not fit into the world as it was defined but which could apparently not be abolished either. The idea was that if they could not be abolished, they could at least be isolated and thereby kept from contaminating the lucidity of their ontologically legitimated counterparts. Therefore, the elements of the three dichotomies share a close family relationship, a relationship emphasized by the frequent use of one of the three terms on one side of the ontological split to define its brothers. Thus, to be objective is to be factual, and being rational means to be objective. And on the other side, taking a subjective approach means to let one's emotions and values become involved. The formal parallelism and substantive overlap of these dichotomies—their family relationship—is of course no accident, since they are all the offspring of the same seventeenth-century outlook which we have been describing.

It should, of course, take no great feat of inference to see the way in which this objectivist world view with its numerous interrelated dichotomies provides the background of the contemporary bifurcation of political theory into the empirical and the normative. The relationship is not only logical and historical but linguistic, with the conception of normative theory as value theory. The difficulties of empirical theory and the absurdities of normative theory when they are conceived in this way are ultimately a product of the inadequacies of the flawed presuppositions which gave rise to them. The objectivist cluster of ideas about knowledge, language, and norms, while only one feature of the face of contemporary political theory, has had a pervasive and distorting impact. A brief sampling of that impact, both historical and contemporary, is our next concern.

Notes

1. Many of these concerns, and the high hopes which the prospect of overcoming the mentioned deficiencies aroused, can be seen in the report of Karl Lowenstein, "Report on the Research Panel on Comparative Government," *American Political Science Review*, XXXVIII (1944), 540-549.

2. David Easton, *A Framework for Political Analysis* (Englewood Cliffs, N.J.: Prentice-Hall, 1965), pp. 17-18.

3. David Truman, "The Impact on Political Science of the Revolution in the Behavioral Sciences," *Research Frontiers in Politics and Government* (Washington, D.C.: Brookings Institution, 1955), p. 212: "By way of preliminary summary, the developments in the behavioral sciences over the past quarter century . . . appear a good deal more revolutionary in the realm of technique than in that of validated and expanded theory."

4. Easton, pp. 8-10.

5. Gabriel Almond and G. Bingham Powell, Jr., *Comparative Politics: A Developmental Approach* (Boston: Little, Brown, 1966): "Historically, comparative government and political theory had been closely connected. . . But in the early decades of the twentieth century the two fields separated, with political theory becoming an essentially historical subject matter, and comparative or foreign government becoming a formal and descriptive study of the great powers of Western Europe . . ." (p. 4). "[Recent trends in comparative theory] point in the direction of a unified theory of politics. Thus, the classic relationship between comparative government and political theory is in the process of being re-established" (p. 9).

6. Cf. Heinz Eulau, *The Behavioral Persuasion in Politics* (New York: Random House, 1963) and Robert Dahl, "The Behavioral Approach in Political Science: Epitaph for a Monument to a Successful Protest," *American Political Science Review*, LV (1961), 1763-1772.

7. "Penumbra" is a term used by some linguistic analysts to designate the connotations and family terms that cluster around a particular word.

8. The term is Glendon Schubert's. He contrasts "behavioralism," which he identifies as interested in theory construction, with "empiricism," which he identifies as interested in collecting facts and refining methodology without much interest in theory construction. Presumably, though, if theory must be either empirical or normative, he would clearly include behavioralism in the former camp. Cf. *Judicial Behavior* (Chicago: Rand McNally Co., 1964).

9. Charles F. Cnudde and Deane E. Newbauer, *Empirical Democratic Theory* (Chicago: Markham Publishing Co., 1969), pp. 1-3.

10. Schubert, p. 4.

11. The usual interpretation here is that Aristotle was partly empirical, but not wholly so. He was not aware of the gap between empirical and normative theory, the argument goes, and at times mixed his descriptions of reality in with other kinds of statements which did not really belong there. With the advantage of our own wisdom, though, so the argument goes, we can separate the wheat from the chaff by our standards. Cf. Harold Lasswell

and Abraham Kaplan, *Power and Society* (New Haven: Yale University Press, 1950).

12. This approach is based upon assumptions about the working of the intellect which run counter to the implications of much modern thought, the father of which, appropriately enough in this conext, was Descartes. Descartes stands as the prime example of one who propounded revolutionary ontological notions while focusing on ostensibly methodological problems. In actuality, changes in epistemology cannot escape their foundations in a change view of reality, even where the impetus for the change lies partly in the demonstrated fruitfulness of a new method. As Karl Mannheim has said, "Although epistemology claims to furnish a standard in terms of which the truth of metaphysical systems can be judged, it turns out itself to have its basis in definite metaphysical positions" (*Essays in the Sociology of Knowledge*, Paul Kecskemeti, ed. [New York: Oxford University Press, 1952], p. 112).

13. Perhaps it is misleading, strictly speaking, to talk of a common origin, since each of the features of empiricism mentioned had its precursors. For example, seventeenth-century nominalism clearly had a forerunner in the theological nominalism of Duns Scotus and William of Occam. As a group, possessed of a clear familial relationship and articulated as a gestalt, however, these ideas did arise together.

14. The term is Polanyi's (cf. op. cit.). I have also discovered the use of this term by Friedrich von Hayek, although it has several connotations in his hands that are not intended here; cf. *The Counterrevolution of Science* (Glencoe, Ill: The Free Press, 1952). In contrast, Polanyi's use of the term and my own are virtually isomorphic.

15. Alfred North Whitehead, *Science and the Modern World* (New York: Mentor Books, 1948), p. 56.

16. Besides Whitehead, the following works are extremely helpful accounts of various facets of the seventeenth century's intellectual revolution: Alexandre Koyré, *From the Closed World to the Infinite Universe* (New York: Harper Torchbooks, 1958); Basil Wiley, *The Seventeenth Century Background* (Garden City, N.Y.: Doubleday, 1953); Edwin A. Burtt, *The Metaphysical Foundations of Modern Physical Science*, 2nd. ed. (London: Routledge & Kegan Paul, 1959); and Milio Capek, *The Philosophical Impact of Contemporary Physics* (Princeton, N.J.: Van Nostrand, 1961).

17. Aristotle *Physics* V.2.225b: "In respect of substance there is no motion."

18. Ibid. V.1.225a.

19. Ibid. III. 1.200b.

20. Ibid. V.6.229b: "For rest is the privation of motion and the privation of anything may be called its contrary."

21. Cf. Herbert Butterfield, *The Origins of Modern Science*, rev. ed. (New York: Collier Books, 1962), esp. chap. 1.

22. Thomas Kuhn, *The Structure of Scientific Revolutions* (Chicago: Pheonix Books, 1962), p. 77.

23. Thomas Hobbes, *English Works*, William Molesworth, ed. (London: John Bohn, 1839), I, viii.

24. René Descartes, *Rules for the Direction of the Mind*, E.S. Haldane and G.R.T. Ross, trans., Great Book Series, vol. 31 (Chicago: University of Chicago Press, 1952), p. 23.

25. Butterfield, p. 15: "Of all intellectual hurdles which the human mind has confronted and has overcome in the last fifteen hundred years, the one which seems to me to have been the most amazing in character and the most stupdendous in the scope of its consequences is the one relating to the problem of motion."

26. Technically, the world was seen by most seventeenth-century thinkers as "indefinite" or "indeterminate" rather than as strictly "infinite." Cf. Koyré. This distinction is irrelevant to our present concern, however.

27. Hobbes, *English Works*, I, viii.

28. Aristotle, *Physics* III.1.200b.

29. Cf. A. Schwegler's observation that "Der Ausdruch 'Substanz' hat in der modernen philosophischen Terminologie seit Spinoza eine Bedeutung gewonnen, die dem Begriffe der artistotelischen 'ousia' fast gerade entgegengesetzt ist." Quoted by Joseph Owens in *The Doctrine of Being in the Aristotelian Metaphysics*, 2nd ed. (Toronto: Pontifical Institute of Medieval Studies, 1963), p. 139.

30. Hobbes, *Leviathan*, Everyman ed. (New York: E.P. Dutton Co., 1950), p. 3.

31. Cf. *Essay Concerning Human Understanding*, II, 23, 2. As in so many cases, however, Locke keeps one foot in the older world even as he advances into the new. In this context, he continues to talk about substances as realities intermediate between simple ideas, which are unequivocal and natural, and mixed modes, which are quite arbitrary categories of things. How these substances are grounded in a world of primary qualities remains less than clear.

32. Aristotle *Metaphysics* II.2.994b: "Further, those who speak thus [i.e., to the effect that essences are reducible] destroy science; for it is not possible to have this till one comes to the unanalyzable terms." Descartes, Hobbes, et. al. would have agreed with the latter half of this contention. However, they had a radically different view of what was unanalyzable; and this difference was a function of their different cosmology.

33. Ibid. XII.3.1070a.

34. Ibid. I.3.983a.

35. This explanatory impotence had become an object of derision with the decadence of scholasticism. Moliere parodied the scholastic aspirant who was applauded for explaining that opium made you sleepy because of its "dormative properties," and Hobbes snorted that "for physiques, that is, the knowledge of the subordinate and secondary causes of natural events, they render none at all, but empty words" (*Leviathan*, p. 597).

36. Hobbes, *English Works*, I, 16.

37. Ibid.

38. Ibid., p. 17.

39. Whitehead, p. 101: "Evolution is reduced to the role of being another word for the description of the changes of the external relations between portions of matter. There is nothing to evolve, because one set of external

relations is as good as any other set of external relations. There can merely be change, purposeless and unprogressive."

40. *Discourse on Method*, E.S. Haldane and G.R.T. Ross, trans. Great Books Series, vol. 31 (Chicago: University of Chicago Press, 1952), p. 52.

41. *Rules for Direction*, p. 24.

42. Ibid., p. 25.

3 The Legacy of Objectivism—Part 1

The objectivist model of reality and its corollaries are not simply matters for the curiosity of antiquarians, for the tenets of objectivism persist to the present day in the form of basic presuppositions about the nature of reality and knowledge which have had an important structuring influence on various schools of contemporary thought. As Whitehead observed, in some ways the assumptions of the seventeenth century "are still reigning." Before moving to an analysis of the impact of the objectivist cluster of assumptions on contemporary political theory, it might be helpful to substantiate Whitehead's contention on a somewhat more general level.

The most rigorous attempt to formulate the implications for social theory of the new thought modes of the seventeenth century came in the work of Thomas Hobbes. In this respect, he may justly be considered the first systematic political theorist of modern times. Machiavelli sometimes has been considered to be the first modern theorist, but his modernity is essentially negative; that is, it consists in the discarding of the ethical setting within which the classical theorists had viewed political life. Moreover, in important respects, Machiavelli's basic paradigms were derived from centuries long past.[1] Hobbes, with conscious constructive originality, apprehended the deep implications of the new world view to which Galileo's thought-experiments had led and set out to develop its consequences for the understanding of politics.[2] Since the seventeenth-century world view which inspired Hobbes's efforts has remained influential into the twentieth century, some striking formal similarities can be found between some of his key assumptions and problems and the assumptions and problems of very recent thinkers.

An exhaustive analysis of these formal similarities would be a truly monumental task, far beyond its utility in the context of the present essay. The central analytical contention, however, need not await such an exhaustive analysis, but can instead be illustrated from selected instances. Those schools of thought which have most consistently and persistently tried to maintain the basic features of the objectivist paradigm are those which are broadly styled positivism and behaviorism. The parallel between some of Hobbes's conceptions and some of the ideas of the preeminent expositors of these outlooks is quite striking indeed. Moreover, since the objectivist model possesses some characteristic difficulties, there is a parallel similarity in the conceptual dilemmas faced by the modern positivists and behaviorists and their positivist-behaviorist forerunner.

The relationship between the outlooks of Hobbes, positivism, and behaviorism is one of overlap, not of identity. Each has its own distinctive ideas and concerns which distinguish it from the others. At least some of the fundamental assumptions of the objectivist tradition are operative in each case, however. The family relationships of these diverse intellectual schools, which span three centuries, have been noted elsewhere. Robert Dahl, for example, remarks in passing that "Hobbes's psychological assumptions bear a remarkable resemblance to the modern school of psychology often called Behaviorism."[3] And A.J. Ayer explicitly locates himself within the same intellectual tradition as Hobbes:

> When we consider that Hobbes and Bentham were chiefly occupied in giving definitions, and that the best part of J.S. Mill's work consists in a development of the analysis carried out by Hume, we may fairly claim that in holding that the activity of philosophizing is essentially analytic we are adopting a standpoint which has always been implicit in English empiricism.[4]

The transformed cosmological paradigm which lies behind the various tenets of objectivism in Hobbes was characterized, as the previous chapter noted, by an ontological homogeneity. The propositions of nominalism, the dichotomy of facts and values, the model of interacting appetites, and so on, all grew from the root model of a unidimensional world. When Hobbes physicalized, and thus eviscerated, Aristotle's idea of substance, he failed to formulate any framework for distinguishing different forms of reality and different forms of motion, the basic function which the rejected Aristotelian concept had performed. Since "substance" and "body" signified the same thing, as Hobbes put it, and since body was mathematicized space, Hobbes left himself with the task of finding a place for politics in a humanly empty world.

Logically, this self-appointed task was an impossibility. A world devoid of human substance simply cannot yield the necessary content which is the stuff of politics. In his early book on Hobbes, Leo Strauss captured the essence of the problem rather well:

> As traditional moral and political philosophy was, to some extent, based on traditional metaphysics, it seemed necessary, when traditional metaphysics were replaced by modern natural science, to base the new moral and political philosophy on the new science. Attempts of this kind could never succeed: traditional metaphysics were, to use the language of Hobbes's successors "anthropomorphistic and, therefore, a proper basis for a philosophy of things human; modern science, on the other hand, which tried to interpret nature by renouncing all "anthromorphisms," all conception of purpose and perfection, could, therefore, to say the least, contribute nothing to the understanding of things human, to the foundation of morals and politics.[5]

The new idea of motion introduced by Galileo nevertheless exerted some real influence on the way that Hobbes envisioned political life. This impact was formal and structural rather than substantive, more mythological than logical. The model of motion provided a principle of limitation, not content, but this contribution was extremely significant.[6] Strauss is quite correct, however, in pointing out the logical flaw which Hobbes never escaped—the impossibility of finding any human, political content in the model of reality which he adopted. This dilemma is one of the characteristic impasses of objectivism, and Hobbes resolved it in a manner which is also fairly characteristic. He simply resorted to his own observations and beliefs about human psychology and drew upon them to provide the substance of his model.[7]

Practically, such a step was almost unavoidable. Logically, however, this stratagem was quite illicit under the ground rules which Hobbes set for himself. Accordingly, this common attempt at escaping one of the characteristic conceptual dilemmas of objectivism might be termed the illicit infusion of human substance into an otherwise empty framework. In the case of Hobbes, the principal components of this infusion were the emotions of vainglory and the fear of violent death. These emotions were then conceived as operative in a fashion analogous to motions per se, and Hobbes had the basis from which he went on to develop his justification of Leviathan.

To maintain the homogeneity of his picture of human behavior, Hobbes conceived human actions and emotions in one of two ways. Those features which he accounted a part of reality he conceptualized on a continuum of appetite and aversion located on a unidimensional plane of inertial motion. Life, or "vitality," Hobbes concluded, drawing upon Harvey's discoveries about circulation, is "but a motion of limbs." The appetites and aversions are themselves "motions of the heart,"[8] and the will is essentially identical with appetite.[9] All of the realities of the human world are hammered into a single dimension. Those features not accounted real he consigned to the status of ghosts, or "phantasms." The homogeneous clarity of the world was thereby preserved.

This relentless reduction of reality to a single homogeneous plane, and the attendant problems, are also features of the twentieth-century psychological behaviorism of John Watson and B.F. Skinner. These psychological theorists explicitly endorse this ontological homogeneity, in which all of life's actions may be interpreted as more or less complicated manifestations of a single set of simple principles. The unidimensional construct basic to behaviorism, quite similar to Hobbes's appetite-aversion model, is that of the stimulus-response pattern. The basic position is expressed concisely in Watson's statement that "life's most complicated acts are but combinations of the simple stimulus-response patterns of behavior."[10] Those aspects of reality which cannot be assimilated to such a model are, as in Hobbes, given short shrift. Consciousness, mind, and will are seen as purely mythical fabrications which have "no functional significance, either in a theoretical analysis or in the practical control of behavior."[11]

The assumption of the homogeneity of the world brings with it corollary linguistic and methodological prescriptions. Such a congruence of substance and method is, of course, not peculiar to any one mode of thought, but the recognition of the relationship is important. Such recognition is especially important where, as in the case of positivism, a denial is made that any ontological views are implied at all. In Descartes and Hobbes it remained fairly clear that the intellectual method of "resolution" was related to a view of the world which saw it as resolvable into simple components. Similarly, if the world is viewed as ontologically homogeneous, then a single method and a single language[12] will be seen as adequate—in fact, as normative. The methodological and linguistic monism is stated by Skinner, then, when he says that "the events affecting an organism must be capable of description in the language of physical science."[13] As the linguistic form of the prescriptive "must be" reflects here, this injunction is contingent upon the predicated cosmology of "physical science." Otherwise, the prescription would have no foundation. The methodological monism, in turn, of course, serves in reciprocal fashion to buttress and confirm the ontological postulates which gave rise to it in the first place.

> Science supplies its own wisdom. It leads to a new conception of a subject matter, a new way of thinking about that part of the world to which it has addressed itself. If we are to enjoy the advantages of science in the field of human affairs, we must be prepared to adopt the working model of behavior to which a science will inevitably lead.[14]

The ontological unidimensionality shared by Hobbes and behaviorism, and the methodological-linguistic counterpart of this unidimensionality, lead to another characteristic confusion of objectivism. This confusion, which might be designated semantic conflation, involves the use of a single term to designate disparate phenomena, thereby attempting to reduce the whole group to a common level. To cite only one example of this ploy which can be found in Hobbes's writings, consider the following formulation:

> So that pleasure, love, and appetite, which is also called desire, are divers names for divers considerations of the same thing . . . . The name "lust" is used where it is condemned; otherwise it is called by the general word "love": for the passion is one and the same indefinite desire of different sex, as natural as hunger.[15]

The single terms "appetite" or "indefinite desire," Hobbes contended, were reflective of a real identity, whereas any "divers" names were essentially misleading.

The classic example of this semantic conflation in behaviorism is the very basic concept of response, upon which so much of the behaviorist superstructure rests. The basic model of the stimulus-response reflex arc is the equal and opposite reaction of physical objects in mathematically conceived space. It is essentially a mechanistic model, in other words. As Skinner reports, "a mechanical toy which imitated human behavior led to the theory of what we now call reflex action."[16] And Watson states, "The behaviorist is a mechanist? Yes, utterly."[17] This is basically what Hobbes meant when he conflated the concept of life into the concept of motion.[18] As a methodological prophylaxis against using any nonmechanist concepts in understanding behavior then, Clark

41

Hull's suggestion is "to regard, from time to time, the behaving organism as a completely self-maintaining robot, constructed of materials as unlike ourselves as may be."[19]

Thus the unidimensional signification of a mechanist reflex is insinuated into any situation of response. In everyday language, however, "response" is a "family" word,[20] serving to designate similarity between different realities. Insofar as there is a common element to responses, they are all forms of "answer" more than forms of reflex; but in any case there are clearly numerous forms of response which can hardly be satisfactorily conflated into a single dimension. "Response" may indeed refer to a reflex, as in "motor response" and "learned response."[21] But "response" in music refers to the chorus. In ecclesiastical language it refers to a liturgical verse sung or spoken in answer to the priest. In law "response" refers to accountability, as in "respondent" or "responsible." Etymologically, in fact, this latter meaning is perhaps most basic, since the Latin root *spondere* means "to promise" or "to pledge one's self." This kind of "response" implies an affirmative personal commitment and would actually be negated by an implication of automatic external causation. There are various types of response, then, which may be mechanical, chemical, nervous, intellectual, personal, or emotional. The behaviorist, however, exemplified by Skinner, wants to draw all of the uses of "response" into the single language-game of mechanism, and he accomplishes his purpose by a hegemonic linguistic operation that embodies a prior cosmological homogeneity.

The tactic of semantic conflation can also be viewed as one special instance of a more generalized tactic of objectivism—namely, the making of propositions under the guise of simply giving definitions. Actually, as we shall argue later on, the giving of definitions often performs propositional functions, a fact of which Aristotle was well aware, even if he gave it a distorted significance. The nominalism of the objectivists, however, obscures and denies this propositional function of definitions. The result is a habit of making propositions on fraudulent grounds; that is, synthetic statements are made in the form of analytic ones. Such a practice is characteristic of the objectivist tradition from Hobbes to the present day; and it has the added polemical bonus of denying an opponent legitimate grounds for disagreeing, since all that is conceded to be in question are presumably analytic definitions whose relationship to reality is purely a matter of convenience. Ayer's disclaimer about the synthetic functions of his undertaking runs as follows:

The validity of the analytic method is not dependent on any empirical, much less metaphysical, presupposition about the nature of things. For the philosopher, as an analyst, is not directly concerned with the physical properties of things. He is concerned only with the way in which we speak about them.[22]

If this were in fact the case, no one could have any quarrel with the positivist analyst, and Ayer in fact believes that there should be no divisions among philosophers, since theirs is wholly an analytic task.[23] In practice, however, the ostensive analysis turns out to be as much linguistically prescriptive as descriptive. The everyday usage of words is often confused and sometimes contradictory, and the culmination of the logical positivist's analysis turns out, therefore, to be advice about what should be done with certain words or forms of statements. This recommendation is made in the name of logical clarity.[24] What in fact happens is that the application of logical analysis to language for the sake of clarity very swiftly moves beyond the realm of pure analysis. In the name of clarity, the ostensive analyst suggests the advisable "proper" way to use or understand a word or statement which he claims to have been confused. The basis for this advice, quite properly, is a perception of the function which the word or statement performs; but a perception of function is implicitly an empirical—that is, synthetic—proposition, and the supposedly empirically neutral analytic enterprise winds up making significant ontological claims.[25]

The appeal to clarity is, in effect, a form of the Cartesian appeal to "clear and distinct ideas" as validation for particular views. And now, just as then, such an appeal represents the certainty of a mind unaware of its own presuppositions. The "translations" recommended by objectivists like Hobbes, Ayer, and Skinner are ultimately a linguistically clothed request to "see things my way," and this potent recommendation cannot legitimately wear the innocuous garb of logical analysis. Contrary to the positivist claim, the tasks of "defining knowledge, classifying propositions, and displaying the real nature of material things" are not "purely analytic,"[26] when "analytic" is taken to mean "purely logical."

Therefore, the entrée for many of Hobbes's contentions comes under the offering of definitions. For example, "the definition of injustice is no other than the not performance of covenant."[27] And, "Liberty or freedome, signifieth properly the absence of opposition; (by opposition, I mean externall impediments of motion;) and may be applied no lesse to irrational, and inanimate creatures, than to rational."[28] The basic point here is simply the potency of these definitions in juxtaposition with the nominalist's contention that names are simply "signs of our conceptions" and manifestly "not signs of the things themselves."[29] As a result, all of the critical interpretative decisions made in understanding the world are left quite groundless. What fills the vacuum, of course, are the views of the one who gives the definitions, but these views are presented in a way which obscures their status and thereby tries to preserve them from criticism. It is hard to find grounds to criticize views which themselves are presented without grounds.[30]

To cite a couple of contemporary examples of potent empirical claims offered in the form of linguistic clarification, consider Ayer's claim:

> To ask what is the nature of a material object is to ask for a definition of "material object," and this, as we shall shortly see, is to ask how propositions about material objects are to be translated into propositions about sense contents.[31]

In this instance, while we may gain some real insight into what we mean by "material object" by engaging in the process of translation which is enjoined, it is by no means clear what grounds exist to compel such a translation. Although phrased as a description, the above injunction is actually neither analytic nor verifiable. It becomes reasonable to suspect, then, that underlying this claim is the belief in the ontological primacy of sense-contents, represented by the hallmarks of alleged simplicity and clarity. Or consider Skinner's barbaric rendering of the injunction to "love thy neighbor":

> "You ought to love your neighbor" may be converted into the two statements: 1) "The approval of your fellow men is positively reinforcing to you" and 2) "loving your fellow men is approved by the group of which you are a member," both of which may be demonstrated scientifically.[32]

Such a translation, of course, simply destroys the traditional meaning of the key terms "love" and "ought" altogether.

The concept of reinforcement alluded to here by Skinner serves as an appropriate introduction to another conceptual dilemma strikingly characteristic of objectivism. The first dilemma reviewed was the problem of constructing social theory in the context of a humanly empty conceptual framework. The strategem resorted to in order to escape this dilemma was the illicit (in terms of objectivism's own ground rules) infusion of human substance on the basis of common sense experience. The second dilemma was the groundlessness of definitions, names, and concepts in a relentlessly nominalistic world. This dilemma, however, was simply taken as an opportunity to make important contentions on fraudulently innocuous grounds. Prominent among these linguistic feats was that of semantic conflation dictated by objectivist unidimensionality. The dilemma to be considered now is the explanatory lacuna which grows out of the utter rejection of any form of teleology.

One central feature of the seventeenth-century rejection of its scholastic tradition was the rejection of the Aristotelian notion of four kinds of causality. The complex of formal, final, material, and efficient causes which Aristotelian thought saw as determinative of particular events was reduced to efficient and material causes alone. As Hobbes put it, "The writers of metaphysics reckon up two other causes besides the efficient and material, namely, the essence, which some call the formal cause, and the end, or final cause; both of which are nevertheless efficient causes."[33] This rejection had important consequences in the area of social and psychological theory.

Whatever the weaknesses of the Aristotelian formulation, the concept of final cause served to explain the rather common fact of experience that biological developments do seem to have a kind of destination. Similarly, it expressed the widely experienced truth that most human action seems to be guided by some end or purpose. Because this kind of purposefulness was seen as characteristic of nature,[34] it made sense to speak of natural law as relevant to social and political order. Man was by nature a social animal, in the sense that his end, his completion, his fulfillment was possible only in and through society. Human order was oriented toward the final cause of the summum bonum and the strivings of political action were not considered to be adequately explicable without such a postulated perfection of social life.

A thorough objectivism, in renouncing final causality completely, rejects these political aspects of the Aristotelian notion along with the physical aspects. This pattern of rejection is consistent from Hobbes to the present day, and it results in some striking views about the nature of political action and in some equally striking explanatory lacunae.

Hobbes, with the lucidity of his relentless mind, recognized the consequences for social theory of the abandonment of any kind of concept of final cause quite clearly. Human motivation was, for him, to be understood on the same model as physical motion; that is, it was inertial. Man was not striving toward an end in his view, but was driven endlessly.[35] There was no place left for the summum bonum in his psychology since there was no place for it in his cosmology. "But for an utmost end, in which the ancient philosophers have placed felicity, and disputed much concerning the way thereto, there is no such thing in this world, nor way to it, more than to Utopia."[36] The image of human striving which emerges from this view Hobbes

45

expressed with great power in his metaphor of the race. As he saw clearly, to be consistent he must picture this race of life as endless, as having no goal or finish line.

> The comparison of the life of man to a race, though it hold not in every part, yet it holdeth so well for this our purpose, that we may thereby both see and remember almost all the passions before mentioned. But this race we must suppose to have no other goal, nor other garland, but being foremost. . . . [37]

This rejection of final causality in the area of social theory left two important explanatory lacunae which the final causal concepts of the summum bonum and natural law had filled in the Aristotelian and scholastic models. The first of these arises in the context of human political striving. The natural tendency of men toward the summum bonum ("as toward a divine likeness," according to Aquinas) served to explain their motivations, at least in significant part. That is, men behaved as they did because they were impelled by the final cause of their own as-yet-unattained perfection. Once this view is abandoned, the question becomes Why do men strive, when there is nothing to strive for? Or in the context of Hobbes's race, the question might be simply put, Why run? I think it has to be conceded that Hobbes's answer to this problem, his attempt to fill this explanatory gap, was another instance of what was referred to earlier as an illicit infusion of substance. That is, he answered the question of motivation by postulating that "restless desire of power after power," but the source of this answer was his common sense observations of human life rather than his cosmology.

The second gap had significant policy implications. One function of the final-cause notions in the classic tradition was to explain the sources of political order. If one asked for the sources of political order, the first reference of an Aristotelian would be to the fact that political order was a part of nature's fulfillment and that therefore significant natural forces were at work in its behalf. There is, of course, a certain optimism implicit in this view, an optimism reflected in the contrast between the view of political society held by the Aristotelian Aquinas and the considerably less sanguine view held by the Platonic and Manichean-influenced Augustine. Hobbes, also in contrast with Aristotelianism, was a cosmological pessimist, in the sense that so far from seeing nature as "everywhere the cause of order"[38] he saw it as a formless chaos. This chaotic aspect of nature he expressed in his image of the "state of nature," which was the now famous "war of all against all." To fill the gap which the loss of final causality left, then, Hobbes turned to that mortal god, the Leviathan. The source of political order had to be seen as entirely artificial, since there was no order in a nature bereft of final causes.

These conceptual developments are significant and intriguing in their own right and worthy of more attention than such a hasty overview. However, the immediate purpose is not to explore them exhaustively but to demonstrate the persistence of the same basic conceptual pattern and resultant problems into contemporary modes of thought. In the case of behaviorism, this persistence is especially striking.

The first explanatory lacuna left by the abandonment of any conception of final cause was, as exemplified in Hobbes, in the area of accounting for human motivation. The concept developed by behaviorism to fill this lacuna is the notion of reinforcement. Reinforcement, an idea which Skinner takes over from Pavlov, refers to "all events which strengthen behavior."[39] Essentially, this concept was developed as a replacement and functional equivalent within the limits of efficient causes for final causes. The Aristotelian tradition had used final causality as an empirical theory to explain the fact that men clearly find some experiences much more satisfactory than others and will therefore respond positively to them and seek them in the future. In Aristotelian terms, this phenomenon was the process of a man striving toward his *telos* as a mature human being. What this *telos* was could be found by an empirical inquiry into the satisfactions of a mature man, and why there was a *telos* was answered by the hypothesis of final causes in nature.

The rejection of teleology in all forms removes the theoretical basis for such an explanation without removing the realities of human motivation that gave rise to such an explanation. The concept of reinforcement represents the behaviorist response to this conceptual dilemma, but that it is not a very adequate response becomes evident when Skinner faces up to the problems: "What Events are Reinforcing?" and "Why is a Reinforcer Reinforcing?"[40] In answering the first question, Skinner concludes that "the only defining characteristic of a reinforcing stimulus is that it reinforces."[41] And in seeking to answer the question of why a reinforcer reinforces, Skinner really runs into problems engendered by the prohibition against references to final causes. He realizes that a common sense version of teleology seems to be the logical answer, but he also realizes that such an answer would be illicit under his premises.

> Why does reinforcement reinforce? One theory is that an organism repeats a response because it finds the consequences "pleasant" or "satisfying." But in what sense is this an explanation within the

framework of a natural science? "Pleasant" and "satisfying" apparently do not refer to physical properties of reinforcing events, since the physical sciences use neither these terms nor any equivalents.[42]

After casting about for a satisfactory answer to his dilemma, Skinner concludes with an a priori attempt to give reinforcement a biological source, while conceding that he really can't answer his own question.

> A biological explanation of reinforcing power is perhaps as far as we can go in saying why an event is reinforcing. Such an explanation is probably of little help in a functional analysis, for it does not provide us with any way of identifying a reinforcing stimulus as such before we have tested its reinforcing power upon a given organism. We must therefore be content with a survey in terms of the effects of stimuli upon behavior. [43]

Ironically, then, the total avoidance of any concept of final cause results in the same form of explanatory impotence as the inappropriate use of final-cause explanations in Aristotelian physics. Hobbes expressed the seventeenth-century derision of Aristotelian final-cause explanations in physics by complaining:

> If you desire to know why some kind of bodies sink naturally downwards toward the earth, and others goe naturally from it; the school will tell you out of Aristotle, that the bodies that sink downward are heavy; and that this heaviness is it that causes them to descend: But if you ask what they mean by heavinesse, they will define it to be an endeavor to goe to the center of the earth: so that the cause why things sink downward, is an endeavor to be below: which is as much to say, that bodies descend or ascend, because they doe.[44]

Paraphrasing Hobbes only slightly and making the appropriate substitutions, one could say that if you desire to know why some human experiences are sought after, the behaviorists will tell you that it is because of reinforcement. But if you ask what they mean by "reinforcement," they will define it by making a survey of those experiences which are sought after. Which is as much to say that some experiences are sought after because they are.

The second explanatory lacuna left by the abandonment of final-cause explanations is, as already seen in Hobbes, related to the problem of the sources of political order. If nature has no ends, then political authority can, and in Hobbes's view must, become unlimited. That is, political authority can be unlimited, for there are no natural limitations set by natural order. And for Hobbes, because there is no political order by nature, the artificial Leviathan must create it by fiat. Skinner's behaviorist utopia, Walden Two, seems at first to proceed upon the same premises. The picture of a situation of total social control must be premised upon the absence of natural ends and limits on the actions of both conditioner and conditioned. The conditioner steps outside of nature for the sake of determining what human nature shall henceforth mean; and the object of conditioning sinks beneath the level of nature to become a pure artifact. Such seems to be the envisioned situation at Walden Two.

> When we ask what Man can make of Man, we don't mean the same thing by "man" in both instances. We mean to ask what a few men can make of mankind. And that's the all-absorbing question of the twentieth century. What kind of world can we build—those of us who understand the science of behavior?[45]

The lack of a source of political order in a nature bereft of final causes is to be filled by the will and expertise of the behavioral scientist acting as a social programmer.

However, Skinner apparently finds it impossible to maintain his own objectivist ground rules rigidly. For it is one of the interesting features of the conceptual substratum of Walden Two that occasionally limitations on the will of the social programmer are mentioned and are implicitly conceived in a way that would do justice to an Aristotelian or to a Shakespearean Elizabethan. At one point the reader is asked to "look at the monasteries, lamaseries, and other forms of unnatural societies."[46] And the founder of Walden Two insists at another point that "Walden Two must be *naturally* satisfying."[47] These injunctions go a long way to soften the tyrannical implications of the relationship between the conditioning manipulator and the conditioned artifact, but they are not really intelligible injunctions in the context of Skinner's explicit rejection of natural ends. Skinner humanizes his political vision, but at the cost of logical consistency. Once again, an illicit infusion of substance has been made into the objectivist framework, this time to fill the vacuum left where final causality had once provided a natural source and limit to political order.

Notes

1. Cf. Herbert Butterfield, *The Statecraft of Machiavelli* (New York: Collier Books, 1962).

2. A more complete account of the impact of the new cosmology on Hobbes is contained in Thomas A. Spragens, "Thomas Hobbes: The Politics of Motion," (University Press of Kentucky, 1973).

3. Robert Dahl, *Modern Political Analysis* (Englewood Cliffs, N.J.: Prentice-Hall, 1963), p. 113.

4. A.J. Ayer, *Language, Truth, and Logic*, 2nd ed. (New York; Dover Publications, 1946), pp. 55-56.

5. Leo Strauss, *The Political Philosophy of Hobbes* (Chicago: Phoenix Books, 1963), p. ix.

6. Cf. Spragens.

7. In explaining why he could publish *De cive* before *De corpore* and *De homine*, which treated the fundamental principles of his philosophy and which should logically have come first, cf. Hobbes, *English Works,* William Molesworth, ed. (London: John Bohn, 1839), II, xx: "Therefore it happens that what was last in order, is yet come forth first in time. And the rather, because I saw that, grounded on its own principles sufficiently known by experience, it would not stand in need of the former sections."

8. Ibid., I, 401.

9. Ibid., 409: "The same thing is called both will and appetite."

10. John B. Watson, *The Ways of Behaviorism* (New York: Harper Brothers, 1928), p. 3.

11. B.F. Skinner, *Science and Human Behavior* (New York: Macmillan Co., 1953), p. 181.

12. I use "language" here in the sense that Wittgenstein uses the term— to refer to an interrelated pattern of verbal conventions which are based upon a single matrix of grammatical rules. These grammatical rules then determine the meanings of the words which play the language-game which they have created, and also determine the range of what is meaningful at all. Cf. Ludwig Wittgenstein, *Philosophical Investigations*, G.E.M. Anscombe, trans. (Oxford: Blackwell's, 1953).

13. Skinner, *Science and Human Behavior*, p. 36.

14. Ibid., p. 6.

15. Hobbes, *English Works*, IV, pp. 32, 48, respectively.

16. Skinner, *Science and Human Behavior*, p. 46.

17. Watson, p. 42.

18. Although not crucial to our central concern here, it is interesting and perhaps a helpful genetic explanation to note that the common position of Hobbes and behaviorism is an inversion of a pattern established by Aristotle, who divided movements into natural movements and spontaneous movements. The former had a cause (i.e., a final cause) whereas the latter were "happenings" that we uncaused, (i.e., directed by no *telos*). These spontaneous, uncaused movements were called *to automata*. With the destruction of final causes in the seventeenth century, automaticity became the hallmark rather than the antithesis of nature, and spontaneous motion became an antithesis rather than a synonym for *to automata*. But since anything outside the realm of automatic (i.e., efficiently caused) movement became inconceivable, "spontaneity" became a meaningless concept. Therefore, Hobbes could claim that automata have a kind of life, and Skinner clearly states the inefficacy of the notion of spontaneity: "But arguments for spontaneity, and for the explanatory entities which spontaneity seems to demand, are of such form that they must retreat before the accumulating facts. Spontaneity is negative evidence; it points to the weakness of a current scientific explanation; but does not in itself prove an

alternative version. By its very nature, spontaneity must yield ground as a scientific analysis is able to advance" (*Science and Human Behavior*, p. 48).

19. Clark Hull, *Principles of Behavior* (New York: Appleton-Century-Crofts, 1943), pp. 27-28.

20. Cf. Wittgenstein.

21. Even here, the imputation of a univocal and automatic reflex is probably misleading. Cf. Maurice Merleau-Ponty, *The Structure of Behavior*, Alden L. Fisher, trans. (Boston: Beacon Press, 1963).

22. Ayer, *Language, Truth, and Logic*, p. 57.

23. Ibid., p. 133.

24. Cf. A.J. Ayer, "On the Analysis of Moral Judgments," in *Philosophical Essays* (London: Macmillan & Co., 1954), pp. 232-233: "Now when a philosopher asserts that something 'really' is not what it 'really' is, or 'really' is what it 'really' is not . . . it should not always be assumed that he is merely making a mistake. Very often, what he is doing, although he may not know it, is to recommend a new way of speaking, not just for amusement, but because he thinks that the old, the socially correct, way of speaking is logically misleading, or that his own proposal brings out certain points more clearly. . . . When one considers how these ethical statements are actually used, it may be found that they function so very differently from other types of statement that it is advisable to put them in a separate category altogether. . . . This may seem to be an arbitrary procedure, but I hope to show that there are good reasons for adopting it. . . . The only relevant consideration is that of clarity."

25. Stuart Hampshire has noted this phenomenon, and he expressed it this way: "Philosophy as linguistic analysis is therefore unwillingly lured into a kind of descriptive anthropology. The principle of individuation, by which one use of language is distinguished from another, has to be founded upon some division of human powers and activities that is external to language itself" (*Thought and Action* [New York: Viking Press, 1959], p. 234).

26. Cf. Ayer, *Language, Truth, and Logic*, p. 52.

27. Hobbes, *Leviathan*, Everyman ed. (New York: E.P. Dutton Co., 1950), p. 119.

28. Ibid., p. 177.

29. Hobbes, *English Works*, I, 17; cf. p. 16: "How can any man imagine that the names of things were imposed from their natures."

30. The grounds, such as they are, are "clarity." The only response then becomes What clarifies things for you doesn't do so for me. And this is a reasonable rejoinder. What never gets squarely confronted is the question, Why?

31. Ayer, *Language, Truth, and Logic*, p. 52.

32. Skinner, *Science and Human Behavior*, p. 429.

33. Hobbes, *English Works*, I, 131.

34. Aristotle *Metaphysics* I.3.984b: "When one man said, then, that reason was present—as in animals, so throughout nature—as the cause of all order and all arrangement, he seemed like a sober man in contrast with the random talk of his predecessors."

35. Hobbes, *Leviathan*, p. 79: "I put for a generall inclination of all mankind, a perpetuall and restless desire of Power after power, that ceaseth only in death."

36. Hobbes, *English Works*, IV, 33.

37. Ibid., pp. 52-53.

38. Aristotle *Physics* VIII.1.252a.

39. Skinner, *Science and Human Behavior*, p. 65.

40. These are chapter titles in *Science and Human Behavior*.

41. Ibid., p. 72.

42. Ibid., p. 81.

43. Ibid., p. 81.

44. Hobbes, *Leviathan*, p. 597.

45. This is the founder of Walden Two speaking, in Skinner *Walden Two* (New York: Macmillan Co., 1948), p. 135.

46. Ibid., p. 172.

47. Ibid., p. 175.

4   The Legacy of Objectivism—Part 2

Twentieth-century positivism has adopted the view that facts and values are utterly dichotomous, a view that was a logical outgrowth of seventeenth-century cosmology. Part of its program has, in fact, been an attempt to articulate and specify more fully the precise nature and limitations of statements of fact and statements of value. The attempt to specify the characteristics of what shall qualify as factual statements led to a quest for an ideal language and to the famous verifiability principle of meaning; and the attempt to understand value statements more fully led to the equally well known emotive theory of ethics. In both cases, positivism has remained true to the logical implications of objectivist epistemological and ontological assumptions. And in both cases, the result has been some highly vexing conceptual problems and explanatory dilemmas.

The objectivist epistemological program was a superficially paradoxical dialectic of total doubt and absolute certainty. It was presumed that the former served as a means to the latter. This belief is quite clear in the writings of Descartes, of course, who was the original proponent of the methodological principle of doubt. Said Descartes;

> It is now some years since I detected how many were the false beliefs that I had from my earliest youth admitted as true, and how doubtful was everything I had since constructed on this basis, and from that

time I was convinced that I must once for all seriously undertake to rid myself of all the opinions which I had formerly accepted, and commence to build anew from the foundation. . . .[1]

This program of doubt seems to be quite radical: one must rid himself of all the opinions which he formerly held. But the final outcome of this process was not seen by Descartes as final doubt. So far from being a purveyor of epistemological despair, Descartes saw himself as prophetically pointing the way to indubitable and unshakable truth. "And finally," he said, "it [the method of doubt] makes it impossible for us ever to doubt those things which we have once discovered to be true."[2] The "radical" doubt of Descartes was in full context only a brilliantly illuminated grace note in what was a melody of supreme certitude.

One feature of this promised certitude would be the development of an ideal language—ideal in that it expressed the unambiguous clarity of the new "clear and distinct" universe. Such a language, obviously, should be modeled upon the language of mathematics, which possessed the desired attributes.[3] Many of the representative giants of the seventeenth and eighteenth centuries concerned themselves with this quest, among them Newton, Descartes, and Robert Boyle. Since it was a logical outgrowth of objectivist presuppositions, the search for an ideal language extended into the twentieth century along with the assumptions which gave rise to it. It found new life and inspiration in the work of Bertrand Russell, especially.

The achievement of Russell and Whitehead, in the *Principia Mathematica*, of reducing complex mathematical propositions to inferences from a relatively small number of logical axioms led to the hope that this feat could be replicated in the context of language. The early analytic movement in philosophy which Russell led was, as he said, "a kind of logical doctrine which seems to me to result from the philosophy of mathematics."[4] Those who shared this hope felt, then, that "Russell had provided the paradigms of success for all to imitate, and had provided the technique and the skeleton of a perfect language, the language of *Principia Mathematica*, in which to do it."[5] As John Wisdom recalls it, "We who were the bright young things of the logico-analytic era welcomed the change from the absurdity of exploring the universe in an armchair to the pleasure of a dance beneath the brilliant lights of *Principia Mathematica*."[5] The Cartesian-objectivist linguistic program continued with new zest. Through the linguistic translation of complex and ambiguous entities into their presumably simple, clear, and distinct components, the final goal was to be the attainment of an irreducible residue of real linguistic symbols.

In the period since the onset of the logical empiricist quest for a perfect language, the analytical enterprise has undergone a radical transformation. Since, however, the tradition has remained integral and in many cases the practitioners the same, the deep character of this transformation is sometimes not fully appreciated by those outside the tradition. In a certain sense, the British philosophers of language continue to pursue the goal of clarity by means of analysis. But this continuity should not be allowed to obscure the wholly different justification, rationale, and approach that is now taken, for central to the development from logical atomism to logical positivism and from logical positivism to contemporary analysis has been the abandonment of the objectivist notion of a single real language of wholly specifiable components.

One of the stumbling blocks which led to this abandonment was the development of alternative calculi that were as correctly formed as that of the *Principia*. This development made it rather difficult to continue to regard the calculus of the *Principia* as the skeleton of a perfect language, mirroring the basic structure of the universe. Perhaps more important, however, was the realization that Russell's early successes in resolving dilemmas by translating statements such as "The king of France is bald" into component propositions simply were not replicable in other areas. As Wisdom observed;

> And when the philosophical problems were recast in the linguistic mode "Can sentences of sort X be translated into sentences not of sort X?" it seemed essential to find sentences not of sort X which meant neither more nor less than sentences of sort X. But these translations could not be found. And this was not because of the accidental paucity of the English, French, or German language. It was no accident at all. . . . in other words, a typical metaphysical difficulty about what is expressed by sentences of sort X cannot be met by translating those sentences into others. [7]

The result of the failure of the enterprise of reductive analysis left the analytical school with two apparent options. The first was to cling to the ideal of logical purity, therefore abandoning ordinary language altogether, and to construct artificial languages which possessed the desired qualities. This option was taken by some Continental positivists. British philosophers, on the other hand, chose the second alternative, which was to seek to clarify ordinary language and to abandon the notion that the goal of such clarification was reduction of this language to simple reports of experience. The philosophical task is still analytic, but it is a very different kind of analysis than the old form, which was heir to the objectivist epistemological method of resolution. It is extremely important that this fact be appreciated by the outsider, for what in fact has occurred here is the rejection as illusory of one perennial component of the objectivist doctrine.[8]

Intertwined with this downfall of one of the components of the objectivist tradition were the vicissitudes of the positivist verifiability criterion of meaning. Once again, this formulation was a continuation and attempt to elaborate upon the empiricist tradition. Specifically, the verifiability criterion was an attempt to specify more fully what shall qualify as a factual proposition in the context of presuppositions which dichotomize facts and values. The standards which it sets up are clearly an elaboration of Hume's position on what was meaningful and what was not.[9]

The verifiability criterion has seen several incarnations, each modification resulting from an attempt to meet an objection raised against it. Essentially, however, it states that a proposition is meaningful only if steps can be taken to verify its truth or falsehood. One must be able to formulate in the case of a genuinely meaningful statement "what observations would lead him to accept the proposition as being true, or reject it as being false."[10] This basic criterion was designed to perform two functions. In the first place, it was to serve as a criterion of demarcation, or test for determining what kind of assertions could be admitted as meaningful. Second, the criterion was to designate a procedure for determining what the meaning of a proposition was. This procedural aspect of the verifiability principle was embodied in the operationalist doctrine that the meaning of a concept was no more and no less than the physical operations performed by the experimenter when he utilized the concept. In short, a proposition was meaningful if, and only if, it could be, within limits, verified or falsified; and the meaning of a proposition was the mode of its verification or falsification.

Today, the verifiability criterion has been either radically reinterpreted or attenuated to the disappearing point in both of its original functions. Some of the modifications have been relatively minor and technical.[11] Others are major and more substantive. In its function as a criterion of demarcation, the verifiability principle was in the embarrassing position of being nonsensical on the basis of its own principles. That is, it was neither verifiable nor tautological according to its own ground rules and hence was meaningless. Since the verifiability principle was clearly not an empirical generalization about the customary usage of language and was also clearly not a tautology, it had to be seen as an a priori rule of language. By positivism's own standards, however, such rules were purely conventional and purely arbitrary. No one was logically compelled to accept the rule unless he felt like doing so.

This paradox of the verifiability principle and the attempt to resolve it was one of the avenues which led to the abandonment of positivism in favor of linguistic analysis. In this way the principle's difficulties reinforced the momentum created by the failure to devise any kind of single perfect language. Analysts such as John Wisdom, J.L. Austin, and C.L. Stevenson began to argue that the verifiability principle as a criterion of meaning really functioned as an observation about differences between various types of statements, together with a preference for one particular type.[12] This new understanding gave the principle cognitive status, but at the price of amending its originally intended significance quite radically. Viewing the verifiability criterion in this way indeed made it meaningful, but it did so only by recasting the whole notion of meaningfulness altogether. Considered both referentially and reflexively, the newly interpreted criterion suggested that the meaning of propositions had to be understood through their function. Referentially, the transformed verifiability principle served to acknowledge the difference in functioning between different kinds of grammatically identical propositions. Reflexively, the principle itself received its new meaning by reference to its own functioning to point out these differing linguistic functions. The outcome was the now famous dictum Don't ask for the meaning, ask for the use.

In its operationalist guise as a procedure for the attribution of meaning, the verifiability principle underwent an almost equally radical transformation, in this case by becoming attenuated virtually to the vanishing point. It soon proved impossible to maintain in any direct sense the principle that the meaning of a concept or proposition is simply the means of its verification if the principle is to have any real plausibility vis-à-vis scientific theories, for the theoretical concepts of science are generally related to experience only indirectly. Some writers attempted to counter this difficulty by introducing the concept of symbolic operations, but this revision involves attenuating the original position so greatly that very little remains. As Abraham Kaplan put it, "Once 'symbolic operations' are included, the operationalist principle is so watered down that it no longer provides methodological nourishment. To find what a scientific concept means, examine how you apply it, or how you apply other concepts related to it. But what else has any one ever done? Indeed, what else is there to do?"[13]

Reinforcing these logical difficulties is the recognition by thoughtful historians of science that the positivist model of verification does not depict the actual practice of advances in scientific theory. As Kuhn observes, "To the historian, at least, it makes little sense to suggest that verification is establishing the agreement of fact with theory. All historically significant theories have agreed with the facts, but only more or less."[14]

As a result of these developments, verification must now be seen as a proximate kind of validation and not as a satisfactory, ultimate answer to epistemological problems. A scientist may verify or falsify certain hypotheses but only relative to some criteria of order which for the moment he does not doubt. For example, a psychiatrist could verify by operational tests that a patient was suffering from an unresolved oedipal conflict, but in order to do so he would have to tacitly affirm criteria of interpreting reality which sustain the particular concept he is testing. He could conceivably in turn subject each of these criteria to a process of verification, but he could never subject the entire complex of mutually constituting concepts to verification against some neutral reality. His verification can be only serial and proximate, not all-at-once and ultimate.

The abandonment of the quest for an ideal language and the drastically revised assessment of verification represent an excision from some of the fundamental postulates of objectivism. These developments indicate that the traditional epistemological paradigm of the West since Descartes is "somehow askew"[15] and in need of replacement. This recognition shall be our point of departure for the constructive suggestions in the final chapters of this essay. For the moment, however, it is enough to emphasize the significance of these developments in the context of the objectivist assumptions which we have been discussing, for what is manifested here is the collapse of the linguistic and methodological components of the objectivist concept of factuality. The search for an ideal language was a logical outgrowth of the model of the factual world as unequivocal and unidimensional. The failure of the search reflects the inadequacy of its premises. The verifiability principle was a logical result of the belief in the certitude with which such facts could be known. The outcome of the objectivist program predicated upon its model of factuality, however, has been neither an ideal language nor certitude but rather a set of conceptual dilemmas not resolvable on objectivism's premises.

The corollary to the objectivist model of factuality was a distinctive interpretation of statements involving norms, or what were called, in positivist terminology, values. Standards of performance, ideals, potentials, obligations, and so on literally had no place within the spatial cosmos of objectivism. Accordingly, statements involving such standards or concepts had to be interpreted as something other than descriptive. That is, such statements had to be seen as pseudopropositions on a priori grounds. There are many manifestations of this theoretical assumption of objectivism. The diligence of behaviorism in prohibiting any explanations of human behavior involving concepts like satisfying, which we examined earlier, is one of these manifestations. The paradigmatic case of the objectivist interpretation of values, however, is probably the positivist view of statements about obligation and goodness.

The basic objectivist position on the significance, or lack thereof, of concepts of obligation and goodness was clearly articulated by Hobbes centuries ago. Essentially, this position holds that normative statements cannot be descriptive of facts, since there is no tension of potential and actual, no hierarchy and heterogeneity, in the world of homogeneous body. Therefore, statements predicated upon these rejected assumptions must be interpreted as having a reference somewhere other than in objective reality. This reference is found to be, then, to the emotions of the speaker making the value statement. Therefore, a normative statement must be seen as an announcement of one's feelings rather than a proposition about the world, and any grammatical similarity between such announcements and genuine factual propositions must be seen as fortuitous and misleading. Hobbes's formulation of this principle runs as follows:

> But whatsoever is the object of any man's appetite or desire; that is it, which he for his part calleth good; and the object of his hate, and aversion, evill; and of his contempt, vile and inconsiderable. For these words of good, evill, and contemptible, are ever used with relation to the person that useth them: There being nothing simply and absolutely so; nor any common rule of good and evill, to be taken from the nature of the objects themselves.[16]

Several centuries later, Ayer approached the issue in virtually an identical way: "But in every case in which one would commonly be said to be making an ethical judgment, the function of the relevant ethical word is purely 'emotive.' It is used to express feeling about certain objects, but not to make any assertion about them."[17]

More careful consideration of the actual use of normative language, in conformity with the approach of the newer linguistic analysis, has indicated that this emotive theory of ethics, which is implied by the objectivist fact-value dichotomy, is simplistic and misleading. Normative language functions in many, many ways, some of them clearly descriptive rather than emotive. Any attempt to do justice to this complex topic would constitute a major digression from our central purposes, but an example of the difficulties of the emotive theory may be cited to illustrate further the pattern of conceptual dilemmas which derive from the various aspects of objectivism.

One fairly common form of assertion in everyday discourse

contrasts the imperative of obligation with personal preferences. An example would be, "I ought to go home and play with the kids, even though I would prefer to play nine more holes of golf." The emotive theory, which interprets value statements involving "ought" and "good" as statements of preference, runs into great difficulty in simply trying to explain why such an assertion should be meaningful at all. Positivism would, for the sake of clarity, have value statements translated into statements taking the form of "I prefer X." Applying that rule of translation in the present instance, however, would result in the truly nonsensical formulation "I would prefer to go home and play with the kids, even though I would prefer to play nine more holes of golf." A relatively intelligible contrast is transformed by positivist dictum into an identity that does not permit contrast. Either the user of our exemplary assertion must be accused of extraordinary confusion or else the emotive theory needs considerable revision.

One might imagine a positivist feeling that one "ought not to say things" like our example—which on positivist principles could be translated that the positivist would prefer that such statements not be made, which, in turn, would probably be true. Less whimsically, an attempt could be made to save the emotive theory by distinguishing different kinds and levels of preference, to preserve the intelligibility of the grammatical contrast while maintaining the basic thesis. This approach would solve a relatively simple case where, let us say, the presence of a strong-armed and strong-willed wife is an unarticulated assumption. In this case our original statement might mean: "I would prefer playing golf to playing with my kids, but if I do that my wife will belt me one and I would prefer that even less." In other instances, however, such a simple solution is hardly possible. The speaker may simply be referring to his sense that he stands responsible for the legitimate needs of his children and that he is therefore morally bound to act in a certain way. Any attempt to translate this situation into preference language either is inadequate and reductive or else must imply some ontological grounds for distinct and hierarchical kinds of preference, grounds that cannot be found in the positivist image of the factual world. Put simply, the positivist view of value statements cannot account for the fact that obligation and preference stand more often as antagonists than as identities.

The last chapter and the present one have covered a considerable number of topics which are all related to the objectivist paradigm. The following outline should help to recapitulate the argument to this point, and to indicate the logic of relationship within it (cf. Figure 1.)

Figure 1

Feature of Objectivist Viewpoint	Subsequent Conceptual Dilemma:	
	A. Theoretical Failure or Incapacity	B. Fraudulent solution
spatial cosmology	Humanly empty world	Illicit infusion of human substance
radical nominalism	Groundlessness of complex definitions	Prescription and description under guise of analysis
all causes are efficient — no final causes	Explanatory lacunae in accounting for aspects of human motivation	Reinforcement
unidimensional cosmos	Failure to account for heterogeneity	Semantic conflation (permitted by nominalism)
unidimensional cosmos: and clarity, certitude, and univocality of facts	Failure in quest for ideal language	
fact-value dichotomy	Failures of verifiability principle	
A. Clarity and certainty of facts	A. Reflexive inconsistency as criterion of demarcation	
	B. Radical attentuation as a procedural guide	
	C. Misleading account of scientific theory status and formulation	
B. Purely emotive significance of value statements	Inability to account for meaningfulness of intelligible sentences	Misleading reduction of obligation to preference

Our basic thesis has been that the objectivist complex of presuppositions which grew out of the cosmological transformation attending the scientific revolution has resulted in numerous and related conceptual dilemmas from which it cannot extricate itself. Figure 1 capsulizes the principal grounds for that generalization. The spatiality of the cosmos as *res extensa* results in a human vacuum and therefore in a lack of criteria for human and political order. This failure is often compensated for by an infusion of human substance from experience, but this infusion is theoretically illicit. The homogeneity of the world leads to a radical nominalism, which in turn results in a lack of any basis for definitions of complex entities, that is, of any reality whose nature is more than mathematical. This nominalism then permits exhortations to translate, which are in fact covert descriptions and prescriptions rather than the pure analyses they are claimed to be. The abandonment of all conceptions of fulfillment or final causes leads to explanatory impotence in some areas of human motivation. This impotence is sometimes recognized, as in the case of Skinner; but only the most feeble and inadequate attempts at overcoming it are made, probably since it is not too profitable to spend much effort on patently unsolvable problems. Nominalism and the unidimensionality of the objectivist cosmos beget the phenomenon of semantic conflation to give a homogeneous accounting for heterogeneous realities. The belief in a world of Cartesian facts leads to a quest for a perfect language that turns out to be a mirage. The same basic belief underlies the construction of a verifiability principle which fails to perform any of its assigned functions. The view of all normative language as only having significance as an emotional discharge leaves the meaningfulness of various kinds of quite intelligible statements a total mystery. In all these ways the various doctrines derived from the objectivist paradigm have resulted in dead ends.

Before turning to a consideration of the constraining and distorting impact of residual objectivism upon the theoretical enterprise of political science, brief mention should be made of two fairly popular methodological stances which represent attempts to avoid the worst weaknesses of objectivism. Both of these positions escape the most blatant incompetencies of objectivist empiricism in social theory, but neither succeeds in reaching a fully satisfactory replacement at a fundamental level. That is, both stances modify objectivism in salutary ways, but never escape the basic conceptual weaknesses which necessitated their creation. The first of these epistemological and methodological halfway houses is the modification of positivism into a kind of neopragmatism. The second is the transformation of the fact-value dichotomy from an ontological principle to a more modest principle of methodological restraint.

Caught between the human vacuity and other failures of objectivism, on the one hand, and the inadequacies of classical cosmology, on the other, many political scientists have taken refuge in a neopragmatic conception of science.[18] This viewpoint loosens the positivist ideal, which was frustrated in its search for indubitable truth, and finds the standard of theoretical adequacy to be "what works," what is most "useful," or most "simple." Any attempt to find any deeper basis for theoretical adequacy in the nature of reality is condemned as metaphysical. By making what works the test of theoretical adequacy, these political scientists are freed to handle political realities with a rough and ready ad hoc style of theorizing. This understanding of the status of theory and of concepts escapes the most crippling features of the pure objectivism which it replaces, and it has permitted the construction of some illuminating and fruitful theoretical models. Nevertheless, the neopragmatic view of political theory, while perhaps satisfactory for the present, has defects which make it unlikely to withstand future developments.

In the first place, the pragmatic, or instrumentalist, view of theory is misleading when offered as an account of the status and meaning of theories rather than as an enumeration of some of the characteristics of good theories. To say that a scientific theory is convenient and simple and nothing more is correct in what it affirms but not in what it denies. Certainly, scientific theories are useful and convenient, and these are important signs of a good theory. But signs should not be offered as substance. It seems ludicrous and incongruous with the intellectual passions involved in scientific inquiry to suggest that scientists are merely concerned with convenience. The fact that a theory works serves to indicate its service in the mind's apprehension of reality. As Abraham Kaplan puts it, "If following a certain rule of action, employing a certain concept, is useful for us, or even just 'convenient,' the reason is that something in the real world answers to our purposes. ... The notion of a 'useful fiction' is strictly speaking self-contradictory: just in so far as it is useful it is not fictitious."[19]

The impetus behind the neopragmatists' rather strained effort to characterize a true theory without any use of the notion of truth actually arises out of the inability to fulfill the criteria of truth laid down by the objectivist tradition. That is, the ideal of Cartesian critical reason represented truth as something utterly indubitable, wholly demonstrable, and ascertainable on impersonal grounds. Since this ideal has proven chimerical, it seems necessary under the existing premises to abandon the whole notion of truth altogether.

The only way to escape this misleading practice of defining truth by its indices while denying it as a concept is to transcend the epistemological premises of objectivism altogether. The outline of such a transformed view, the construction of which has begun in the work of Michael Polanyi, Thomas Kuhn, and others, will be sketched in the final chapters.[20]

The second disadvantage of a strictly pragmatic view of theory is that it encourages an overproliferation of conceptual models which may have little or no relationship or compatibility with each other. By designating as a theory any model of metaphor which has any suggestiveness (heuristic value) or utility, the threshold of the realm of theory is lowered drastically. All theories may have a metaphorical element to them, but to call any suggestive metaphor a theory poses a threat to the conceptual tissue of the discipline. It takes only a limited feat of the imagination to conjure the prospect of an aspirant theorist offering his "apple theory" of the state: it has a self-propagating core and a red fringe. Or similarly one might devise a "theory" of political development which employed Freud's developmental categories, so that "less developed" countries would be designated "oral" polities, while "mature" countries were "genital" polities, responsive to the desires of the populace. Most political scientists are becoming aware of these dangers on a practical level, and conscientious attempts are being made to preserve some conceptual coherence to relate and direct the growing quantity of empirical investigations being conducted. This effort could be greatly enhanced by a reconstructed understanding of the status of a theory which corrected the instrumentalist's excessive casualness on this score.

A final problem with the pragmatic understanding of theory is this: if the only status and significance which a theory has is based entirely upon its usefulness or convenience, then the real possibility emerges that theory becomes an agent of ideology or political interest. Such a subordination of theory to political utility may not be, and indeed generally is not, intentional; it is instead likely to be wholly unconscious. It is no less real.

The status of theoretical constructs and perceptual norms in pragmatist theory is grounded entirely upon the utility of these constructs and norms to the theorist. The individual theorist, of course, is part of a larger community of scholars—the discipline— which is in turn part of a larger, political community. All of this cultural setting of theoretical constructs is proper and necessary and unavoidable in any case. However, there is an important ambiguity in the pragmatist interpretation which can open the way to the improper subordination of the theoretical enterprise to political partiality. The pragmatists' view is that "what is observable . . . is what a community of speakers and inquirers takes to be observable."[21] As an empirical fact about the activity of knowing, this constitutes an unexceptionable observation that the objectivist tradition tended to obscure. However, the pragmatist elides this empirical observation that theoretical constructs are cultural artifacts with his justification of these constructs. The practical origin of a theory is presented as if it constituted sufficient grounds for accrediting the theory, or at least as if no further grounds were discernible—that is, the theory is developed because it is useful, and if it is useful, there is nothing more that needs to be said. On this formulation, the tension of the knower and the known, the element of obligation or bondage of the theorist to a reality which lies beyond him, is dissolved. When scientific theory, which undeniably grows as a cultural artifact becomes understood as merely a cultural artifact, no barrier remains in principle to keep political theory from being merely an articulation of political culture.

A culture is the only possible soil of scientific understanding; therefore, the culturally derived component of knowledge must be accepted, and accepted without despair, as a positive good. On the other hand, the same culture that serves as an irreducible substratum of knowledge serves also as a limitation upon it; therefore, it must not be accepted with complacency. The instrumentalist view of theory, unfortunately, condones this complacency and therefore threatens the de facto relativizing of theory.

The other modification of objectivism in the context of social-science methodology which clearly arises from and has affinities to positivism while nevertheless altering its postulates somewhat is what has been termed scientific value relativism. This approach is basically that of the great Max Weber and has been carried on as an articulated tradition more recently by Arnold Brecht. Unlike its predecessor objectivism, which could be called ontological value relativism, the scientific value relativism of Weber and Brecht does not deny all cognitive significance to value statements or metaphysics on a priori grounds. As Weber put it, "We are furthermore completely free of the prejudice which asserts that reflections on culture which go beyond the analysis of empirical data in order to interpret the world metaphysically can, because of their metaphysical character, fulfill no useful cognitive tasks."[22] However, this kind of reflection, Weber and Brecht insist, must clearly be distinguished from science and be seen as speculation. Normative statements are not characterized as cognitively meaningless, but they must be seen as "absolutely heterogeneous in character" by contrast with "empirical propositions."[23] Basically, then, scientific value relativism maintains the objectivist insistence on the utter dichotomy of facts and values while at the same time changing the basis of the dichotomy from an ontological to an epistemological principle of exclusion and granting a speculative worth to value statements.[24]

Maintenance of the fact-value dichotomy by the scientific value relativist comprises two features. In the first place, empirical and normative statements (synonymous with "facts" and "values," respectively, in this view) must be seen as quite distinct in kind and status. Second, this heterogeneity of status leads to an insistence that the two kinds of statement are quite separate—that is, logically unrelated. In fact, however, Weber and Brecht are never really able to keep their judicious analysis of particular cases consistent with these general propositions.

Take, for example, Brecht's treatment of the epistemological status of fact statements and value statements.[25] Brecht correctly observes that there is a real difference in the extent to which "intersubjective transmissibility" and agreement can be reached in cases of relatively unequivocal fact and in cases of what he calls ultimate value judgments. Yet Brecht then goes on to concede, first, that what he calls value judgments are dependent upon a kind of knowledge about reality and second, that even the more unambiguous levels of scientific factual research are shaped by social culture and are not fully verifiable.[26] By his own characterization, then, both kinds of statements represent a kind of knowledge and neither is absolute, indubitable, and wholly impersonal. Nevertheless, Brecht wants to say, in order to preserve the model of the unbridgeable gap between facts and values, that there is "more than a merely quantitative difference in the difficulty of verifying factual statements and value judgments."[27] However, Brecht is unable to specify what this difference in kind rather than quantity is. His general proposition does not really grow out of his specific characterizations of concrete statements but is imposed from the outside as an a priori tenet which he cannot abandon. The specific analyses he offers actually suggest a continuum rather than a gulf. All parts of the continuum represent knowledge, while no parts can match the Cartesian ideal of indubitable knowledge. At one end of the continuum are fairly unambiguous interpretations of relatively simple realities; at the other end are more debatable interpretations of complex realities. Despite Brecht's attempt to speak in dichotomous generalities, the picture he presents is one of more subtle gradation, with the problem being where to draw the line for various cognitive enterprises, keeping in mind that the price of greater transmissibility is a loss of comprehensiveness of vision.

Just as the notion of absolute heterogeneity of epistemological status between the opposed halves of the alleged fact-value dichotomy does not survive detailed examination, so also the corollary belief in their "unconditional separation"[28] proves impossible to sustain. The unbridgeable hiatus implied by the postulated logical heterogeneity is in fact crossed in both directions. Take first the impact of facts upon values. Weber suggests as a general proposition that values are ultimately "demonic," not subject to rational determination. In other words, facts are not determinative of values. This thesis is consistent, of course, with the basic conception of the absolute heterogeneity of the two. However, Weber says that "the primary task of a useful teacher is to teach his students to recognize inconvenient facts—I mean facts that are inconvenient for their party opinions."[29] This wise observation about one of the tasks of a good teacher is, strictly speaking, incompatible with Weber's stated position on the status and relationship of facts and values, for if values are truly demonic, then no fact at all could be more convenient or inconvenient than any other. On the other hand, if the meaningfulness of the notion of inconvenient facts is maintained, then the model of an unbridgeable gap must be surrendered. Weber's own work suggests the latter option.[30]

Weber's own practice, as contrasted with his methodological speculations, also suggests that the gap between values and facts is crossed from the other direction as well. That is, not only are values heavily structured by facts, but facts are shaped by values. (Of course, this whole mode of discourse is awkward and misleading, for what is really being suggested cannot be framed in terms of fact-value language at all, since this language-game is predicated upon assumptions which must themselves be transcended. This terminological awkwardness is systematic and intentional in this context and should be seen as reflecting the fundamental inconsistencies between Weber's theory and his practice.) To cite only a few of the value-laden factual terms which Weber finds useful in his own characterization of social reality, consider the phrases "sublime religious thought," "perfection that is nowhere surpassed," "incomparable grandeur," "humbug," "voluptuaries without heart," and "miserable monstrosities."[31] Arnold Brecht tries to apologize for Weber's utilization of these terms by saying that no scientific value relativist would condemn such concepts "whenever they are used within a clear frame of reference as descriptive in accordance with known standards, as long as these standards are not themselves at issue." He continues, "Whenever the latter is the case, then indeed, according to Scientific Value

Relativism, it is scientifically not correct to continue using one's own standards as though their absolute validity had been proven."[32] The simple rejoinder to this defense is that such standards are, cognitively speaking, at issue whenever they are used. From the point of view of epistemology, whether they are practically at issue—in the sense of subject to disagreement or controversy—is strictly accidental.

Brecht's argument is essentially faithful to Weber's own attempt to save himself from some grave difficulties of his formulations, an attempt which is, however, subject to the same basic defect as Brecht's argument. Weber recognizes the relevance of values to facts in the sense that values determine the selection of facts to be analyzed. "Without the investigator's evaluative ideas, there would be no principle of selection of subject-matter and no meaningful knowledge of the concrete reality."[33] And by using the phrase "point of view" Weber approaches the recognition that the question is one of the structure of perception and not merely of the principle of data selection. The obvious conclusion here is that objective knowledge is wholly contingent upon subjective factors. Weber virtually makes this concession, but he feels an area of objective validity can still be preserved.

> In the method of investigation, the guiding "point of view" is of great importance for the *construction* of the conceptual scheme which will be used in the investigation. In the mode of their *use*, however, the investigator is obviously bound by the norms of our thought just as much here as elsewhere. For scientific truth is precisely what is *valid* for all who seek the truth.[34]

This distinction between construction and use of a conceptual scheme does not constitute a satisfactory prophylaxis to the problem of scientific validity, however. Such a view would make the problem of scientific validity meaningful only within the context of an accepted paradigm and not extend it to the adequacy of the paradigm itself. Yet it is the latter problem which is most fundamental and crucial. It is the construction of a conceptual scheme which governs the identities and limits of the realities to be investigated; the use simply governs the relationships between these realities. If the construction of a conceptual scheme is based on values and values are essentially demonic, it almost begins to look as though facts must ultimately be seen as demonic as well. Perhaps this is why Weber speaks of the "hair-line which separates science from faith"[35] and why Leo Strauss claims that Weber succumbed to "historicism."[36]

What in fact happens to Weber and to other sophisticated

representatives of scientific value relativism is that their own research and their own methodological analyses simply shatter the boundaries of the general viewpoint with which they begin and with whose categories they try to speak. They begin by taking over the objectivist fact-value dichotomy while transferring it to a modified epistemological, as opposed to ontological, emphasis. Yet they continually find that neither facts nor values behave quite as they should by definition. They are defined as utterly heterogeneous but seem to function as complements as much as opposites, with each being based in part upon the other. On the one hand, increasing factual knowledge seems to narrow significantly the range of value options. On the other hand, facts seem to be constituted only in the context of values functioning as principles of selection and as perspectives. The objectivity that is left is of a contingent rather than an ultimate nature, much as the verifiability principle is now seen to function only contingently.

Ultimately, however, the nature and status of whatever it is upon which the limited objectivity is contingent becomes quite problematic. That is, the status of the criteria of order which perform the function of the scientific paradigm becomes mysterious, at best. Weber is in practice and persuasion clearly not the epistemological nihilist that Strauss claims he ultimately is in theory; but he is not capable of explaining why he is not. To do so, he would have had to reexamine the assumptions with which he began and which he effectively broke apart while trying to apply them conscientiously.

Notes

1. René Descartes, *Meditations*, E.S. Haldane and G.R.T. Ross, trans., Great Books Series, vol. 31 (Chicago; University of Chicago Press, 1952), p. 75.
2. Ibid., p. 72.
3. As Isabel Knight summarizes the view of the pursuers of an ideal language: "All languages ought to approximate the language of algebra, and insofar as they succeed, they will resemble one another in the perfection of their clarity" (*The Geometric Spirit: The Abbé de Condillac and the French Enlightenment* [New Haven: Yale University Press, 1968], p. 175).
4. Bertrand Russell, "The Philosophy of Logical Atomism," cited by J.O. Urmson, *Philosophical Analysis* (Oxford: Clarendon Press, 1956), p. 149. Urmson remarks, "We may recall that Descartes, too, based his methods and doctrines on his mathematical successes."
5. Urmson, p. 150.
6. John Wisdom, "The Metamorphosis of Metaphysics," in *Paradox and Discovery* (Oxford: Blackwell's, 1965), p. 61.

7. Ibid., p. 64-65. Urmson's characterization of the dilemma is comparable and quite concise: "So the analysis which for both the logical atomist and the logical positivist had been the central activity of philosophers was seen, after and as a result of the most patient efforts, to be impossible of achievement except in comparatively trivial cases, outside the field of mathematical logic in which Russell had scored his successes. The view of philosophy as having its task in the reductive analysis of the puzzling statements of our ordinary everyday language to the simple atomic reports of immediate experience had to be abandoned. This could not be the way to reveal either the structure of the world or the structure of our language" (op. cit., pp. 159-160).

8. Urmson, p. 161: "The ancient doctrine of British empiricism that all non-simple concepts are complexes of simple concepts must finally go. We have not merely to think of a new justification of traditional analysis, we have to get a new conception of philosophy which we may or may not call analysis. This was the alternative which, in one way or another, most English philosophers chose."

9. David Hume, *An Enquiry Concerning Human Understanding*, XII, 3.

10. Ayer, *Language, Truth, and Logic*, 2nd ed. (New York: Dover Publications, 1946), p. 35.

11. A summary may be found in the preface to Ayer, *Language, Truth, and Logic*, 2nd ed., or in C.G. Hempel, "Problems and Changes in the Empiricist Criterion of Meaning," *Revue Internationale de Philosophie*, XL (1950), 41-63.

12. Cf. C.L. Stevenson, "Persuasive Definitions," *Mind*, XLVII (1938), 331-350; and John Wisdom, "Metaphysics and Verification," ibid., 452-498.

13. Abraham Kaplan, *The Conduct of Inquiry* (San Francisco: Chandler Publishing Co., 1963), p. 42.

14. Thomas Kuhn, *Structure of Scientific Revolutions* (Chicago: Phoenix Books, 1962), p. 146. As for the version of the positivist thesis that emphasizes falsification, Kuhn says, "I doubt that [falsifying experiences] exist" (p. 145).

15. Ibid., p. 120.

16. Thomas Hobbes, *Leviathan*, Everyman ed. (New York: E.P. Dutton Co., 1950), p. 41.

17. Ayer, *Language, Truth, and Logic*, p. 108. It follows that, since words such as "good" have no objective meaning but rather signify approval, two people could use normative terms in apparently contradictory ways without actually contradicting each other. "It is, indeed, true that in a case where a person A approves of X, and another person B approves of not-X, A may correctly express his attitude towards X by saying that it is good, or right, and that B may correctly use the same term to express his attitude toward not-X. But there is no contradiction here" (Ayer, "On the Analysis of Moral Judgments," in *Philosophical Essays* [London: Macmillan & Co., 1954] pp. 232-233).

18. The term "pragmatic" is here used in a colloquial sense to refer to the position that "it's true if it works." The ideas and insights of those com-

monly called pragmatists have often transcended this simple, in-strumentalist position, however. In fact, as Morton Kaplan has pointed out, C.S. Peirce was driven to coin the term "pragmaticism" precisely to dissociate his ideas from what he saw as the misconceptions implicit in what was commonly coming to be known as pragmaticism. Cf. Morton Kaplan, *Macropolitics* (Chicago: Aldine Publishing Co., 1969), p. ix.

19. Kaplan, *The Conduct of Inquiry*, p. 47.

20. Cf. Michael Polanyi, *Personal Knowledge*, (New York: Harper and Row, 1964) and Kuhn.

21. Marx W. Wartofsky, *Conceptual Foundations of Scientific Thought* (New York: Macmillan Co., 1968), p. 117.

22. Weber, "Objectivity in Social Science and Social Policy," in *The Methodology of the Social Sciences*, Edward Shils and Henry Finch, eds. and trans. (Glencoe, Ill.: The Free Press, 1949), p. 59.

23. Weber, "The Meaning of Ethical Neutrality in Sociology and Economics," ibid., p. 12.

24. At times it should be noted, Weber falls back upon traditional ob-jectivist terminology in his distinctions between empirical and normative contentions. Thus, the former are seen as appealing to the "analytical understanding" and the latter to the "sentiments" (ibid., p. 60). The latter are "personal" in presumed contrast to the impersonality of the former. And normative contentions are sometimes characterized as "preferences" (ibid., p. 9). Weber's famed characterization of ultimate value judgments as demonic also suggests an exercise of will unrelated to reason.

25. Cf. Arnold Brecht, *Political Theory* (Princeton, N.J.: Princeton University Press, 1959).

26. Ibid., p. 298.

27. Ibid., p. 299.

28. Weber, "The Meaning of Ethical Neutrality," p. 11.

29. "Science As a Vocation," excerpted in *From Max Weber*, Hans Gerth and C. Wright Mills, eds. (New York: Oxford University Press, 1958), p. 147.

30. One need not agree with Eric Voegelin's own interpretative stance to appreciate his observation that "In so far as Weber was a great teacher, he gave the lie to his idea of values as demonic decisions." And after surveying Weber's treatment of Marxism, Voegelin observes: "It would seem that demonism is a quality which man possesses in inverse proportion to the radius of his relevant knowledge." (*The New Science of Politics* [Chicago: Phoenix Books, 1966], pp. 16, 19, respectively.)

31. These phrases, and others like them, were noted by Leo Strauss, *Natural Right and History* (Chicago: Pheonix Books, 1965).

32. Brecht, *Political Theory*, p. 265.

33. Weber, "Objectivity in Social Science," p. 82.

34. Ibid., p. 84 (emphasis in original).

35. Ibid., p. 110.

36. By "historicism" Strauss means a kind of historical relativism in epistemology which he feels to be ultimately nihilistic. Cf. *Natural Right and History*.

5   The Dilemmas of Empirical Theory

The fundamental assumptions of objectivism have led, we have argued, to the growth of insoluble conceptual difficulties in fields of inquiry ranging from the philosophy of language to the psychology of motivation. A similar pattern of conceptual confusions bred by conscious or habitual adherence to the constraints and distortions of objectivist preconceptions can be discerned in the recent history of political theory. These problems have arisen in several areas of recent theorizing, and often no one has been more acutely aware of their existence than the practitioners themselves. As within other disciplines cited in previous chapters, however, a lack of understanding of the source and depth of the difficulties prevents the growth of effective solutions. The purpose of the following section is to contribute to such an understanding, which in turn can permit the continued growth of the contemporary theoretical enterprise, unimpeded by a faulty foundation and misconceived limitations.

In order to establish the coherence of the following analysis and its continuity with previous chapters, it might be helpful to outline the contours of our argument before elaborating it. Among the most significant components of the objectivist sensibility which grew out of the scientific revolution's transformed weltanschauung were nominalism, the myth of total detachment of the knowing subject, the notion of the absolute heterogeneity of facts and values, a belief in the fundamental homogeneity of knowledge and of the world, and an essentially static ontology. All of these features, sometimes acting in concert, have been responsible for the growth of problems in various areas of contemporary political theory.

The principal deficiencies which grow from the various facets of objectivism include a tendency toward idiosyncratic fragmentation of the theoretical enterprise, a cavalier approach to the basic concepts used by the discipline, ethnocentrism, a general naiveté and confusion about the political overtones of theoretical stances, a narrowing of the range of political substance to the vanishing point, and an implicit conceptual conservatism. Nominalism is largely responsible for the conceptual fragmentation of so much of our inquiry, and together with the myth of knowledge as a kind of detached spectation it permits the insinuation of ethnocentric preconceptions into theoretical models. The myth of detachment joins with the belief in the absolute heterogeneity of facts and values to cause the naive belief in the possibility of total theoretical neutrality and the unfortunate political repercussions of this naiveté. The belief in the absolute heterogeneity of facts and values, together with objectivist monism, results in the narrowing of the scope of the political to an extent which omits some of the most important aspects of politics. And objectivism's static ontology has contributed to an implicit conservative bias in some areas of theory. The manifestation of these problems can be found in the areas of democratic theory, in the theory of political development, in the limitations of the Eastonian systems model, and in the arbitrariness of some methods of concept formation in the discipline.[1]

These patterns of conceptual influence may be capsulized in Figure 2, which is of course a vast oversimplification.

The tendency of nominalism to contribute to the difficulties of reaching conceptual coherence in political theory should require less elaboration than some of the other facets of the objectivist impact. The simple fact of the proliferation of conceptual models, the interrelationships of which are far from clear, does not require documentation to anyone conversant with contemporary political science. This conceptual diffusion may in part legitimately be considered the manifestation of a transitory stage of exploratory thought, but there is a source of diffusion that lies deeper and is less easily perceived. This is the nominalist abandonment of the conceptual coin of the discipline to the essentially arbitrary artifices of the individual mind. It is reflected in the peculiarly anomalous position occupied by the attempts to perform consciously the absolutely central task of determining the definitional concepts and criteria of relevance for particular inquiries.

Figure 2

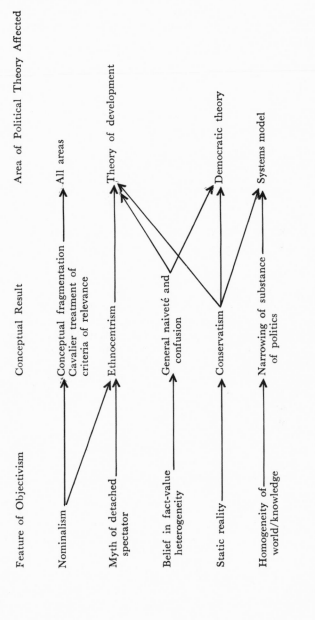

Feature of Objectivism | Conceptual Result | Area of Political Theory Affected

Nominalism → Conceptual fragmentation
Cavalier treatment of criteria of relevance → All areas

Myth of detached spectator → Ethnocentrism → Theory of development

Belief in fact-value heterogeneity → General naiveté and confusion → Democratic theory

Static reality → Conservatism

Homogeneity of world/knowledge → Narrowing of substance of politics → Systems model

Take, for example, the rather widely known enterprise of Harold Lasswell and Abraham Kaplan in *Power and Society*.[2] A substantial part of this work consists in the giving of definitions which are to guide political inquiry and theoretical understanding. However, the status of these proffered definitions remains far from clear. Lasswell, in accordance with the conventional wisdom about the disjunction of political theory into empirical and normative halves, has said that political science "states conditions" and political philosophy "justifies preferences."[3] To begin with, the task which he assigns political philosophy is nonsensically self-contradictory, since the logic of preference and the logic of justification are actually incompatible. More centrally in the present context, this definition of political science raises a question rather than settles the issue— political science states conditions, but conditions of what? How are the variables whose conditions are to be stated identified? The epistemological status of this task, a task which Lasswell undertakes in *Power and Society*, is not examined, although it is clearly crucial. To put the problem another way, most of *Power and Society* is a work neither of political science nor of political philosophy by Lasswell's own definitions. What, then, is it? Basically, it is an attempt to fill the vacuum left by objectivism and nominalism in the area of concept formation and definition. Why the particular concepts and definitions put forward should be adopted in preference to others is not fully explained; nor could it be fully explained under the assumptions in effect, since nominalism leaves the grounds for formulating definitions wholly unspecified.

A similar and closely related manifestation of nominalism's tendency to obscure the nature and status of the discipline's conceptual tissue is the approach taken in formulating criteria of relevance for research. The problem of formulating criteria of relevance is largely approached as though it were purely a methodological one. The philosophical chasms that lie beneath are obscured and ignored. Similarly, problems of classification and categorization of data are approached as basically technical problems. One has to think to remind oneself that the differences between Plato and Marx, for example, can be seen as the expression of different criteria of relevance. Such differences, of course, can hardly be resolved at a technical level, since they represent fundamental differences in what is seen to be real and meaningful.

The suggestion that sunspots might be considered relevant to political outcomes is offered in one symposium concerned with criteria of relevance as a facetious counterexample.[4] However, the reasons for holding fanciful either this suggestion or one that witchcraft or black magic might possess political potency are not technical and procedural but rather substantive. That is, the selection of appropriate criteria of relevance, classificatory schemes, and the like is a function of ontology, not of methodology. Ever since Descartes packaged revolutionary ontological contentions in an essay which he chose to title *Discourse on Method*, this fact has been obscured; but it must be recognized if the status of theoretically significant definitions is to be properly understood and if the real grounds of political theory are to be appreciated. Both the clarity and the unity of the theoretical enterprise should be enhanced by such a development.

Beyond this basic impact upon the approach to concept formation in general, the derivatives of objectivism have brought confusion and misunderstanding into several important areas of contemporary political theorizing. In turning to an elaboration of this contention, it should be kept clearly in mind that the following observations are made selectively in the service of a particular argument. If the analysis seems one-sidedly critical, this imbalance must be understood as the result of a distinct selective bias which is not intended to supply a comprehensive assessment of the theoretical areas under consideration. In fact, it is because the areas of development theory, democratic theory, and systems analysis are so central and productive that attention is devoted to them. Our concentration upon the constraining effect of the objectivist legacy, therefore, should in no way be construed as a denial of the basic vitality of the areas of theory in question.

As Gabriel Almond observed in his presidential address to the American Political Science Association in 1966, "the emerging analytical framework in contemporary political theory is the concept of system." The concept of system, he continued, is a "new paradigm" that "represents a genuinely important step in the direction of science."[5]

Within the discipline of political science, the foremost expositors of systems analysis have been David Easton and Morton Kaplan.[6] Easton and Kaplan differ in their approach, both in inspiration and application. Easton is in the tradition of Parsons and Levy in sociology, and he centers his application of the systems model upon the analysis of intranational political processes. Kaplan receives his theoretical inspiration from W. Ross Ashby's *Design For a Brain*, and his applications center upon the interactions of nations.[7]

Our concern in this section is not with the utility of the systems concept per se, which may be taken as established, nor with the differences between theorists such as Easton and Kaplan. Instead, we shall focus upon some of the problems which have arisen from the attempt to use Easton's substantive definition of the political system as an exhaustive framework for political analysis, for when it is conceived as a sufficient theoretical framework for the analysis of politics, Easton's widely adopted definition of the political system eventuates in a narrow and limited vision of political life.

Easton himself seems somewhat ambivalent as to whether his systems model has legitimate hegemonic aspirations. He modestly and wisely observes at one point that "no one way of conceptualizing any major area of human behavior will do full justice to all its variety and complexity."[8] And at times he makes quite candid statements of some of the explanatory incompetencies of his model: "My approach to the analysis of political systems will not help us to understand why any specific policies are adopted by the politically relevant members in a system."[9] Yet at times, Easton seems to suggest that his model is capable of serving as a comprehensive matrix for the entire range of empirical theory. For example, he says in one place that "these steps lead to efforts to construct a useful and comprehensive framework of concepts for the analysis of political systems."[10] And he asserts that his framework will "indicate the part of reality to be included within a systematic study of political life."[11]

It is in this latter and highly ambitious guise that the systems model is capable of generating some misleading substantive implications and explanatory incompetencies. In the absence of clearly understood limitations upon the scope of the competence of systems analysis, what begins as a highly useful methodological tool has a tendency to be transformed into a kind of ontology of political life. There is nothing unique about this transformation in scientific theory.[12] What happens is simply that, as one philosopher of science has put it, "any abstractive methodological framework generates its own ontology."[13] Concepts originally introduced on an instrumentalist basis become transformed into definitive guideposts as to the nature and limits of the real world.[14] In the case of systems analysis, this tendency is encouraged by the congruence of its substantive implications with the predilections of objectivist ontology, reflected especially in the central use of the unidimensional noun "values" to represent all manner of political ends and purposes.

When it is deemed to be a legitimate comprehensive framework for a description of politics, Easton's systems analysis functions not only as a format but as a designation of the substance of politics. It results in giving an implicit and profoundly influential answer to that theoretically crucial and primary question, What is the realm of the political?[15] Sheldon Wolin has carefully and persuasively pointed out the centrality of this basic question of definition in his

78

Politics and Vision, observing that watersheds in the history of political theory can be conceived as reflecting shifts in the answer given it.[16]

The substantive identity of any system and of its constituent acts or functions, as distinguished from the pure form of a system, is determined basically by the postulated end of the system. In the systems framework, then, political acts and functions attain their general status as political by their relationship to the defined *telos* of the political system, and they attain their particular identity by how they are related to this goal. The designation of this *telos,* then, constitutes the establishment of a theoretical *axis mundi,* which in turn becomes the source of order within the conceptual universe thus established. Proceeding upon the presumption that "the fundamental fact confronting all societies is that scarcity of some valued thing prevails," a fact which "leads inevitably to disputes over their allocation," Easton establishes the "authoritative allocation of values" as the *axis mundi* of the political universe. "What distinguishes political interactions from all other kinds of social interactions is that they are predominantly oriented toward the authoritative allocation of values for a society."[17]

As a substantive delimitation of the realm of the political, this formulation is not wholly adequate. By narrowing the conception of politics rather severely, it carries with it some questionable implications and also fails to provide the basis for some quite productive explanatory concepts. To begin with, it can legitimately be argued that the allocative functions of a polity are relatively secondary features of political life rather than its fundamental defining features. Hobbes was probably correct in designating the creation of order as the fundamental feature and task of politics, for it is only within some kind of order that a process of allocation could be instituted or could be considered authoritative. And another political task which possibly precedes the process of allocation is the attribution of some meaning and significance to the order which has been constituted. As Eric Voegelin has reminded us, human society is "a cosmion, illuminated with meaning from within by the human beings who continuously create and bear it as the mode and condition of their self-realization. . . . The self-illumination of society through symbols is an integral part of social reality, and one may even say its essential part."[18]

The conception of politics which emerges from the Eastonian orientation toward authoritative allocation of values narrows and distorts our vision of political reality. Even if the decision-making process is deemed definitive of politics, the characterization of the results of this process as an allocation of values can be systematically misleading. The image suggested is that of a kind of universalized pork-barrel politics in which the sole and central concern is dividing up the public coffers. While it can be protested that this is too confining an interpretation of what Easton intends to convey by the notion of value, this narrowness is invited by Easton's own terminology and its philosophical background. The term "value," when it is used as a noun that can be preceded by the indefinite article, is of positivist origin, and the implied homogeneity does not provide the basis for distinguishing between distinct kinds of political ends and distinct kinds of and bases for political decisions. The term "allocation," moreover, clearly invites this interpretation. In any case, a political scientist would certainly have to transcend Easton's definition of politics simply to make a distinction between pork-barrel decisions and more profound political choices. Even if it is uncharitable to interpret the substantive orientation of Easton's systems model as a universalization of the pork-barrel, then, the model does not possess the conceptual resources to distinguish this form of politics analytically from other forms.[19]

It is also clearly extremely important in analyzing a polity to understand the setting and limits within which the allocative process functions. And obviously, an analysis which begins at the boundary of the process which presumably identifies the realm of politics cannot deal with this question. The consequence is either a misleading inference derived from a truncated analysis or else a failure of explanation, for if no mention is made of the setting and limits of the allocative process, one possible inference might be that it has no limits but in fact does represent the whole of the political life of the polity in question. From the systematic failure to mention the limiting context, it becomes easy to infer a picture of politics which bears real resemblance to Hobbes's race—a relentless quest for power after power that has no end. As a consequence, there arises some real logic behind Lasswell's designation of Napoleon as "close to the true political type," since he embodied a rather pure form of motivation toward power as an end in itself.[20] So conceived, politics becomes essentially an exercise in psychopathology.

Again, even if this substantively misleading inference is not made, there remains as best an explanatory incapacity. That is, within the resources of the systems model of politics as an allocative process, one cannot distinguish polities in which the politics of allocation has no bounds from polities in which clear limitations upon it are present. In fact, it is not really possible to distinguish between an effective political order and a kind of war of all against all in which allocations are made by depradation and authority is defined by the will of the stronger.[21] Whether the politics of allocation is contingent rather than absolute and how it is contingent are important considerations in distinguishing between differing forms of political order. One of the distinctive features of constitutionalism, for example, is the contingency of allocative political functions. This contingency, or limitation of scope, is part of the "effective, regularized restraint" which Charles McIlwain saw as the key to constitutionalism. In a slightly different context, Lucian Pye has also noted the importance of this element of contingency:

> The evolution of stable, creative politics requires that a citizenry come to believe that in their political system there are certain fundamental institutions which stand apart from immediate partisan conflict, which can be fully trusted and respected, and which can *limit* but also give *meaning* to the entire realm of politics.[22]

In order to incorporate such significant analytical distinctions, either the systems model must be transcended or else the substantive orientation which Easton designates for it must be broadened.

The a priori establishment of what a political system is and does by definition also results in a significant narrowing of the possible range of comparative analysis. In fact, it sets very distinct limits upon the very notion of comparison. Once the methodological assumption is made that there is a fundamental identity between all political systems as to their basic properties,[23] the analyst may be left with very little to compare. Comparison becomes simply a matter of quantitatively ordering objects already held to be structurally identical by assumption. As one thoughtful analyst notes, "two objects being compared must be of the same class."[24] By this time it begins to appear that the more interesting and crucial questions come at the level of classification, but it is not clear by what criteria classifications are to be made.

The essential sameness of structure which is postulated for all political systems contains an important component of ethnocentrism, moreover. In deciding what social interactions are to be deemed political functions, a model of politics which is rather clearly that of secular Western pluralism is used. Genuine comparative insight may consequently be lost at the very outset of analysis. When the raison d'être of the political order is seen to be the conversion of inputs into outputs, the notion of system begins to assume analogical as well as analytical significance—the analogy being that of technical production, with the systemic components identified in technical and functional terms. While this conceptual framework may be quite appropriate to the modern Western secular political arena which is a neutral battleground for a pluralistic society, it may result in a very misleading view of a more traditional or totalitarian society. In these societies, the behavior of the political system may be a result of considerations of a different order than the postulated intramundane rationality of functions directed toward value allocation. As David Apter has noted in his *Politics of Modernization*, the modern Western image of political functions may be quite different from a traditional view of political roles:

> Today an analysis of society proceeds in terms of professionalization, skill, technology, rationality, and functionality—all terms that we associate with modern society. We identify these abstractions in terms of particular strategic roles in the society, e.g. the civil servant, the hydraulic engineer, the community development expert, the university lecturer. How sharp is their contrast to traditional roles—the chief, the priest, the queen-mother, the bearer of the king's patrimony.[25]

The imposition of our modern functional categories upon more traditional societies, where they are less applicable, may obscure some critically important features of the political system through its a priori definition of the nature of a political act. (In fact, the imposition of these categories as a comprehensive framework may also obscure our understanding of modern systems as well, where more traditional features persist than we often recognize.) For example, Apter found that a crucial determinant of the response which African traditional societies made to modernizing forces was whether they were consummatory or instrumental societies.[26] Yet this important distinction already transcends the conceptual resources of the Eastonian paradigm which, by identifying political acts on the basis of their functional significance vis-à-vis the allocation of values, conceives them to be instrumental by definition.

Another area where the Eastonian model needs at times to be transcended for purposes of adequately explaining political behavior is that of political motivation. The rules which govern the behavior of certain functional components of the Eastonian system are very often not determined by the principle of order of the system itself. That is, many political actions derive their meaning and direction from some source other than the postulated end of influencing the allocation of values. The rationality of these actions is not the rationality of the political game so conceived. For many conceptual and explanatory purposes this distinction may be irrelevant; it may suffice to consider the actions as defined solely by their functional significance vis-à-vis the designated *axis mundi* of value allocation. At other times, however, it may be critical to know the nature and extent to which the sources of political motivation are external to the narrowly defined realm of politics. To take such considerations into account, the conceptual resources of the systems model would once again have to be transcended.

Considerable empirical evidence suggests that the whole behavior pattern of a political society may be shaped by the extensive influence of such extrapolitical (in the sense of transcending and perhaps even running counter to the politically rational goal of attaining power over value allocation) motivations. Understanding the predominance of one or another pattern of political motivation may therefore be quite important in analyzing a single political system and in comparing political systems. To cite one example, it would seem to be important in understanding and explaining difficulties in the interest-aggregation function of the Indian political system to recognize that extrapolitical considerations often dominate the behavior of party elites. Because the disruption of older achievement hierarchies has intensified the use of political standing for the attainment of personal status in India, party workers often are "more concerned with maintaining the identity of their group and its ideology than in increasing their prospects for achieving political power by working more closely with others."[27] The resulting militancy and tendency to shun identity-blurring compromise is, of course, important to the political system as a whole.

Finally, mention must be made of an important theoretical concept which has generally been associated with systems analysis—the notion of equilibrium. Any thorough consideration of the history and significance of this concept in social theory would go far beyond the scope of this essay, but it is important to consider the basic nature of the concept itself in this context.[28]

Equilibrium is a genuinely descriptive concept. It refers to an empirical situation in which a system has reached at least a relative state of balance. It is also a normative concept; that is, it involves a perception of order, coherence, and satisfactory adaptation which is functionally superior to a state of disequilibrium. The concept, especially in the context of social theory, has been subject to numerous confusions and obfuscations, since the whole notion of concepts that are both normative and descriptive is anomalous within objectivist assumptions. The persistent pattern in the rise of equilibrium analysis, consequently, has been as follows: someone uses the concept of equilibrium in a social theory; someone else attacks him for making surreptitious prescriptions; he, in turn, issues an indignant denial that he was covertly ideological and insists that he was being empirical and scientific.[29] The argument then degenerates into irascible charges and countercharges, since both disputants are right in what they affirm while they both share the objectivist-derived faulty assumption that if they are right, then their opponent must be wrong. In fact, this kind of argument is paradigmatic whenever normative descriptions arise and not simply in the case of the concept of equilibrium.[30]

The present tendency of equilibrium analysis is to imply a kind of conservatism. At least, contemporary criticism of the normative implications of the equilibrium concept feel this to be the case,[31] and there is some real justification for this view. Historically, however, the normative implications of equilibrium models have been varied. Russett speaks of the model's "capacity to encapsulate several quite different versions of Utopia."[32] Throughout its history, however, one feature of the concept of equilibrium has remained quite consistent—namely, its perception as an essentially desirable situation. Such diverse figures as Comte, Spencer, Ward, Pareto, Bentley, and Catlin have agreed on this.[33]

This historical consistency has to be recognized, I think, as representative of the status of the equilibrium concept as legitimately descriptive and legitimately normative at the same time rather than as an unfortunate lapse of logic that somehow almost always occurs. In the absence of the strong objectivist prejudice against any relationship between the normative and the descriptive, the consistent intertwining of these allegedly distinct functions in the use of the equilibrium concept by some of the best minds in social theory would seem to constitute a fairly strong de facto case for seeing an intrinsic logical connection between them. This inference is substantially accurate, I think, and can be rendered cognitively respectable by the coming revision of our outmoded Cartesian epistemology, a revision outlined in the final chapters of this essay. Consideration of much of what has been, according to objectivist prejudices, considered the normative debris of classical thought will reveal that it was a form of equilibrium analysis itself. The Platonic notion of *dike*, for example, represents a profound analysis of a normative equilibrium. And the normative functioning of the Aristotelian concept of nature was the logical product of viewing the natural situation as a form of equilibrium—a state where a substance (one might even say a system) reached a state of rest through becoming actualized. Putting aside its substantive ontological errors, which are logically separable, we might find it worthwhile to consider the possibility that the classical tradition was far clearer about the epistemological relationship of norms and descriptions than the modern tradition.

The conclusion to be drawn from the preceding criticisms is not that the systems model is a failure as a tool of analysis. Far from it. The service which it has rendered political scientists in conceptualizing the interrelationship of political phenomena is irreducible and indispensable. The problems discussed arise not from any inherent impotence or falsity of the systems approach but from the attempt to use it as a comprehensive theoretical matrix, a function which it cannot perform without giving rise to explanatory incompetencies and misleading implications. The real problem is the theoretical vacuum which allows the systems model to be expanded into this inappropriate role by default.

The sources of this theoretical vacuum, in turn, are the objectivist assumptions which obscure the nature and grounds of theory construction: the nominalist view of concept formation, the bias toward ontological homogeneity, the blindness to the interaction of norms and description. The systems model is an extraordinarily productive approach within its realm of competence. However, a great deal of important empirical analysis remains to be done beyond the capacities of systems analysis; and one of the steps necessary to facilitate this development will be the recognition and abandonment of the faulty constraints placed on the theoretical enterprise by objectivism. These constraints can be further illuminated by considering the more concrete theoretical areas dealing with political development and democracy.

The paradigmatic pattern of objectivist constraint and distortion of the theoretical ordering of political reality is quite clear in the study of political development. Nothing should be more obvious than the essential descriptive function of norms—criteria of political order and efficacy—in conceptualizing the meaning and process of political development. Because this conceptual function of norms is not understandable or justifiable under the assumptions of objectivism, however, this part of the construction of a theory of political development is ignored and repressed. Whenever an essential component of the human economy, intellectual as well as sexual, is repressed, of course, the result is not elimination of the function it performs but rather a pervasive contamination from the failure to give the repressed component its legitimate attention. In the conceptualization of political development, the cognitively irreducible functions of norms have tended to be performed by a rather vague ethnocentrism and other unexamined philosophic premises which enter by the back door.

To someone interested in the conceptual structure of the field of political development, its most striking feature is the extraordinary evanescence of its central concept. Reams have already been written about political development, but there seems to be little clarity or unanimity about what "political development" really means. S.N. Eisenstadt understates the situation considerably when he observes that "the meaning of political development has not yet been precisely or clearly established."[34] Students of political development seem to have discovered a great deal about how it comes about without clarifying what it is. While there are some good practical reasons for this, the situation remains rather unusual from the theoretical point of view.

In the absence of a generally accepted understanding of the meaning of "political development", it has been the general practice for every man to define the term to his own satisfaction.[35] There is considerable overlap between the different definitions, but there are some variations as well. From time to time, moreover, the predominant view of what constitutes political development has seemed to shift. In its early stages, the concept of development was closely allied with the concept of social mobilization. Perhaps because of the relative amenability of the latter concept to the emerging quantitative techniques,[36] there was not much attention given to the highly problematic quality of the nexus between development and mobilization. This relationship becomes especially problematic when it is recognized that one critical component of the process of mobilization is actually the breakdown of established patterns of political order. For example, Deutsch has defined "social mobilization" as "the process in which major clusters of old social, economic, and psychological commitments are broken and people become available for new patterns of socialization and behavior."[37]

This designation of a breakdown of traditional order as a step toward political development is partially a reflection of a bias against traditional polities and a predilection for our own modern secular forms of political orientation. This bias may or may not have justification in an appreciation of the superior proficiencies and capabilities of modern political forms, but since this justification is rarely attempted, the whole theoretical matrix of development theory has often been permeated by an unexamined semiconscious ethnocentrism. The suspicion that an ethnocentric hypostasization of the political forms of the contemporary Western world has provided much of the content for the model of development is heightened by the intertwining of the terms "development" and "modernization." Some political scientists have recognized the dangers and limitations which a fusion of the concepts modern and developed brings and have counseled against it;[38] however, the tendency toward such a fusion, or at least a heavy overlap, is quite widespread. For example, Lucian Pye asserts that "the essence of contemporary political development is the realization of that extraordinarily complex human institution, the modern nation-state, which in turn was originally produced within the European state

86

system."[39] Others, like David Apter, make modernization and development related but distinguishable concepts, which can be placed on a continuum.[40] The modern phenomena of a contract society and a secularized political order are also very widely accepted as aspects of political development.[41] And many would probably assume with John Spanier that political development and democratic government are almost synonymous.[42]

This confluence of the concepts of development, mobilization, and breakdown of traditional order, besides reflecting an admixture of ethnocentric bias, also incorporates a tendency to assume a relatively easy and spontaneous path toward a viable modern political order. Although rarely, if ever, stated explicitly, a kind of quasi-Enlightenment belief in the spontaneity of progress seems to have been partly responsible for the very casual treatment of the immense positive task of development in the early stages of dealing with that problem.[43] In any case, the focus upon the passing of the traditional order in tandem with complacent talk of development certainly is congruent with one of the fundamental weaknesses of Enlightenment political theory—the notion that a dissolution of existing constraints will be virtually a sufficient cause of a new modern order that will develop naturally or under the benevolently guiding hand of history.

This theoretical shortcoming may have also contributed to a faulty perspective in the creation of our political stance vis-à-vis the underdeveloped nations. Our underestimation of the great depth of the positive task of political development may have helped lead us to an overestimation of our powers abroad, with some costly consequences both to ourselves and to the objects of our intended beneficence. As Senator Fulbright has observed,

> Far from being bumbling, wasteful, and incompetent, as critics have charged, American government officials, technicians, and economists have been strikingly successful in breaking down the barriers to change in ancient but fragile cultures.
>
> Here, however, our success ends. Traditional rulers, institutions, and ways of life have crumbled under the fatal impact of American wealth and power but they have not been replaced by new institutions and new ways of life, nor has their breakdown ushered in an era of democracy and development. It has rather ushered in an era of disorder and demoralization. . . .
>
> With every good intention we have intruded on fragile societies, and our intrusion, though successful in uprooting traditional ways of life, has been strikingly unsuccessful in implanting the democracy and advancing the development which are the honest aims of our "welfare imperialism." [44]

Recently, theorists of development have begun to recognize some of these theoretical weaknesses and descriptive inaccuracies of the original concept of development. Part of the occasion for this critical reassessment has been the unfortunately evident failure of some of the developing nations to develop much more than strong-man rule, anarchy, and coups d'etat. Samuel Huntington, notably, has written a rather thorough critique of the misleading implications of the notion of development in his article, "Political Development and Political Decay."[45] There he writes that the identification of development with social modernization makes the concept too parochial, too vague, and misleadingly unilinear. He also observes that almost anything occurring in developing countries has become conceptualizable as a component of political development and that the concept of development "thus loses its analytical content and becomes simply a geographical one."[46] As a result, "things which are in fact occurring in the 'developing' areas becomes hopelessly entwined with things which the theorist thinks should occur there."[47] The outcome, he continues, is a Webbist concept which is ethnocentric and has no provision for reversibility or "political decay." In fact, he notes, as some earlier theorists such as Plato, Aristotle, and Machiavelli had recognized, social mobilization has a tendency to be politically disintegrative in the absence of adequate, effective political institutions.

Huntington's criticisms are directed principally at the descriptive failures of the early use of the concept of development. These failures are not purely fortuitous or simply the result of technical problems or even of limited samples of data, although the latter has been partly responsible. One of the underlying reasons for these difficulties must be located in the lack of attention devoted to the nature and status of the concept of development itself. That is, political scientists have shied away from asking what kind of concept the model of development is and what assumptions must be made in order to legitimate its use. This inattention is partly a result of the urgency of the problems for which the concept of development has been created. However, some of this inattention has probably been a result of an implicit recognition that close examination of the concept of development would show its philosophical foundation to be extremely weak. Specifically, the types of theoretical assumptions necessary to legitimate the concept of development are admissable within the framework of objectivism; and it is decidedly easier, if less intellectually honest, to repress this problem than to face the deep theoretical dilemmas which it raises.

The theoretical anomaly of the concept of development in the context of some of the philosophical assumptions inherited from objectivism has been noted by Lucian Pye. As Pye observes, a definition of empirical theory which completely separates it from a consideration of norms does not accommodate very well the conceptualizing of political development.

> The emergence of the problems of development also caught political science at a time when the discipline thought that it was successfully breaking from its earlier and strongly normative tradition. Modern political science, in seeking to become an empirical discipline, has been anxious to be highly realistic and to deal with conditions and processes as they actually occur in life. This fundamental trend again seems in some respects to conflict with the orientation necessary for working on the problems of development. [48]

One specific feature of a theoretical backdrop formed by the scourging of norms from the scene—namely, a thorough cultural relativism—seems particularly incongruous with the idea of development, says Pye. Faced with the practical need to deal with problems of development, however, Pye continues, the tendency has been to repress this whole dilemma rather than to refashion the fundamental theoretical principles until they are adequate to support the concepts being used. [49]

No one should take issue with the desire "to be highly realistic" or to "deal with conditions and processes as they actually occur," in Pye's characterization of the motivations behind the quest for empirical theory. To demand that descriptive theory be realistic is to pose a question, however, not to supply an answer. Pye, for example, in noting the incongruity of the notion of development with the objectivist component of the conventional understanding of empirical theory, does not mean to suggest that development is in any way unreal. The real problem arises from objectivism's substantive assumptions about the nature and range of political reality. The critical insufficiency of the conventional understanding of empirical theory to sustain the concept of development has its origin in a concept of reality which denies the existence of those phenomena which Aristotle understood through the concept of *horme*—the tendency of various creatures to seek actualization. This is essentially the same incapacity which caused Whitehead to note the incongruency between objectivism and the idea of evolution. It is the ingrained theoretical inclination to picture the forces behind change as inertial rather than as aspiring that clashes with the need for a theory that is both empirical—that is, about reality—and capable of conceptualizing development.

An implicit recognition of this situation is what has led Gabriel

Almond to suggest that some kind of concept of teleology—a notion proscribed by objectivism and therefore widely disdained by moderns—may need to be employed in an adequate theory of political development.

> Natural law notions have little resonance in contemporary political theory and political science. And yet implied in the idea of a spreading "world culture" and "demonstration effect" is the proposition that confronted with similar stimuli and opportunities human beings seem to come up with very similar responses and solutions. . . . Surely there is implied in the notion of modernization and development some teleological element, not that of divine purpose, but the pressure of human aspiration and choice toward a common set of goals employing similar instrumentalities. If this be teleology, then make the most of it.[50]

In the absence of a teleology of this sort, the ostensive realism of objectivism in practice results in an implicitly conservative theoretical bias. That is, a failure to give theoretical status to forces and aspirations toward development, because these are held to be illicit incursions of idealism or teleology, leads to a basically static paradigm of political behavior which conflicts with the perspective of development theorists. Pye once again has perceived this anomaly: "The spirit of empiricism . . . had given a certain sense of legitimacy to the ongoing workings of any political process, which in turn had left political scientists with the feeling that reformism was slightly naive."[51] This form of theoretical conservatism is more a function of what empiricism's relativistic and realistic formulations do not say than of what they do say. The perception of the conservative bias noted by Pye is, therefore, a kind of argument from silence. In this context, however, there is considerable justification for this generally risky form of argument, for the systematic omission of an alleged phenomenon—in this case, a tendency toward development—constitutes an effective denial of its existence. The plea of the empiricist that he is simply being descriptive fails to reach the real issue, for the complaint of people such as Pye and Almond in this context is not that empirical theory has failed by not being prescriptive but that its failure is its presentation of a dogmatically [52] truncated description as if it were a complete description.[53] And once again, the underlying source of the conceptual confusion is the narrowness and static bias of entrenched objectivist presuppositions about what may be accredited as real.

After making these insightful criticisms of the theory of development, or lack thereof, however, neither Pye nor Huntington offers any very helpful positive contributions toward the construction of a more satisfactory theory. Pye follows his recognition of the "need for theory" in the study of development with a survey of some of the standard sociological distinctions between traditional and modern societies. These distinctions are, of course, quite helpful in understanding some of the social transformations which industrialization tends to bring to the emerging nations. But as Huntington has argued, the process of modernizing is not necessarily one of development. Huntington himself offers the proposition that the level of political development is determined by the level of institutionalization. While this view is a welcome corrective to the previous tendency to ignore the crucial role of effective institutions in the creation of political order, the criterion of institutionalization alone is hardly sufficient to bear the theoretical burden which Huntington places upon it. It may be, as he suggests, that there is a lot of truth in the idea that "what's good for the Presidency is good for the country"; but turning this colloquial half-truth into the test of political development is surely to reverse the proper relationship of the two, for if the bolstering of a particular institution is to be "good for the country," it must have embodied an appropriate organizational response to a genuine need of the polity in the first place. Otherwise, the strengthening of the institution may be at the expense of the larger body politic rather than in its behalf. The simple test of institutionalization per se begins to lose some of its plausibility if one asks whether what was good for the Hitler Jugend was good for Germany, whether what was good for Kwame Nkrumah was good for Ghana, or whether what is good for Congress is necessarily what is good for the United States. A degree of plausibility is built into the Huntington test of development by reference to institutionalization per se because of the tendency of dysfunctional institutions to be discarded or overthrown, whether they are tyrannical or simply ineffectual. But this circumstance is an empirical phenomenon rather than a theoretical criterion; it needs to be explained as much as it explains. By itself, then, a measure of the level of institutionalization is not a sufficient test of political development.[54]

Even those most aware of the conceptual dilemmas and descriptive deficiencies of the theory of development, then, have not really undertaken a full-scale attempt to establish the development concept on a firm theoretical foundation. The reason for shrinking from a task logically implied by their own criticisms is probably a recognition that the necessary revision does indeed strike at some very deep-rooted assumptions of the discipline. Any adequate, comprehensive, and explicit model of development, for example, would require abandoning the notion that normative and empirical theory are mutually exclusive. And this abandonment in turn would threaten the cherished ideal of total epistemological objectivity established since the seventeenth century. These assumptions and the cluster of presuppositions which surround them are, however, critical components of the self-characterization which contemporary social science has developed in the context of its aspirations to be a genuine science. They cannot be jettisoned without creating a kind of identity crisis in many social scientists; and thus there exists an understandable reluctance to precipitate the antipathy and controversy which following the problem to its source will undoubtedly generate. Especially is this reluctance understandable when those who perceive the anomalies in the established paradigm most clearly have no ready substitute to provide. It is for this purpose that the final two chapters of this essay are offered—to sketch an alternative paradigm of political knowledge which can permit forthrightly facing such problems as we have been discussing.

Unless the theory of development is to persist in its present inchoate and logically confused state, political scientists who wish to use the concept must assume the philosophical burden necessary to legitimate a model of development. The whole idea of a developed polity clearly requires the use of some kind of norms, but there are several possible levels of normative depth and complexity at which the concept of development could be meaningful and legitimate. All of these levels of significance have their usefulness, depending upon the questions which are under consideration. It is not necessary, then, to choose one of these levels for all time, rejecting the others totally; all that is necessary is that the level at which the concept is functioning be understood and specified and that the philosophical burden necessary to legitimate the concept's use be assumed.

This concept of levels of normative depth and complexity can perhaps best be elaborated by illustration from some extant uses of the development concept. The most shallow and least complex use of the development concept is to signify the sheer size and extent of politicization of a society. The norm at this level is basically quantitative: a society would be considered politically developed in this sense when political activity within it had reached a certain threshold of salience. Or perhaps more subtle comparative measures would be useful. This essentially quantitative developmental norm is suggested by those who emphasize mobilization as the critical feature of development. Perhaps this is also the proper level at which to understand Harold Lasswell's characterization of development as a "sequence of approximations toward a self-sustaining level of power accumulation."[55]

A second, somewhat deeper and more complex meaning of

political development might refer to the sheer productive ability of a political system to convert inputs into outputs. This standard would be basically a criterion of technical efficacy and is suggested by "capabilities analysis," by the whole language of "conversion functions," and also by some of Huntington's tests of institutionalization. "Development" in this sense would refer to the establishment of a viable modus vivendi between a system and its environment, a modus vivendi which enables the system to persist and to perform its intended functions. In a way, this understanding of "development" would make the term analogous to the biological concept of adaptation and to the psychological notion of adjustment. The probable result of analysis at this level would be a multilinear model of development on the basis of which it would be possible to speak of developed tribal societies and developed totalitarian regimes as well as of developed secular liberal societies.[56]

At its most profound level, the theory of development should have considerable affinity with the classic inquiry into the nature of the good society. In this sense, a developed polity would be conceived of as one which effectively provides for the genuine social needs of human beings. This understanding of development in its fullest sense would incorporate the more limited meanings of that term discussed above—mobilization and efficiency—but would also go beyond them to substantive characterizations of the order produced by political systems. The ultimate basis of categorization and assessment of stages of development would be a model of the social potential of human beings; in other words, the criteria of philosophical anthropology—the study of human nature—would be determinative in development concepts of this order, as they were in somewhat different form in classical theory.[57]

Basically, this is the far-reaching model of development which J. Roland Pennock is moving toward in his article, "Political Development, Political Systems, and Political Goods."[58] As he says there, advocating that political outcomes should be a crucial test of a developed polity, *"A priori, the test of anything in terms of what it produces seems to make sense."*[59] The importance of a modern version of philosophical anthropology in this perspective is reflected in Pennock's statement that "we are indeed still dealing with the attainment of political goals, but the focus of attention is upon those goals that satisfy 'needs'—not just needs of the state, as such, matters that will enable it to persist, but human needs whose fulfillment makes the polity valuable to man, and gives it its justification."[60] A truly developed polity, as he suggests, is one capable of producing such goods as security, justice, liberty, and welfare for its members.

Attempting to utilize a model of political development at this most profound level of analysis would, of course, break some of the conventionally prevailing ground rules and prejudices of recent political science; but these are, as we have suggested all along, rules and prejudices that can very profitably be broken. In the first place, as suggested by Pennock's concerns with such traditionally important outcomes as justice and liberty, the confinement of political analysis and developmental categories to matters of process alone would have to be transcended. The policy content of decisions—their impact on the structure of the members' lives—would have to be taken into account and theoretized to supplement characterizations of patterns of political power and influence.

Second, a total relativism would have to be abandoned as incompatible with any serious concept of development, as Pye has tentatively indicated. A modified relativism could survive in the guise of a multilinear model of development, but this would be a conscious, empirical theoretical option rather than the product of the faulty objectivist understanding of scientific neutrality. It is altogether possible that several competing theoretical perspectives on development may result, for while even the most complex concept of development outlined here is an empirical concept, its formation, like the formation of all high-level scientific concepts, involves an element of personal judgment. In this sense, Harold Lasswell is correct in seeing that full-scale models of political development must be "explicitly preferential."[61] However, it is misleading to understand this necessity in the positivist language of preference, for what is involved is not a subjective, emotive imperative but rather an interpretative judgment about the objective realities of political order. Lasswell's positivist understanding of the theoretical situation precludes the examination and analysis of ultimate, and hence unprovable, theoretical norms even while admitting their necessity.[62]

Finally, pursuit of a model of political development in its most profound sense would offer the possibility, even the necessity, of interaction and mutual inspiration of normative and empirical theory. This interaction would greatly enhance both kinds of theory, which would be recognized as related aspects of an integrated theoretical enterprise rather than utterly foreign areas of inquiry whose habitation in the same discipline is something of a mystery. Normative theory could with better self-understanding turn to its legitimate task of interpreting and evaluating the performance of political systems in the light of the human needs they were created to fulfill. It would no longer be focally an enterprise in intellectual history, although it would require a solid grounding in the work of those who previously labored on its recurring problems. Nor would it find its alleged positive task to be the intrinsically anomalous one of justifying preferences.

Empirical theory, on the other hand, would have to shed some of its more utopian epistemological fantasies; but disillusionment in its literal sense, however temporarily painful, is a productive process. Basically this process of disillusionment would consist in recognizing as illusory the goal of a comprehensive model of development which will arise automatically from an accretion of wholly unambiguous data. Such a goal is based on a faulty understanding of scientific theory construction and has been abandoned by knowledgeable philosophers of science anyway. In exchange for this sacrifice, the clarity of the empirical theoretical enterprise would be vastly improved, since no longer would it be forced to rely upon the intrusion of subliminal ethnocentrisms to give some coherence to the landscape of theoretical confusion generated by the spell of objectivism. It might also become possible to rediscover the empirical relevance of some of the classical political theorists—or at least better to understand the nature of their inquiries. For example, the different schemes of political morphology employed by Plato and Aristotle could be seen as analogous to the contrast between a unilinear and multilinear model of political development.[6 3]

Objectivist presuppositions have, in multiple ways, had an impact upon theories of democracy. In the first place, they have led to some misleading attempts to identify the logic of democracy with the structure of an empiricist world. Second, they have contributed a conservative cast to the theoretical formulations of contemporary empirical analysis of democratic government. Third, they have led to a truncation of the theoretical criteria employed in conceptualizing democracy.

The first of these developments takes place within the context of what would normally but inadequately be termed normative theory; it is actually a form of empirical inquiry, not a statement of preferences. Specifically, what is at issue is the congruence or lack of congruence of the structure of democracy with the structure of the natural order of the world. Are the underlying postulates of democratic political order compatible with or in contradiction with the basic nature of reality? Objectivism has contributed to a distinctive set of answers to these questions; but the answers provided are not logically sound, and the rationale of democratic government has been left in a rather shaky condition. This situation provided the background for Paul Tillich's observation a few years back that "the intellectual defense of Anglo-Saxon civilization against Fascist ideologies is extremely weak."[6 4]

This precarious balancing of democratic commitment upon an understanding of reality which does not finally possess the resources for sustaining it is not, of course, a twentieth-century novelty. Ever since the rise of the seventeenth century's revolutionary cosmology, the same basic pattern has replicated itself in several contexts. Locke, the classic democratic liberal, exhibited the mismatch of cosmological assumptions and political conclusions rather dramatically, in that his belief in natural right floated in a philosophical vacuum. In Locke and in the thought of such later democratic adherents of the new cosmology as the English deists and various Enlightenment figures,[65] the fundamental incapacity of the objectivist outlook to sustain a political tradition was hidden by the massive carry-over of classical and medieval ideas into political thought and political reality. However, a combination of time and analytical acid has gradually worn away much of the residue of the classical and medieval legacy which sustained democratic liberalism at its outset. The incapacity of objectivist philosophy to sustain the democratic tradition has become more apparent to careful thinkers, and the practical consequences of the incapacity have also begun to manifest themselves.[66]

Perhaps because of the natural liberalism produced by America's historically dominant sociological patterns, however, this problem has remained largely unrecognized in this country.[67] The dominant tendency is to assume that a combination of pragmatism, science, and common sense leads to unassailably democratic conclusions. The result is an often latent, but sometimes quite explicit, distortion of the interpretation of contemporary democracy by objectivist presuppositions. Generally, this tendency takes the form of an assumed correlation of democracy with an objectivist interpretation of science, linked by the presumed common denominator of relativism.

Sometimes, this alleged affinity of democracy and science is simply taken for granted, issuing into the comfortably pretentious belief that the rationality of democracy is scientifically certified. For example, consider the assertion of one philosopher of science of a positivist persuasion that "there is an important common element in mature thinking (as we find it in science) and mature social action (as we see it in democracy)."[68] He goes on to conclude that

a mature humanism requires no longer a theological or metaphysical frame either. Human nature and human history become progressively understood in the light of advancing science. . . . Naturalism and Humanism should be our maxim in philosophy and in education. A Scientific Humanism emerges as a philosophy holding considerable promise for mankind—if mankind will at all succeed in growing up.[69]

To cite another example of this easy assumption of the congruence of science and democracy, social scientist Daniel Lerner has argued that "the great current issue for Social Science is how to increase democracy's chances for survival in our time."[70] The widespread currency of such an outlook lends credence to Joseph La Palombara's observation that "it is difficult to imagine how the social scientists in the United States would now go about rebutting the reiterated Russian claim that Western social science is not much more than thinly veiled bourgeois ideology."[71]

Insofar as there is logic as well as ethnocentrism behind such claims for the correlation of science and democracy, it rests upon a presumed congruence between scientific relativism and democratic tolerance. An attempt to spell out the logic of this relationship, which in the context of America's sociologically grounded certitude is often simply assumed rather than examined, was once made by the German thinker Gustav Radbruch under the duress of the rising threat of Nazism. Radbruch's basic thesis was that objectivist relativism leads to the conclusion that values should not be forced on a people against their will; from this he goes on to infer the validity of many of the traditional natural rights.[72] The problem here is that this argument presumes some worth to a person's or a people's will, and this presumption in turn presupposes the very natural right which Radbruch wanted to ground autonomously in relativism.

There are actually two analytically distinguishable varieties of relativism, both of which have been justified on the basis of objectivist assumptions by their more intellectually self-aware adherents. But neither is in fact capable of serving as the basis for a commitment to democratic tolerance. The first form of relativism is the epistemological relativism which Brecht calls scientific value relativism. This epistemological relativism simply holds that science is intrinsically incapable of making statements about values. As Brecht notes, this form of relativism cannot prescribe democratic tolerance or constitutional liberties, for it can in fact prescribe nothing. It can only insist that no political order be imposed on the authority of science.

The attempt to bolster democracy by relativism fares no better, moreover, if the relativism is ontological relativism, the position that all patterns of human order are in fact of equal worth and significance, in contrast to epistemological relativism's assertion that science cannot say one way or the other; if no political goal, no political preference, is better than any other, it is equally as logical to impose an arbitrary order on society as it is to prescribe tolerance. In fact, political nihilism is one perfectly viable option consequent upon ontological relativism, for there remains no barrier against the conclusion of Dostoyevsky's paradigmatic nihilists that "all is permitted."[73] The hidden premise which bridges the logical gap between ontological relativism and tolerance is the assumption that the positivist principle of equality ("all preferences are equal") represents an equality of worth rather than a parity of worthlessness. This assumption, of course, is not a logical correlate of relativism per se.

Moreover, the lack of substance in this formal principle of equality renders it relatively impotent in the context of scarcity and interrelationship which characterizes politics in the real world. The perennial political situation, in other words, is a collision of preferences, and ontological relativism, even including its narrowed principle of human worth and equality, provides no criteria to regulate this situation. Suppose that the preference of one is a desire for domination over others or for possession of a disproportionate share of a scarce resource or for the creation of a political arrangement which relegates some to slavery? What sort of status does this kind of preference have? Is it, too, equal, or should it be distinguished from legitimate preferences? And if so, where does ontological relativism find the criteria for making the distinction? Obviously, it cannot find such criteria within itself; rather, it tends to assume with the ingenuousness of classical liberalism that some political analogue of Adam Smith's "invisible hand" will convert pursuit of private preference into common good.

The converse of the argument that objectivist relativism implies democracy—that is, that democracy presupposes relativism—has also been argued. Anyone who believes in the existence of autonomous standards of human morality, as in the natural-law tradition, this argument runs, will logically insist upon the authoritarian enforcement of these standards in politics. The relativist, in contrast, will logically affirm the principle of democratic majority rule. Hans Kelsen once stated the basic thesis quite clearly: "For, just as autocracy is political absolutism—which is paralleled by philosophical absolutism; so democracy is political relativism—which has its counterpart in philosophical relativism."[74]

Such a formulation misconstrues the crucial distinction between philosophical positions that justify autocracy and those that do not, for the critical dividing line is not between philosophical relativists and philosophical absolutists, but between those who feel that an absolute truth exists which can be known with certainty by finite men and can be imposed by authority without distortion and all others, relativist or not, who deny these claims. A philosophical position which accredits the reality of autonomous moral standards that are transcendent (not capable of full embodiment in history) and which has the epistemological humility to realize that these standards are never fully and certainly vouchsafed to some select group of finite men (whether an ecclesiastical hierarchy, a philosopher-king, or a historical vanguard) will suggest quite a different political conclusion than absolutism. In fact, from such a viewpoint, it becomes a form of blasphemy to ascribe absolute worth to, or to demand absolute allegiance to, any political order. Rather than sustaining political absolutism, then, such a philosophically absolutist outlook may be highly compatible with democratic government. The principal insistence of this outlook would be, as McIlwain has suggested, that the scope of governmental power be limited to keep it from arrogating to itself authority and functions to which it is not legitimately entitled. In short, philosophical absolutism of this sort is incompatible with totalitarian pretentions of any kind and compatible with limited government, including constitutional democracy.

This issue, of course, has many more complications which cannot be discussed in detail here. It is sufficient for present purposes simply to draw from this argument the conclusion that there is no necessary link between democracy and the relativist tenets of objectivism, as many have wanted to suggest or to assume. Neither epistemological nor ontological relativism by itself leads to a democratic political stance, nor need an adherent of democracy be committed to relativism. In short, one consequence of objectivism and its derivative relativism vis-a-vis democratic theory has been to impede a realistic appraisal of the philosophic grounds of democratic constitutionalism by offering an illusory foundation of its own.

Another interesting problem which derives from objectivist assumptions about reality and therefore about what is permissible in theory-building is the question of whether recent empirical theories of democracy have been guilty of a conservative bias. The problem of objectivist conservatism is not confined to democratic theory, as the earlier discussion of equilibrium analysis attests; however, it was in the context of democratic theory that a recent prominent and suggestive dialogue took place which was stimulated by claims of the presence of such a conservative bias.

This particular dialogue was initiated by Jack Walker's argument in "A Critique of the Elitist Theory of Democracy."[75] Briefly, Walker's criticsm of recent attempts to construct an empirical theory of democracy is that, first, the realism of the revisionist efforts have transformed democracy from a radical to a conservative doctrine and, second, the bias of the revision leads to the neglect of some important contemporary political developments. Robert Dahl, in response, makes a fairly simple rejoinder: namely, that Walker does not seem to understand that the revisionists' empirical theory of democracy is descriptive, not normative. In Dahl's words, "One central difficulty with Professor Walker's paradigm is, I think, that he insists upon interpreting as if they were normative or deontological certain writings that were mainly if not wholly intended to set out descriptive, empirical theories."[76]

Setting aside as peripheral the occasional intrusion of prescriptive statements in the work of the revisionists, the central issue is thus clearly joined. And Dahl is, on the surface at least, quite justified in his basic position that there is a difference between description and prescription and that revisionist or elitist theories of democracy are descriptive rather than prescriptive. However, Walker's "reply to the rejoinder" makes an observation worth quoting at some length:

> Ideas and beliefs have manifold consequences, some intended and others wholly unexpected; writings meant by their author to be purely descriptive may still lead their readers to draw normative conclusions, and it is quite possible to study these conclusions without violating the logical distinction between descriptive and prescriptive statements. It would be extremely difficult, perhaps impossible, for any single writer to describe every aspect of the American political system. Each writer must choose among innumerable phenomena which could conceivably be studied. Regardless of the writer's intention, I would argue that the facts he presents and the explanations he proposes may prompt his readers to make certain normative inferences.

Walker cites several examples of such selective interpretations with normative implications, among them the overriding theoretical focus upon stability and continuity of existent regimes.

The Dahl-Walker exchange clearly raises some important and puzzling issues. Two thoughtful and knowledgeable analysts of democracy are in disagreement over the nature, status, and implications of some of the recent theoretical trends in their field. Each provides considerable evidence and logic to support his positive contentions, yet these contentions are apparently incompatible. The most puzzling paradoxes of this discussion, however, could be dispelled if the faulty underlying assumption of a dichotomy between empirical and normative theory were recognized as the source of the apparent anomalies. In fact, both Dahl and Walker are correct in what they affirm—Dahl that the democratic theory in question is descriptive rather than prescriptive, Walker that this description utilizes norms which are not those of classsical democratic theory. The apparent contradiction stems from a faulty identification of the distinction between descriptive and prescriptive statements with the alleged hiatus between normless and normative theory. The possibility of at least beginning to resolve the contradiction can emerge only with the recognition of the irreducible descriptive functions of norms.

These descriptive functions of norms in perception, definition, identification, and explanation will be elaborated in the next chapter. A few anticipatory remarks are necessary, however, to sustain our analysis of the theoretical problem raised by Dahl and Walker. Basically, the objectivist assumptions which prescribe the severance of normative and empirical theory are grounded in a distortedly simplistic view of what is involved in description. The Cartesian postulates of a spatial ontology and the removal of the knowing subject from the known object suggest that the process of description is a designation of spatiomathematical coordinates from an Archimedean vantage point. If this were in fact an accurate model, then it would be correct to deny the need for any descriptive norms beyond the mathematical criteria of order. In fact, of course, the Cartesian model is a wholly fanciful one that bears no resemblance to the process of description by a real human knower in the real world.

A real-world describer must select a particular pattern or group of patterns which he deems significant from an almost infinite number of possible configurations and relationships within which a particular sensible datum could play a part. Whenever it rises above the primitive level of mere pointing, descriptition must proceed on the basis of gestalt, analogy, and metaphor.[7][8] It must rely upon contrast and context. The relationship of a descriptive concept to its background and setting is an effective part of the concept itself. Even perceptually, for example, one does not become aware of a black spot without the contrast of a different shade; and this other-than-blackness is an irreducible requisite of the concepts of black and spot, however tacit its role may be. Similarly, as Wittgenstein has made clear, a word has no meaning apart from its total linguistic context. One cannot define a word in vacuo, for its meaning is the manifold functions it performs within a language game. In describing something, therefore, one must always employ contextual patterns of order, a framework by reference to which the focal concepts are given their full meaning. And this employment is a use of norms, standards and patterns of order which structure the significance of the constituent concepts of a theory.

The conservative implications produced by objectivist limitations on the permissible criteria of order in a theory are principally a result of the rejection of any contextual concepts of potentiality or intentionality. As the common stem of the two concepts suggests, both refer to a situation in which the present is suspended between an origin and a goal. In such a situation, an adequate description of the present requires the use of concepts which reflect its existence in the tension between "has been" and "not yet." It was for this reason that Aristotle designated the *telos* of a movement to be a crucial, if not the crucial, reference point in defining or describing that movement.

The objectivist tradition, however, is radically ahistorical in its spatial orientation. *Res extensa* does not exist in any temporal tension. Time is conceived as an abstraction from space; it is, in Hobbes's word, simply a "phantasm." It is only logical, therefore, that concepts of intentionality and potentiality be denied a legitimate role in an empirical description, since they are clearly time-contingent concepts and must be themselves relegated to the realm of phantasm.

On a priori grounds, therefore, a description adhering to objectivist standards must jettison as unscientific and illicit any concepts which signify the temporal suspension of unfulfilled intentions or potential. Such a rejection, of course, has a profoundly transforming and limiting impact upon description. For example, describing an acorn as an incipient oak tree would be unempirical by objectivist standards—but is the normative reference to an oak really descriptively illicit? Or isn't it necessary to a full description? For another example, consider a tennis shot which lands beyond the base line. Must an objective description be limited to describing where it landed? Or isn't the normative concept of an error, arising from the context of intentionality, part of a full description? In other words, the *telos* of an intention or a potential may not be empirical by objectivist standards, but it possesses an irreducible defining significance, whose omission in a description has manifold consequences.

The conceptual elimination of the tension of intent or potential in the name of empiricism has the effect of hypostazizing the present into the intellectually indispensable role of providing norms or criteria of order. Although this choice of a conceptual *axis mundi* is made in utter good faith as the apparent alternative to the intrusion of subjective norms, the implications are inescapably conservative in the sense of theoretically favoring the status quo. In addition, the definition of the constituent concepts of the theoretical description by reference to standards which rule out the presence of tension gives the system thus created an appearance of completion or self-sufficiency. This is the feature of recent empirical theories of democracy which disturbs Walker. The implication of completion and fulfillment which he finds there is an implication drawn partly from silence—from what the theory does not describe rather than from what it does describe—and is therefore perhaps not fully justified. Arguments from silence are always suspect. Nevertheless, the definition and systematic conceptualization of human, political realities apart from their vectors of intentionality runs contrary to such a deep-seated tacit convention of human discourse that it is not really the reader's fault if, in Walker's words, "writings meant by their authors to be purely descriptive may still lead their readers to draw normative conclusions."[79] Partly because of the conceptual limitations imposed by the objectivist notion of theoretical neutrality, these normative conclusions have been, as Walker suggests, essentially conservative.

As Walker would undoubtedly agree, the problem that puzzles and troubles him is not a function of any positively false contentions by what he terms the revisionist theorists of democracy. The problem is more a function of the presentation of a partial description as if it were fully descriptive, as if anything more to be said would have to employ prescriptive syntax. Generalizing this observation beyond the problem of implied conservatism, we reach the third impact of objectivist assumptions upon democratic theory—an effective truncation of theoretical description. Essentially, this is a result of the application of objectivist-empiricist ontological criteria to determine what shall be admissible in a theoretical description. Any theoretical distinction or concept which cannot be framed on the standards of empiricism is ruled out as illicit. The outcome is a theoretical descriptive reduction of the dimensions of politics to fit the limited dimensions of an objectivist view of reality. If the resultant model were presented as an expression of philosophic conviction, few problems would arise. But it tends to be presented as the only possible description that is scientific, as if to be empirical in the general sense of descriptive one had to be a philosophical empiricist or as if to be objective in the general sense one had to be objectivist. At this point, with its presentation as a general theory, the empiricist model becomes misleading.

An example of this sort of dimension reduction of politics to fit empiricist presuppositions can be found in Robert Dahl's influential little tract *A Preface to Democratic Theory*.[80] In that work, Dahl first examines the logic of Madison's defense of the Constitution, before proceeding to give his own characterization of the limits of democracy. He first notes that Madison's view that the growth of a "majority faction" is hindered by a large electorate with diverse interests tends to detract from his justification of separation of powers as a defense against tyranny.[81] And Dahl also argues that no merely constitutional safeguards would really be adequate to prevent tyranny in the context of the avaricious self-interest of all parties which Madison pictures.[82] Both of these criticisms are well taken, if not wholly novel.[83] What is more significant in the context of our present concern is a third criticism which he makes of Madison.

Much of the burden of Madison's constitutional effort was directed toward the prevention of tyranny and against the deleterious effects of "faction." Admittedly, Madison's attempt to engineer constitutional mechanisms that would effect the sort of prophylaxis he desired was, considered by itself, an impossibility. Dahl observes that "no modern Madison has shown that the restraints on the effectiveness of majorities imposed by the facts of a pluralist society operate only to curtail 'bad' majorities and not 'good' majorities; and I confess I see no way by which such an ingenious proposition could be satisfactorily established."[84] In other words, wholly procedural measures cannot guarantee substantive results, even if they can prevent particular abuses. However, Dahl's criticism of Madison's references to tyranny and faction runs deeper than the observation that the concepts were not effectively translated into practice. It also involves the contention that the concept of natural rights upon which the concepts of tyranny and faction depend must be specified from within the political system. In other words, to be meaningful, the idea of tyranny must be definable by some aspect of the system itself.[85] After considering the possible ways in which this might be done, and finding each of them unacceptable, Dahl concludes that Madison's definition of tyranny "seems to have no operational meaning in the context of political decision-making."[86]

Insofar as this criticism trades upon Madison's failure to see that the mechanism of checks and balances acts as a buffer to tyranny only because it is a buffer to political action generally, it is essentially justified. Insofar as it is a general criticism of the function of the concepts of tyranny and natural right within the context of American democracy, however, it depends upon certain assumptions about the specification and functioning of norms. And Dahl does extend his assessment that tyranny and faction are operationally meaningless to a general principle, since, in his words, "the assumptions that made the idea of natural rights intellectually defensible have tended to dissolve in modern times." Use of such a concept "involves a variety of assumptions that at best are difficult and at worst impossible to prove to the satisfaction of anyone of positivist or skeptical predispositions."[87] Accordingly, Dahl finds no use for natural right and derivative concepts in his constructive efforts which follow his critique.

These constructive efforts, therefore, proceed within the confines of exceedingly minimal criteria of order. This conceptual narrowing exceeds even the limitations counseled by scientific value relativism. It is not a case of simply refusing to commit oneself to propositions about human order which transcend widespread intersubjective transmissibility; rather, these propositions cannot even be considered as part of the empirical data because they do not fit the dimensions of empiricism. The objectivist model of human order as merely a complex of homogeneous preferences must consider a concept such as natural right as no more than a self-deluding rationalization. Recalling Dahl's words about natural right, its rationale "involves a variety of assumptions that at best are difficult and at worst impossible to prove to the satisfaction of anyone of positivist or skeptical predispositions."[88] Hence, to be scientific, to be empirical, one should interpret the polity as a network of preferences, which need not be distinguished by content, because they are essentially interchangeable on positivist presuppositions. This interpretative procedure could be termed aggressive empiricism because it insists that political phenomena be identified and interpreted only on the basis of criteria of order acceptable to an empiricist, regardless of whether or not these are the criteria of interpretation used by the committed spokesman for the political order itself.

Once the objectivist assumption of the homogeneity of preferences dissolves criteria of human order into an indistinct agglomeration of interests, nothing remains except patterns of influence. The entire scope of empirical theory, consequently, becomes an attempt to trace these patterns of influence—that is, to find out who governs. The sociology of power, which is undeniably a valuable and legitimate intellectual enterprise, presumes to claim that its boundaries are coincident with those of all empirical theory. And in fact, the constructive part of Dahl's *A Preface to Democratic Theory* is devoted precisely to the task of defining "democracy" in terms which do not exceed these boundaries.

The rejection as meaningless of concepts such as natural right which do not fit the conceptual dimensions of empiricism actually results in a dogmatically narrowed—that is, narrowed on a priori philosophic grounds—theoretical scope, which cannot deal with some fairly obvious empirical realities. For example, it seems fairly clear that the idea of natural right has had a very profound operational significance in the context of limitations on governmental power, civil liberties, and so on which American courts have imposed and guaranteed. It also has had operational significance in the nation's political culture. Any empirical theory of democracy which does not incorporate such realities would strike many of us as rather inadequate.

At even the simplest level of theoretical description, therefore, political theory might do well to emulate the strategy of contemporary linguistic philosophy when it abandoned its dogmatic positivist phase and adopted its present approach. In its positivist phase, linguistic analysis kept stumbling over propositions that it was forced to dismiss as meaningless on the basis of its postulated criteria of meaning. When it became clear, however, that many such statements could not be dispelled by translation and seemed reasonably intelligible to their users, a new analytic stance seemed necessary. So instead of delimiting the range of meaningful concepts a priori, analysts began to look for the meaning of a linguistic expression in its use. By examining the functions of a word, statement, or phrase, analysts found themselves able to find meaning in expressions which they previously were forced to dismiss out of hand. In effect, by leaving behind the dogmas of logical empiricism, they were enabled to be more empirical. Political scientists who are forced to truncate their empirical theories because of their empiricist prejudices would do well to ponder this lesson.

Notes

1. Almost none of the criticism of features of these theories which follows is altogether novel. Most of the components appear in one form or another in the following works: In democratic theory, Lane Davis, "The Cost of Realism: Contemporary Restatements of Democracy," *Western Political Quarterly*, XVII (1964), 37-46; Jack Walker, "A Critique of the Elitist Theory of Democracy," *American Political Science Review*, LX (1966), 285-305; Peter Bachrach and Morton Baratz, "Two Faces of Power," ibid., LVI (1962), 947-962; Charles McCoy and John Playford, eds., *Apolitical Politics* (New York: Thomas Y. Crowell, 1967); and William Connolly, ed., *The Bias of Pluralism* (New York: Atherton Press, 1969). In the theory of political development, Samuel Huntington, "Political Development and Political Decay," *World Politics*, XVII (1965), 386-430; Gabriel Almond, "Political Development," *Comparative Political Studies*, I (1969), 447-470; J. Roland Pennock, "Political Development, Political Systems, and Political Goods," *World Politics*, XVIII (1966), 415-434. In systems analysis, Paul Kress, "Self, Systems, and Significance: Reflections on Professor Easton's Political Science," *Ethics*, LXXVII (1966); 1-13; Robert Dowse, "A Functionalist's Logic," *World Politics*, XVIII (1966), 607-622; Christian Bay, "Politics and Pseudo-Politics," *American Political Science Review*, LIX (1965), 39-51.

Related observations can also be found in Joseph La Palombara, "Decline of Ideology: A Dissent and an Interpretation," ibid., LX (1966), 5-16; and William Connolly, *Political Science and Ideology* (New York: Atherton Press, 1967).

What needs to be realized, however, is that the problems discussed in these works are not wholly isolated cases, but are in part related difficulties which arise logically from some common preconceptions. Once this fact is appreciated, these problems can be consolidated to some extent, and a unified reassessment of the nature and status of empirical and normative theory will be possible.

2. Harold Lasswell and Abraham Kaplan, *Power and Society* (New Haven: Yale University Press, 1950).

3. Lasswell, *Politics: Who Gets What, When, How*, 2nd ed., (New York: Peter Smith and Company, 1950), p. 3.

4. Roy Macridis, Richard Cox, et. al., "Research in Comparative Politics," *American Political Science Review*, XLVII (1953), 641-657.

5. Almond, "Political Theory and Political Science," ibid., LX (1966), 875-876.

6. Cf. David Easton, *A Framework for Political Analysis* (Englewood Cliffs, N.J.: Prentice-Hall, 1965), and *A Systems Analysis of Political Life* (New York: John Wiley and Sons, 1965); and Morton A. Kaplan, *Systems and Process in International Politics* (New York: John Wiley and Sons, 1957), and "On Systems," in *Macropolitics* (Chicago: Aldine Publishing Co., 1969), pp. 49-76.

7. Cf. William Ross Ashby, *Design for a Brain*, 2nd ed. (New York: John Wiley and Sons, 1960).

8. Easton, *A Framework for Political Analysis*, p. 23.

9. Ibid., p. 89.

10. Easton, *A Systems Analysis of Political Life*, p. 10.

11. Ibid., p. 12.

12. Biology, for example, has seen important cases of this sort. Cf. J.H. Woodger, *Biological Principles* (New York: Harcourt and Brace, 1929).

13. Marx W. Wartofsky, *Conceptual Foundations of Scientific Thought* (New York: Macmillan Co., 1969), p. 361.

14. One example of this logical pattern was the development of legal positivism in the field of jurisprudence. In Austin, the severance of positive law from questions of natural law, morality, and justice, was originally methodological. Austin did not deny the presence or influence of what he called "the law of God" and "positive morality," but he wanted to bracket them analytically. Later on, however, the almost irresistible tendency to convert a methodological limitation into an ontological one came to fruition in the empirical identification of law with the command of the sovereign.

This tendency is also noted by two astute contemporary sociologists in the context of their own discipline: "A purely structural sociology is endemically in danger of reifying social phenomena. Even if it begins by modestly assigning to its constructs merely heuristic status, it all too frequently ends by confusing its own conceptualizations with the laws of the universe" (Peter Berger and Thomas Luckmann, *The Social Construction of Reality: A*

Treatise in the Sociology of Knowledge [Garden City, N.Y.: Doubleday, 1966], p. 170).

15. In Easton's words, it indicates "the part of reality to be included within a systematic study of political life" (Easton, *A Systems Analysis of Political Life,* p. 12).

16. Sheldon Wolin, *Politics and Vision* (Boston: Little, Brown, 1960); see esp. intro. chap.

17. Easton, *A Framework for Political Analysis,* pp. 50, 53.

18. Eric Voegelin, *The New Science of Politics* (Chicago: Phoenix Books, 1966), p. 27.

19. One aspect of this incapacity, to supply only one example, is the inability of a political scientist working within the limits of Easton's model to distinguish between what Christian Bay has contrasted by the terms "politics" and "pseudo-politics"; cf. "Politics and Pseudo-politics," *American Political Science Review,* LIX (1965), 39-51. Whether Bay's phraseology here is felicitous or not is subject to question, but he was at least trying to rescue the conceptualization of political acts from the analytical vacuity which follows their definition within a homogeneous plane of meaning.

20. Lasswell, *Politics: Who Gets What, When, How,* p. 197: "With his insatiable craving for gestures of deference to his ego from his fellow men, he had no durable interests in the objective processes of nature or the conditions of beauty. He sought the balm of success for his wounded ego, and he was forever licking his self-inflicted mutilations."

21. With systemic interrelationship presupposed methodologically, it in fact becomes difficult to investigate empirically the degree of actual coherence and order in a polity. Even if the concepts used do not prejudice the issue, they at least do not possess the capacity for conceptualizing distinctions between well-integrated systems and systems that are loosely connected at best. As A. James Gregor has recently observed, "When Easton defines a 'system' as 'any set of variables regardless of the degree of interrelationship among them,' one can legitimately wonder when one would be disposed to maintain that a 'system,' political or otherwise, no longer obtains" ("Political Science and Functional Analysis," *American Political Science Review,* LXII (1968), 431. Similarly, the methodologically presumed interrelationship tends to obscure the cross-purpose of various system components by analyzing them solely in relationship to a common end. Probably this speculation is pure fancy, but I sometimes wonder whether some of the students who criticize all social institutions as undifferentiated constituents of a monolithic system might not have been predisposed to this analytical narrowness by absorbing the methodological limitations of systems analysis as if they comprised an adequate empirical description.

22. Pye, *Communications and Political Development* (Princeton, N.J.: Princeton University Press, 1963), p. 79.

23. Almond and James Coleman, *Politics of the Developing Areas* (Princeton, N.J.: Princeton University Press, 1960), p. 11: "The same functions are performed in all the political systems."

Easton, *A Systems Analysis,* pp. 15-61: "Since we would be concerned with the processes underlying all political life, whatever form it takes, we would have to be prepared to test the general utility of concepts by their applicability to systems as small as a band of fifty Bushmen or as large as an international system encompassing hundreds of millions of persons." The crucial questions here turn about the logic of "same" and "whatever form it takes." While for some purposes the presumption of functional similarities among different political systems is fruitful, in other cases it might be crucial to determine whether the functions performed are the "same" and whether the "form" taken by political organizations is significantly different.

24. Arthur L. Kalleberg, "The Logic of Comparison: A Methodological Note on the Comparative Study of Political Systems," *World Politics*, XIX (1966), p. 69.

25. David Apter, *The Politics of Modernization* (Chicago: University of Chicago Press, 1965), p. 60.

26. Apter, "The Role of Traditionalism in the Political Modernization of Ghana and Uganda," *World Politics*, XII (1960), 45-68.

27. Myron Wiener, *Party Politics in India* (Princeton, N.J.: Princeton University Press, 1957), p. 7. Nonpolitical motivations are also important to American party workers, of course, but these motives are largely convivial; cf. Samuel Eldersveld, *Political Parties* (Chicago: Rand McNally Co., 1964).

28. For a good introduction to the manifold uses of the concept of equilibrium in the work of numerous social theorists, cf. Cynthia Russett, *The Concept of Equilibrium in American Social Thought* (New Haven: Yale University Press, 1966).

29. For example, Vilfredo Pareto responded to one such criticism by fuming, "It is a monumental stupidity to say, as one critic said, that when I speak of a state of equilibrium, I am thinking of a state which I consider *better* than another state, equilibrium being better than lack of equilibrium" (cited by Russett, *The Concept of Equilibrium*, p. 99). As Russett remarks, however, "in the face of the available facts stupidity has to be risked, for Pareto did cherish the notion of social equilibrium" (loc. cit.).

30. For example, the same logical pattern is apparent in the very recent exchange, to be considered later, between Robert Dahl and Jack Walker; cf. Jack Walker, "A Critique of the Elitist Theory of Democracy," and Robert Dahl, "Further Reflections on 'The Elitist Theory of Democracy' " *American Political Science Review*, LX (1966), 285-305.

31. For example, cf. James Petras, "Ideology and United States Political Scientists," *Science and Society*, XXIX (1965), 192-216. Karl Deutsch tends to agree that equilibrium analysis has had a conservative cast, but he feels that this tendency is due to a homeostatic model which can be transcended by cybernetics; cf. *Nerves of Government* (Glencoe, Ill.: The Free Press, 1966), pp. 88-91.

32. Russett, *The Concept of Equilibrium*, p. 54.

33. Speaking of the first three of this group, Russett says, "Equilibrium, for all three, was a convenient scientific symbol for cherished social values" (ibid., p. 54). "Curiously, Bentley's mechanical model, with its proscription of external norms, nevertheless terminated in an apotheosis of equilibrium"

(ibid., p. 83). Equilibrium "represented for Pareto a very desirable kind of social stability"(ibid., p. 99). Catlin "invested equilibrium with a meaning that was heavily normative, then used it in such a way as to make clear his personal commitment to political democracy" (ibid., p. 107).

34. S.N. Eisenstadt, in *Bureaucracy and Political Development*, Joseph La Palombara, ed. (Princeton, N.J.: Princeton University Press, 1963), p. 96.

35. Frederick Frey, in *Communications and Political Development*, Lucian Pye, ed. (Princeton, N.J.: Princeton University Press, 1963), p. 299: "Any number of views as to what constitutes political development are in vogue; contemporary consensus seems to be lacking."

36. Karl Deutsch, "Social Mobilization and Political Development," *American Political Science Review*, LX (1961), 493-514: "The main usefulness of the concept (of social mobilization) should be in the possibility of quantitative study which it offers."

37. Ibid., p. 494.

38. Cf. La Palombara, "An Overview of Bureaucracy and Political Development," in *Bureaucracy And Political Development*.

39. Pye, *Aspects of Political Development* (Boston: Little, Brown, 1966), p. 6.

40. Apter, *The Politics of Modernization*, p. 67: "Development, modernization, and industrialization can be placed in a descending order of generality."

41. Cf. ibid., and the criterion which Almond and Powell postulate of "the increased secularization of political culture," in *Comparative Politics: A Developmental Approach* (Boston: Little, Brown, 1966), p. 105.

42. In his *World Politics in an Age of Revolution* (New York: Praeger, 1967), p. 278, Spanier refers to "political—that is democratic—development."

43. Cf. Paul Meadows, "Eschatons of Change: Philosophical Backgrounds of Development Theory," *International Journal of Comparative Sociology*, IX (1968), 41-60; and Ali Mazrui, "From Social Darwinism to Current Theories of Modernization: A Tradition of Analysis," *World Politics*, XXI (1968), 69-83.

44. J. William Fulbright, *The Arrogance of Power* (New York: Vintage Books, 1966) pp. 18-19.

45. *World Politics*, XVII (1965), 386-430.

46. Ibid., p. 390.

47. Ibid., p. 391.

48. Pye, *Aspects of Political Development*, pp. 52-53.

49. Ibid., p. 52: "The very legitimacy of Development is thus brought into question by the spirit of cultural relativism. . . . The manifest urgency of the historical problem of development has in the main forced social scientists to suppress some of their scruples of cultural relativism but has left them without strong philosophical underpinnings to support their involvement in the development problem."

50. Almond, "Political Development," p. 459.

51. Pye, *Aspects of Political Development*, p. 52-53.

52. By "dogmatic" I mean simply that the truncation is a function of a

priori philosophical assumptions rather than the a posteriori result of unprejudiced inquiry. For amplification of this usage, cf. Thomas S. Kuhn, "The Function of Dogma in Scientific Research," in A.C. Crombie, ed., *Scientific Change* (New York: Basic Books, 1963).

53. This same basic pattern is repeated in the Walker-Dahl exchange discussed below.

54. For a thoughtful elaboration of the central role of institutional factors in development, cf. Ralph Braibanti, "External Inducement of Political-Administrative Development: An Institutional Strategy," in Braibanti, ed., *Political and Administrative Development* (Durham, N.C. Duke University Press, 1969), pp. 3-106.

55. Lasswell, "The Policy Sciences of Development," *World Politics*, XVII (1965), 288.

56. Examples of this general approach are Karl de Schweinitz, "Growth, Development, and Political Modernization," ibid., XXII (1970), 518-540; and Warren Ilchman and Norman Uphoff, *The Political Economy of Change* (Berkeley and Los Angeles: University of California Press, 1969).

57. Bay has offered some suggestions about the form of inquiry necessary to sustain this kind of model in the context of contemporary thought; cf. the final section of "Politics and Pseudopolitics."

58. *World Politics*, XVIII (1966), 415-434.

59. Ibid., p. 433.

60. Ibid., p. 420. For further recent examples of this approach, cf. Carl Friedrich, "Political Development and the Objectives of Modern Government," in Braibanti, ed., *Political and Administrative Development*, pp. 107-135; Denis Goulet, "Development for What?" *Comparative Political Studies*, I (1968), 295-312; Mulford Q. Sibley, "Social Order and Human Ends: Some Central Issues in the Modern Problem," in David Spitz, ed., *Political Theory and Social Change* (New York: Atherton Press, 1967), pp. 221-255; Douglas V. Steere, "Development: For What?" in John H. Hallowell, ed., *Development For What?* (Durham, N.C.: Duke University Press, 1964), pp. 213-235.

61. Cf. Lasswell, "The Policy Sciences of Development."

62. As if to illustrate this weakness, Lasswell bases his model on his "explicit preference" for "human dignity" without ever undertaking to examine critically what this "dignity" might be.

63. Another resolution of the conceptual difficulties with the notion of development is also possible. In a very recent article, Samuel Huntington has suggested that the concept be abandoned altogether. "These definitional problems," he argues, "raised very real questions about the usefulness of political development as a concept. Referring to Pye's list of ten definitions, Rustow argued that this 'is obviously at least nine too many.' In truth, however, one should go one step further. If there are ten definitions of political development, there are ten too many, and the concept is, in all likelihood, superfluous and dysfunctional" ("The Change to Change: Modernization, Development, and Politics," *Comparative Politics*, III [1971], p. 303). Huntington offers some sound arguments for the abandonment of the concept of political development as it has been used; and the

111

often unproductive discussions and analytical usage of that specific term may well quietly disappear. However, what will not disappear so easily are the very real conceptual insufficiencies and confusions which the hassle about political development has embodied. These problems, it is safe to say, will reappear under a new name until they are confronted and resolved explicitly.

64. Paul Tillich, *The Protestant Era* (Chicago: Phoenix Books, 1957), p. 153.

65. Cf. Carl Becker, *The Heavenly City of the Eighteenth-Century Philosophers* (New Haven: Yale University Press, 1932).

66. Both the logical progressions and the practical problems of this process have been the concern of Walter Lippman in various of his writings, especially in *Preface to Morals* and *The Public Philosophy.* A similar recognition is reflected in John H. Hallowell, *Decline of Liberalism as an Ideology* (Berkeley and Los Angeles: University of California Press, 1943).

67. For an analysis of America's "natural liberalism" and its impact on political thought, cf. Louis Hartz, *The Liberal Tradition in America* (New York: Harcourt, Brace & World, 1955), and Daniel Boorstin, *The Genius of American Politics* (Chicago: University of Chicago Press, 1953). Americans, in a political replica of Cartesian faith in clear and distinct ideas, have possessed a "sober faith that its norms are self-evident" (Hartz, p. 58). An overly acerbic but nevertheless often insightful study of the impact of this "sober faith" on American political thought can be found in Bernard Crick, *The American Science of Politics* (Berkeley and Los Angeles: University of California Press, 1959).

68. Herbert Feigl, "The Scientific Outlook: Naturalism and Humanism," in Feigl and May Brodbeck, eds., *Readings in the Philosophy of Science,* (New York: Appleton-Century-Crofts, 1953), p. 18.

69. Ibid.

70. Daniel Lerner, "Social Science: Whence and Whither," in Lerner, ed., *The Human Meaning of the Social Sciences,* (New York: Meridian Books, 1959), p. 38.

71. La Palombara, "Decline of Ideology: A Dissent and an Interpretation," *American Political Science Review,* LX (1966), 14-15.

72. For a summary of Radbruch's argument, cf. Arnold Brecht, *Political Theory* (Princeton, N.J.: Princeton University Press, 1959), pp. 336 ff. Or for the original published statement, cf. Radbruch, "Le relativism dans la philosophie de droit," *Archives de philosophie du droit et de sociologie juridique,* IV (1934), 105-110. Radbruch later repudiated his original position.

73. Michael Polanyi, for one, has contended that this logical option has found historical expression in the process which he terms "moral inversion"; cf. *Logic of Liberty* (London: Routledge & Kegan Paul, 1951), and *Beyond Nihilism* (London: Cambridge University Press, 1960).

74. Quoted in Brecht, p. 338.

75. *American Political Science Review,* LX (1966), 285-295. Somewhat parallel contentions had also been made by Davis, "The Cost of Realism;"

and by Graeme Duncan and Steven Lukes, "The New Democracy," *Political Studies*, XI (1963), 156-177.

76. Robert Dahl, "Further Reflections on 'The Elitist Theory of Democracy,' " *American Political Science Review*, LX (1966), 298.

77. Ibid., p. 391 (letter to the ed.).

78. C.S. Lewis, in Max Black, ed., *The Importance of Language*, (Englewood Cliffs, N.J.: Prentice-Hall, 1962), p. 47: "When we pass beyond pointing to individual sensible objects, when we begin to think of causes, relations, or mental states or acts, we become incurably metaphorical."

79. Walker, op. cit., p. 391.

80. Dahl, *A Preface to Democratic Theory* (Chicago: Phoenix Books, 1956).

81. Ibid., p. 30.

82. Ibid., p. 134. In other words, the Enlightenment tendency to see constitutions as the guarantors of a good society, a tendency best exemplified by Kant's remark that a "race of devils" could establish a workable state if they were good legal mechanics, is rather naive.

83. E.E. Schattschneider made the first criticism in his *Party Government* (New York: Holt, Rinehart and Winston, 1942). And as Dahl notes, Machiavelli stressed the dependence of constitutional efficacy upon the habits and attitudes of the society.

84. Dahl, *Preface*, pp. 29-30.

85. Ibid., p. 23: "It is self-evident that the definition of tyranny would be entirely empty unless natural rights could somehow be defined. It can be shown, I think, that we must specify a process by which specific natural rights can be defined in the context of some political society." Unfortunately, Dahl only states that this necessity "can be shown," rather than going on to present this demonstration; for it is in the logic of demonstrating this necessity that the critical theoretical problems arise.

86. Ibid., p. 24.

87. Ibid., p. 45.

88. Ibid., p. 45.

6 The Descriptive Functions of Norms

Our concern so far has been to analyze the nature and origins of some of the central conceptual problems faced by contemporary political theory. We have argued that many of these conceptual difficulties which have emerged grow from the attempt to maintain an unbridgeable gap between empirical and normative theory. Since the presuppositions behind this model of a dichotomous theoretical enterprise are faulty, trying to abide by the ground rules which it decrees seriously hampers the theorist's efforts to understand and interpret political reality. At times the theories produced in accordance with these rules are truncated, at times they are distorted, at times they are misleading because they rely on hidden elements of political substance or norms which have crept in unacknowledged. Sometimes these theoretical dislocations are minor; at other times they are more central and important. They will very likely become more, rather than less, troublesome as political scientists aspire to theories of higher levels of significance and generality.

The presuppositions behind the presumed dichotomy in political theory, we have suggested, are not an idiosyncrasy of political science but have instead been assimilated from the philosophical substratum of Western thought since the scientific revolution of the seventeenth century. Conceptual problems similar to those faced by political scientists, therefore, have arisen in various other fields, from philosophy of language through psychology and on into some of the natural sciences, such as biology and physics. We sketched a few of these problems in earlier chapters to indicate the breadth and basic consistency of the pattern of conceptual anomalies.[1]

Borrowing again Thomas Kuhn's interpretative categories, we may say that we have looked at a basic theoretical paradigm—almost a metatheoretical paradigm, since it governs our understanding of what a theory is—and at some of the anomalies that have developed in its use. The logical task which remains is to indicate the nature of an alternative paradigm which could perform the functions of the previous one while resolving anomalies which the previous paradigm could not handle. In its entirety, of course, this task exceeds the scope of a broad exploratory essay such as this one. However, some suggestions along these lines are virtually compelled by the logic of our thesis. Fortunately, some of the components of a new paradigm have begun to emerge from various sources as the defects of the older paradigm have become apparent, and so, our suggestions need not be manufactured from thin air. Sketching the basic outlines of a new paradigm governing the nature and status of political theorizing, then, will be the concern of the final two chapters.

In this chapter, we shall try to replace the dichotomous model of the theoretical enterprise by arguing that norms perform descriptive functions in theory construction. This contention has been implicit in many parts of the preceding chapters. Here we shall attempt to elaborate the argument in somewhat more general terms. If norms do function in theoretical descriptions, of course, the notion of an unbridgeable gap between normative theory (allegedly dealing with prescriptions) and empirical theory (allegedly dealing with normatively empty descriptions) must be abandoned and the unity of the theoretical enterprise reasserted. In the final chapter, our concern will be with a basic epistemological model which sustains and justifies this view of the role of norms in theoretical description.

The problems surveyed in previous chapters will continue to perplex us until we are able to restructure and rearrange some of our most fundamental epistemological categories. Specifically, the conventional understanding of the meaning and mutual relationship of such concepts as description, normative, empirical, and objective needs to be carefully reexamined and ultimately revised. Such a reassessment requires a fairly sustained effort of the imagination, since it presupposes the suspension of intellectual assumptions which have been uncritically, hence inarticulately, held for more than three centuries. It requires the conscious mind to swim upstream against its own subconscious habits and against the very linguistic patterns within which it has habitually operated.

The dichotomous model of political theory has placed the concepts of empirical, descriptive, and objective on one side of the divide and the concepts of normative, prescriptive, and subjective on the other side. The new paradigm of a reintegrated political theory involves the systematic repudiation of this categorization and a consequent revision of the meanings of the individual terms themselves. We have little direct concern with prescription for the moment, for a theory is a form of description, not of admonition or exhortation, even though it may involve fairly unavoidable prescriptive implications of a general nature. We shall first, then, turn to the concepts of description and norm in order to indicate that they are not heterogeneous but instead are often intrinsically complementary. Recognition of this complementarity will imply, of course, that the conventional understanding of each of the terms is inaccurate and misleading in some respects. And in the final chapter, we shall argue that empirical theory is both objective and subjective in one sense and neither objective nor subjective in the sense that implies their mutual exclusiveness.

The objectivist model of dichotomized theory rests upon two faulty identifications. First, the epistemological distinction between empirical theory and normative theory is identified with the syntactical distinction between description and prescription. Second, political neutrality is confused with theoretical and conceptual neutrality. Neither identification will stand close examination, however. All theory is essentially descriptive, including theory which would be classed as normative by the conventional wisdom. Any theory composed of nothing but syntactical prescriptions would be nonsensical. And all theories to some extent or another have prescriptive implications; but this is a prescription predicated upon the reality principle. For example, Burke's theoretical description of the organic qualities of political society implies that it would be wrong to approach politics as one would approach a purely mechanical artifice. Plato's theoretical description of certain poets as charlatans and image-makers implies that it would be wrong to take them too seriously. A descriptive study of the functionality of political corruption in developing states implies that it should not be approached as if it were a useless aberration.[2] In each case, the prescriptive implication is fully contingent upon what is, both logically and syntactically, a descriptive theory. The theorist may at times draw some of the prescriptive implications himself, but if his theory were pure and unadulterated prescription which had no descriptive basis, no one would pay him a moment's attention.

The belief in neutrality as a theoretical stance akin to political neutrality is similarly mistaken. Neutrality is a possible feature of the practical world of action; it is impossible in the context of constructing and using a theory. A politician may decide to be neutral in a particular dispute, but a theorist can be descriptively neutral only if he refrains from opening his mouth altogether. In practice, the achievement of extensive theoretical neutrality in the name of objectivity is achieved by the use of theoretical models which are patterned metaphysically on some subhuman reality such as that of a mechanism. The neutrality thus achieved is in direct proportion to the human emptiness of the model employed—and is, in fact, heavily committed to the peculiar felicity of that model.

The implicit model which underlies both of these confusions, the identification of the contrast between description and prescription with a presumed hiatus between empirical and normative theory and the alleged "neutrality" of an objective description, is a Laplacean understanding of what is involved in description. Absolute detachment and objectivity would indeed be possible and meaningful within the Laplacean view of knowledge. Knowledge, for Laplace, was the exact determination of all of the particular component atoms of the world in their spatiotemporal location by a mind which was a passive spectator without historical location itself. "Nothing would be uncertain," as Laplace exulted, to such a mind. This is the model of knowing which has sustained the concept of science as utterly objective, normless description to this day. The only difficulty is that the Laplacean model is a complete delusion, resting on absurd premises.

In the first place, there is no such thing as a knowing mind that can simply step outside of history to an Archimedean point and passively register an exhaustive picture of all existent spatiotemporal atoms. Even more important, however, even if such an exhaustive computation of all atomic data could be made and absorbed by such a mind, it could tell us nothing at all of political relevance. Such a mind could perceive a pattern of spatiotemporal relationships between atomic particulars, but it could not infer anything about political patterns from this knowledge.[3] As Michael Polanyi has put it, "The tremendous intellectual feat conjured up by Laplace's imagination has diverted attention from the decisive sleight of hand by which he substitutes a knowledge of all experience for a knowledge of all atomic data. Once you refuse this deceptive substitution, you immediately see that the Laplacean mind understands precisely nothing and that whatever it knows means precisely nothing."[4]

The real-world student of politics is in a quite different situation

118

from the mythical Laplacean observer. To begin with, he exists within and is a product of some of the very political and cultural patterns which he is trying to understand. Moreover, in discerning patterns of political order around him, he gains no sustenance from the purely spatiotemporal coordinates of the mythical Laplacean world. In order to perceive, to define, to appraise, and to explain political reality, the real-world mind must ascertain and employ organizing gestalts to find order in what would otherwise be an empty landscape. That is, a real-world knower, in contrast with the mythical Laplacean observer, uses organizing norms in his descriptive apprehension of political reality.

The basic nature and role of norms needs to be understood in this context; and such an understanding should not be too difficult once the enchantment of Laplace's delusive dream is broken. This proper understanding of norms has been largely obscured in recent years by the insistence that they be located only in the context of prescription. As the dictionary definition of the word indicates, however, a norm is basically a pattern, a type, a standard. Norms serve the general intellectual function of providing criteria of order. Criteria of order may, of course, function in the context of a prescription as ideals, but this is only one possible function. There is nothing syntactically imperative in the use of norms per se. Norms also function as ordering criteria in the context of cognition, perception, description; in fact, I would argue this to be their most essential function. A norm is really more a form of concept than it is a form of imperative. Indeed, it is a gestalt, a shape, a meaning.[5]

The cognitive, descriptive functions of norms have been obscured by the Laplacean model of description, acting in concert with the Baconian view of theory-building. On this understanding of a descriptive theory, an inquiry begins with observation, which is conceived as relatively objective (that is, unbiased and theory-neutral) and unproblematic. A steady accretion of these observables—the data—gradually grows into a pattern, then, which is the theory. Recent, more sophisticated explorations of descriptive theories recognize, in contrast, that there are no such things as Laplacean observables. There are only perceptibles, which are data already selected and structured by criteria of order.

A few citations from noted philosophers of science might be helpful both to elaborate and to document this important point. Norwood Hanson devotes his first chapter in *Patterns of Discovery* to the problematic quality of observation. "There is a sense," he holds, "in which seeing is a theory-laden undertaking."[6] Kuhn argues that a scientific revolution is basically akin to a shift of perception and concludes that the objectivist model of neutral sense-data is no longer acceptable:

> But is sensory experience fixed and neutral? Are theories simply man-made interpretations of given data? The epistemological viewpoint that has most often guided Western philosophy for three centuries dictates an immediate and unequivocal, Yes! In the absence of a developed alternative, I find it impossible to relinquish entirely that viewpoint. Yet it no longer functions effectively, and the attempts to make it do so through the introduction of a neutral language of observations now seem to me hopeless.[7]

Marx Wartofsky writes that "all observation and all measurement that goes beyond blind sensory 'contact' or 'raw feel' is observation that something is the case, and this step beyond pure neural response or 'immediate sensation' (if there is such a thing) is made in virtue of some framework of observation or measurement, in which it attains to significance."[8] And Michael Polanyi points out that "every perception of things" is dependent upon a tacit theoretical context and "involves implications about the nature of things which could be false." If all of these tacit contextual shaping components of perception "could be eliminated by training myself to look at things again with unperceiving eyes, letting their images sweep across my retina like a motion picture which is continuously slipping through the gate of the projecting lantern," he continues, "I would not feel assured of gaining access thereby to a core of indubitable virgin data. I should merely be blotting out my eyesight, just as fakirs do when they go into a trance with open eyes."[9] The study of ethology has made it clear, in fact, that perception is not only theory-laden but that, more radically, perception itself is intrinsically organized by sensory-motor gestalts.[10]

This uneliminable component of organizing patterns on the process of perception has been worth emphasizing because its consequences are enormous. Acceptance of this increasingly accepted and well documented view of perception as the irreducible origin of cognition implies the repudiation of the Laplacean model of description, the Baconian view of theory-formation, the Cartesian program of critical doubt, the empiricist view of sense-data, and the positivist conception of verifiability. In this way, our improved understanding of the nature of perception and its relationship to theoretical frameworks and description is the central source of the rejection of the whole objectivist epistemological program and, at the same time, is the critical source of the epistemological model that must be elaborated to replace it.

This more sophisticated new model of perception-description-theorizing (each shades off into the other) has numerous consequences, of course, for understanding the epistemological status of political theory. In the present context, our principal concern is the light which it sheds upon the relationship between norms and descriptive-empirical theory. As we have said, norms are essentially patterns of order. They serve in the context of description, then, as guidelines which shape perception by providing organizational patterns of coherence. They provide the contextual framework, often tacit, which gives shape to the data which are structured descriptively within it.

As Polanyi correctly insists, it is quite impossible to step completely outside all organizing patterns of perceptual coherence to arrive at some virgin, unstructured landscape of pure data. One would then not see particulars unencumbered by theoretical trappings; one would simply see nothing at all. This is because the particulars of a perception or theory, the focal data, receive their own identity or definition by virtue of their relationship to the total context. They cannot stand completely alone. The situation is directly analogous to that discussed by Wittgenstein when he observes that the meaning of a particular linguistic datum—a word—is a function of its context, the language-game. No game, no words (except for ostensive words such as "this" or "that," and even here the physical context of pointing is essential to their meaning). The uneliminable role of the tacit organizing pattern in cognition is expressed well by Norwood Hanson:

> Organization is not itself seen as are the lines and colors of a drawing. It is not itself a line, shape, or a color. It is not an element in the visual field, but rather the way in which the elements are appreciated. Again, the plot is not another detail in the story. Nor is the tune just one more note. Yet without plots and tunes details and notes would not hang together. Similarly, the organization of [one of Hanson's illustrations] is nothing that registers on the retina along with other details. Yet it gives the lines and shapes a pattern. Were this lacking we would be left with nothing but an unintelligible configuration of lines.[11]

This important observation serves to illuminate the difficulty with the belief that empirical theory is being merely and purely descriptive by refining out or bracketing norms, for these norms perform a cognitive, perceptual, descriptive role as the organizational framework within which the data are seen and understood. As Hanson notes, it is simply incorrect to assume that this contextual framework of order and meaning can be set aside without effecting a positive change in the content of the data themselves.

Refining out all norms, then does not simply cast aside separable, detachable additions to an autonomous picture of reality; rather, such a process changes the whole picture. The constituent elements of the picture are the same in one sense, but in another sense, the sense in which what they are is contextually defined, they are no longer the same.

Suppose, for example, that a relentlessly objectivist analyst were asked to describe a game of tennis and took utterly seriously the admonition that all norms, all standards of order with prescriptive implications, were illicit. Presumably, then, terms such as "fault" and "error" would have to be eliminated as dependent upon norms of performance for their meaning and hence not within his legitimate purview. The use of such concepts would be normative and critical, whereas he was to be objective and purely analytical. It would be quite possible, of course, to describe a tennis game without using the terms in question. The purely objective description using only spatiotemporal norms, would be confined to distinguishing different shots by their relative locations, so that rather than fault, one would merely note the distance that the ball landed beyond the service line, and so on. There would be nothing wrong—in the sense of inaccurate—with such an account. It's simply that the overall picture presented by such a description would seem rather strange to a tennis player, who would imaginatively replace the normative setting to make the description fully meaningful to him. A tennis novice presented with such a description would learn little about the game, it is safe to say, and he would very likely draw some faulty prescriptive conclusions about how one should go about playing. The bracketing of normative concepts results in a transformation of descriptive gestalt that in effect creates a whole new ball game.

This is analogous to the situation which disturbs Jack Walker, Lane Davis, and others when they contemplate the limited description of democracy produced under the ground rules that require bracketing its traditional purposes and significance as normative encumbrances. It is like hearing a story without its plot, or hearing some familiar musical notes placed into the setting of a new tune. They can find nothing positively inaccurate in any of the constituent parts of the new tune or the new story, but the overall general impression seems partial, curiously focused, and in some ways misleading. Somewhat tentatively, they express this sense of disorientation by talking about the "prescriptive implications" which they find to be implicit in the theoretical model presented to them.

The response to these criticisms, by such theorists as Dahl, that the new theories are purely descriptive is accurate but, as our argument above indicates, also too simplistic and misleading. Such a response is simplistic because it does not recognize the complete permeation of data by the organizational norms employed in their perception. It is misleading because it implies that the revisionist theory is the sole description that can be made and that any other account would be a variety of syntactical prescription. In fact, the theories in question are the product of one of several possible theoretical-perceptual orientations, all of which are essentially descriptive.

It is, of course, a perfectly legitimate methodology to bracket the descriptive setting of the norms of intent, potential, or significance for certain analytical purposes. Such a methodological abstraction makes it possible to focus upon particular facets of a political system without being distracted by questions that are irrelevant to one's principal concern. What is not legitimate is to conceive the results of such a methodological abstraction as the sole possible objective description of political reality. To do so is to allow the abstractive methodology to produce its own truncated ontology, with misleading consequences. Reality is not that limited, nor is description that simple.

To recapitulate the basic argument to this point, then, norms are patterns or standards of order that have an important descriptive impact as the organizational matrix of description. This matrix of structuring norms, moreover, is not a detachable window dressing but rather a decisive determinant of the contextually defined data themselves. It therefore cannot be bracketed without producing a positive change of gestalt, and it is consequently not entirely acceptable to consider the resultant picture as theoretically privileged. This argument is quite applicable, moreover, in cases where the normative framework in question is the context of intentionality, potentiality, or meaningfulness—realities which are denied or misinterpreted by the conceptual and ontological limitations of objectivism.

A theoretical description is a reflection, through models either verbal or visual, of a perception of order. This perception of order and coherence in reality is often tacit, but it constitutes an irreducible component of all knowledge and all theory. Norms, as we have said, are part of the family of these epistemologically significant ordering patterns. It is not at all incorrect to say that science begins with these perceptions of order. If you read Aristotle's view that "nature is everywhere the cause of order" as a statement about epistemology rather than as a statement enmeshed in his ontological beliefs, the point is essentially the same. That is, science begins with wonder at or bemusement by patterns of orderliness and coherence which are distinguishable from purely random occurrences.

It is one of the most glaring deficiencies of the objectivist account of knowledge that it is unable to specify the grounds for this fundamental perception of order, which is contrasted with randomness. This incapacity derives from the objectivist model of motion, discussed in previous chapters, which conceived all motion as random. It is also consonant with the objectivist spatial ontology, which envisions each spatial point of reality to be equally related or unrelated to every other spatial point. Perhaps the very omnipresence and irreducibility of the order-discerning operations of the human mind have allowed them, like Poe's famous purloined letter, to go unexplained by epistemology. Any account of theory construction which begins by speaking uncritically about observation, for example, has already ignored this critical feature of the human intelligence. The formulations of Kuhn, Polanyi, Hanson, and Wartofsky cited above represent the recognition of this failure and the attempt to remedy it by contemporary philosophers of science.

Every time a human mind discerns the structure of a complex entity, such as a biological organism, or proceeds to explore a pattern of orderliness in nature, it is utilizing this capacity to discover order in the world and to distinguish it from randomness. Yet this capacity of the human intelligence, which is essential to its capacity to give a theoretical description of anything (anything beyond an empty spatial infinity) remains an anomaly to objectivism. This power is a capacity to find real patterns of order; it is not merely the injection of subjective fantasies into a world of pure spatial objectivity. The reality of the patterns of order is attested by their heuristic powers to illuminate and explain as yet unperceived events or realities. Yet it is also undeniable that the discernment of these real patterns of order requires the operation of human judgment. No computer, no Laplacean eye, could perform such a feat of knowledge unless it was previously programmed to do so by a human intelligence—that is, unless the perception in question had already been made by a cognitive power other than its own wholly contingent power.

This recognition of the role of human judgment in the fundamental and irreducible cognitive act of perceiving order leads to the recognition that acts of appraisal may constitute a part of description.

This appraisal may refer to structure or to performance, but in either case it takes place within the context of descriptive faithfulness to reality. Once again, the objectivist mentality obscures our understanding of this element of much scientific description, since this aspect is anomalous under objectivist presuppositions: in the objectivist view, descriptive appraisals must be interpreted as a confused intermixture of logically distinct and separable halves, one descriptive and the other prescriptive, which can and should be disentangled analytically. The only problem with this account is that the allegedly separable halves cannot be separated without doing violence to the scientific theory in question. The alleged confusion results not from any improper epistemological miscegenation in the theory but rather from the imposed confusions of objectivist categories. If they are suspended, the theoretical and epistemological integrity of descriptive appraisals in scientific theory should be apparent to all except the most dogmatic.

The role of descriptive appraisal in scientific theory can be illustrated from almost any area of science. A few examples, however, should be sufficient to illustrate and substantiate the general contention. In the areas of scientific investigation concerned with suborganic phenomena, descriptive appraisals are of structure rather than of performance, in keeping with the subject matter.

Take, for example, the physical chemist's investigation of the nature of crystals. In the scientific study of crystals, the crystallographer begins with the establishment and elaboration of a system which

> sets up first an ideal of shapeliness, by which it classifies solid bodies into such as tend to fulfill this ideal and others in which no such shapeliness is apparent. The first are crystals, the second the shapeless (or amorphous) non-crystals, like glass. Next, each individual crystal is taken to represent an ideal of regularity, all actual deviations from which are regarded as imperfections. This ideal shape is found by assuming that the approximately plane surfaces of crystals are geometrical planes which extend to the straight edges in which such planes must meet, thus bounding the crystal on all sides. This formalization defines a polyhedron which is taken to be the theoretical shape of a crystal specimen. [12]

Proceeding from this system of structural norms, each crystal specimen is described by reference to its ideal, or regular, polyhedron. The different forms of regularity in crystals were discovered by application of the structural norm of symmetry. By examining the possibilities of combining elementary symmetries into a single polyhedron, a categorization of crystalline formations into thirty-two distinct classes was made. These classes are each themselves standards for a particular kind of orderliness. Moreover, these thirty-two standards may themselves be arranged along a continuum representing a descending order of overall symmetry, "from the highest cubic to the lowest triclinic class. The variation down this series is extensive and only the higher classes possess sufficient beauty to make their specimens valued as precious stones."[13] The heuristic value of this pattern of structural norms was vindicated as a perception of real orderliness (as opposed to a purely subjective imposition of order, as, for example, in the designation of particular clusters of stars as constellations) by the discovery in the twentieth century of the underlying atomic structure of crystals, which was reflected in the macroscopically discerned structural norms. Today, the normative structural categorization of crystals is "regarded as merely indicating the presence of an underlying atomic orderliness, from which the thirty-two classes of symmetry can be rigorously derived."[14]

The essential lesson to be learned from this account of the development of crystallography is that the whole theory of crystal structure turned around a set of structural norms. Without these standards of orderliness, there would have been no theory at all. The norms of symmetry played an essential role in the theoretical descriptions of crystallography.

When science turns to organic phenomena, it still utilizes norms in its descriptive theories. If anything, the role of norms is here even more pervasive. Since organic phenomena are characterized by the performance of various functions, a new kind of descriptive norm develops which relates to the appraisal of these functions. We can designate these ordering standards performance norms, in contrast with the static structural norms used in crystallographic theories. In discussing deviations from these norms, descriptions speak in terms of malfunctions, rather than simply of malformations. The theoretical models of physiology, for example, are replete with such norms of performance and their derivative concepts. The physiological study of an organ begins with the discovery of its purposes within the overall physiological system. The satisfactory performance of these purposes, or functions, then constitutes operational standards which are the basis of descriptive appraisals. In this sense, the theoretical framework of a physiological description is clearly normative,[15] and the bracketing of these norms would dissolve the conceptual structure of physiology altogether.

The normative framework of physiological theory, almost too obvious to belabor, is perhaps clearest in the concepts used to represent deviations from the norm of a satisfactory performance of a physiological task. The whole language of pathology derives its significance from the functional standards which are not being met.

126

Whether the function in question is that of nutrition, digestion, respiration, circulation, perception, or whatever, it is a task with implicit standards of adequacy and failure. Failure or inadequacy is represented in descriptive appraisals such as malnutrition, circulatory occlusion, misperception, motor defect, and so on. The essential thing to notice in the context of epistemology and the understanding of scientific theorizing is that these terms and the conceptual framework behind them represent genuine perceptions of real patterns of order; they are not emotive expostulations which can be disentangled from the objective data. In short, the descriptive empirical theory is a normative theory, and whatever those under the spell of objectivist preconceptions may think, this situation is not confused, anomalous, or self-contradictory.

Despite the most diligent linguistic and conceptual contortions of behaviorism, moreover, the situation is structurally quite analogous in psychological and psychiatric theory. The terminology may fluctuate from time to time or from one school of theory to another, but the concepts of personality patterns are set in a context of descriptive appraisals of performance. The relevant pattern of order may be expressed by reference to normality, sanity, integration, adjustment, genital maturity, harmony, balance, or whatever. In each case, however, whether explicitly or implicitly, a standard of satisfactory psychic performance is invoked. Aberrations may be perceived in terms of abnormality, insanity, maladjustment, neurosis, or even the colloquial "hang-up." In each of these cases, a descriptive appraisal is being invoked to convey a perception of disruption, failure, or inadequacy of psychic functioning. The normative criteria, again, are not subjective value-judgments foisted from the outside upon an unequivocal and autonomous set of objective data. They constitute intrinsic components of the theoretical description.

A final aspect of the descriptive functions of norms worth mentioning is their utility within the context of explanation. Norms may serve an important explanatory role when they are norms of potentiality. That is, certain events in nature or politics may require recourse to norms of fulfillment if their causes are to be intelligible. Explanation by reference to norms of potentiality has been considered illicit by objectivism, in part because such an explanatory form was badly abused by the Aristotelian-based philosophies which objectivism reacted against and supplanted. Yet, as we argued in an earlier chapter, the total rejection of all such explanations leaves some explanatory lacunae that are impossible to fill by other means. The unintelligibility of the behaviorist notion of reinforcement within behaviorist ground rules is one of the best examples of this problem.

Sometimes, this explanatory role of norms may overlap with their role in a descriptive appraisal. One instance of this overlap comes when the external manifestations of a malfunction in a physiological, psychological, or political system are illuminated through the descriptive appraisal implicit in the concept of malfunction. This explanatory procedure is brought into play when a symptom is explained by reference to its cause, which is the implicitly normative concept of physical or mental illness. For example, Freud's theoretical description of the human psyche originated in his attempts to understand and explain the phenomenon of hysteria. The explanation developed by Freud for hysterical symptoms was based upon the concept of repression, which then led to the unfolding of norms of proper psychic functioning to make intelligible the failure implicit in repression.

This overlapping continuum of descriptive functions of norms in perception, identification, appraisal, and explanation has many applications in the context of political science. In the remainder of this chapter, a few of these applications will be suggested for purposes of illustration. These suggestions serve only as examples, of course, and are not intended as exhaustive or definitive analyses of the theoretical problem areas within which they arise. It is hoped that the reader who has absorbed the basic argument will be able to elaborate its implications for his own special area of concern.

The structuring impact of norms upon the definition and iden--tification of basic concepts and important empirical phenomena can be quite significant in almost any area of theory. Take, for example, the absolutely central theoretical task in political science of defining the concept of power and identifying the exercise of power. Power, it can be assumed, is generally agreed to be an empirical reality, one which is of crucial concern to all students of politics. Yet it should be equally apparent that no mere aggregating of wholly unambiguous sense-data can ever add up to a perception of this reality. Power is always contextual. As a result, what will be perceived as an identifiable instance of an exercise of power will hinge upon what is seen as the relevant context.

As its etymology would suggest, one of the important ingredients in the contextually contingent identification and description of power is the norm of potentiality. This potential may be the potential of possibility, or it may be the potential of full actualization of interests. In either case, it serves as an irreducible ordering context in the identification of an instance of power; in either case it is not objectively (verifiably) determinable. Consider Dahl's definition of power:

> My intuitive idea of power, then, is something like this: A has power over B to the extent that he can get B to do something that B would not otherwise do.[16]

Or consider the definition of Parsons:

> Power we may define as the realistic capacity of a system-unit to actualize its "interests" (attain goals, prevent undesired interference, command respect, control possessions, etc.) within the context of system interaction and in this sense to exert influence on processes in the system [17]

In the former case, it is clear that the identification of an instance of power depends upon knowing what B would otherwise do. In fact, the perception of power is mathematically dependent upon this contextual perception, for A's power, we could say, equals the difference between what B did, and what he would otherwise do apart from A's action. Consequently, the epistemological status of the concept of power is no more purely objective than the status of the concept of potentiality, in this case the potentiality of what would have happened otherwise. In the case of Parsons's definition, an identification of power takes place within the context of the continuum of actualization of interests. Once again, the norm of potentiality is critical, almost in an Aristotelian sense.

This dependency of the empirical phenomenon of power upon a contextual setting which is not itself objective in the empiricist sense constitutes something of an embarrassment for the objectivist view of political science. Perhaps for that reason, it has received little systematic attention at the level of epistemology. The theoretical epistemological models of objectivism have, as a consequence, become rather remote from the very real methodological problems faced by power theorists. The practical consequences of the inadequacy of the conventionally accepted, oversimplified understanding of the nature of the concept of power can at times be profound, of course. This faulty understanding leads, in particular, to an inability to account for the rise of rather different views of the power relationships within a particular political arena. The necessity of understanding this intellectual phenomenon should lead to a considerably more sophisticated view of the nature and status of political theory, one which will shed the illusions of objectivism and open the way for reintegrating political theory through its new appreciation of the descriptive role of norms.[18]

The case of the concept of power is an example of the dependence of a central concept on its normative context of potentiality. The structuring impact of perceptual norms may similarly be important in the way that a particular datum or event is characterized. Take, for example, the problem of locating within an empirical theory of democracy an event such as the Hays-Alford congressional campaign and election in Little Rock, in 1958. On that notable occasion, Alford, running as a write-in candidate, defeated the incumbent Hays in an election in which virtually every single member of the electorate was aware of the candidates' identities and their stands on at least one basic issue of public policy. In the context of purely statistical norms of voter awareness and participation, this particular case can clearly be described as an aberration or deviation from the normal pattern. Yet simply to describe it in that way would actually be descriptively insufficient and in some ways misleading. For this particular case, while a deviation from the statistical norm, constitutes an approximation of the norms of intentionality and potentiality. That is, this case approached the actualization of the potentiality of the democratic norms of representation and participation. It therefore needs to be given a privileged place in empirical descriptions of democracy, which it does not deserve on purely statistical grounds. Moreover, such a case, as the revelation of the potential of a system, should serve as an important contextual feature in the description and interpretation of statistically more frequent cases, which must be seen in part as instances where a potential was not fulfilled. That is, an election in which 40 percent of the populace voted and in which this is all that could possibly vote is not the same as an election in which 40 percent of the populace voted and the possibility of total participation existed. In short, the structuring context of possibility and intent exercises an influence on the way that a particular event occurring within that context should be described.

The descriptive utilization of the norm of intent, or purpose, may lead to describing a particular event in terms of appraisal. For example, if the declared purpose of an independent regulatory commission is to serve as a counterweight to strong private political interests in its area of concern and if it then does not serve in this way, it is probably a fair descriptive appraisal to say that it has in some ways been a failure. In a sense, in fact, not to speak in terms of appraisal by reference to the context of intent obscures or denies by implication the presence of the intent.[19] (This is basically the situation that, in the context of democratic theory, disturbed Jack Walker, Lane Davis, et. al. See the discussion in the preceding chapter.)

The direction which the theory of political development seems to be taking will lead it into making descriptive appraisals of a very similar sort a significant part of its task. The element of appraisal which is logically implicit in the whole notion of development is now becoming recognized. Gabriel Almond, for one, has suggested that the task of appraising the performance of political systems must be undertaken explicitly—even though such a program seems to conflict with deep-seated objectivist assumptions—if development theory is to progress. "Surely," he says, "this capacity to measure and evaluate performance is one of the principal goals of political theory. Our conflicts and inhibitions about being normative and evaluative get in the way of this essential concern of political theory."[20]

Overcoming objectivist inhibitions to understand the descriptive functioning of norms in development theory should also help to stimulate a more sophisticated view of the nature and epistemological status of what recently has been labeled normative theory. That is, recognition that norms operate in the context of description and are not merely prescriptive expressions of preference should make more apparent the basically descriptive, one might even say empirical, character of normative theory. The logical structure of normative theory is actually that of a complex description composed of two essential components: a model of human nature and a model of political reality. The distinctive character of normative theory proceeds from the combination of the two descriptive models.

The logic of this form of inquiry can be illustrated by returning to a previous example. Freud, we observed, was faced with the problem of understanding the phenomenon of hysteria. His investigations led him ultimately to perceive this phenomenon as a symptomatic manifestation of a psychic malfunction which he labeled repression. His insight into the causes of hysteria therefore led him to articulate an understanding of the human psychic economy within which the underlying phenomenon of repression was intelligible. When he later turned to examine political reality, admittedly rather sketchily and unsystematically, in *Civilization and Its Discontents*, he viewed/perceived/described that reality in light of his earlier discoveries. His excursion into normative political theory, such as it was, then, consisted of a combination of two component descriptions: his model of the human psyche and his perception of politics. The former component of this complex form of description characteristic of normative theory was in its origin, it should be emphasized, the product of an earlier empirical inquiry. In the context of the normative political inquiry of *Civilization and Its*

Discontents, its status remains the same, but its functions are altered. Formerly the focal result of an empirical inquiry into the functions of the human psyche, this model becomes converted in the new inquiry into a subsidiary perceptual-conceptual framework which serves to structure, illuminate, identify, explain, and interpret the political phenomena which now constitute the descriptive focus.

This understanding of the logical structure of so-called normative theory and of the patterns of discovery which lie behind it is worth emphasis for several reasons. In the first place, the paradigm outlined here can be seen to be quite applicable to most of the recognized classic political theorists. Marx may begin his inquiry by seeking to formulate an explanation for what he perceives as alienation, and Plato may begin with an attempt to explain what he perceives as political disintegration. The form of the inquiry, the logical structure of the resultant theories, and the epistemological status of the resultant theories, and the epistemological status of the whole process are quite similar in each case, however. Second, this analysis makes clear that norms are generally the product of empirical investigation and that they become normative not by virtue of a unique epistemological status but by virtue of their functions in a particular description. What are empirical results in one inquiry can serve as norms in another. The difference is one of role. Finally, this understanding of the structure of normative theory is important because while it is hardly extraordinarily complex, it has been obscured by the prevailing simplistic view of description derived from objectivist presuppositions. This Laplacean notion of description as a simple laying out of discrete, unambiguous data actually rendered the logic of normative theory quite unintelligible. The positivist propagators of this view, when they deigned to consider normative theory, dismembered it into statements which they translated with some grotesqueness into expressions of emotion, which could then be dismissed epistemologically. The analysis offered here should help to save normative theory from such distortion and peremptory dismissal by making it logically intelligible.

Finally, the explanatory functions of certain norms in the context of political science should be noted. The particular kind of norm which is often utilized in this role is the teleological norm, or the norm of potentiality. Under the ground rules of objectivism, teleological norms have been shunned as unscientific. Nevertheless, the explanation of many political phenomena is contingent upon norms of this sort, however much their explicit use is avoided. It should be remembered in this context that the teleological element in Aristotle's thought grew not out of inclinations to be a moralist, uttering prescriptions, but out of what he saw as the necessities of adequate causal explanation. The application of explanation by final causes to the behavior of inanimate objects, such as falling bodies, was a misapplication of the principle, of course; the absurdities engendered in this area led the protagonists of the seventeenth-century intellectual revolution to reject the whole idea of teleology. What is absurd in the context of physical motion is not so absurd in the context of human action, however, and to follow the objectivist proscription of any teleological norm whatsoever would render many political events quite inexplicable.

Explicit recourse to teleological norms in explanation is easily avoided in the social sciences by allowing the reader to fill them in through his common-sense understanding of human behavior. When a social scientist explains a political rebellion with some statement such as "The Lilliputians finally rebelled against the perpetual frustration of their wishes by the colonial agencies," he is implicitly invoking a teleological conception of natural human tendencies, which the reader instinctively supplies to fill in the logic of the explanation. The same could be said of a sociologist's explanation of juvenile delinquency by citing the behavior patterns as responses to deprivation of status by the "straight" society. The reader implicitly understands that there exists a natural tendency of human beings to attain at least a limited position of status, the frustration of which can result in a distinctive behavioral pattern.

These explanations are two examples of the use of teleological norms in social science. Another area where these norms possess considerable explanatory utility is in the explanation of the impetus toward political development. It is to the credit of Gabriel Almond that he has demonstrated both the intellectual perspicacity to recognize this element in the explanatory forms of his field of inquiry and the intellectual honesty to affirm it. "Surely," he remarks, "there is implied in the notion of modernization and development some teleological element, not that of divine purpose, but the pressure of human aspiration and choice toward a common set of goals employing similar instrumentalities. If this be teleology, then make the most of it."[21] This element of final-cause explanation, however latent, actually occupies a logically essential role in great numbers of explanations offered by social scientists. For the sake of intellectual honesty and conceptual self-understanding, the widespread explanatory functions of such teleological norms should be given proper recognition.

To summarize, then, norms must be understood as criteria of order, not as syntactical imperatives. As criteria of order, they play an irreducible role in our perception of reality as the organizational matrix upon which all scientific data rely for their identity and significance. They may be bracketed temporarily for certain purposes, but this expedient effects positive changes in the data themselves, and it cannot be represented as an expression of epistemological objectivity. The theoretical descriptions of political science, at least as much as those of other sciences, utilize, and logically must utilize, norms as they identify, appraise, and explain their subject matter. Recognition of the necessity and legitimacy of these descriptive functions of norms can lead to the reintegration of the theoretical enterprise, clarify and solve some present conceptual difficulties, and facilitate the capacity of the discipline to appraise the capabilities and performance of political systems openly rather than furtively.

Notes

1. We gave our principal attention to philosophy and psychology, which are more clearly related to politics than the natural sciences. For an investigation of parallel problems in physics and biology, cf. Milio Capek, *The Philosophical Impact of Contemporary Physics* (Princeton, N.J.: Van Nostrand, 1961), and Marjorie Grene, *Approaches to a Philosophical Biology* (New York: Basic Books, 1968).

2. Cf. J.S. Nye, "Corruption and Political Development," *American Political Science Review*, LXI (1967), 417-427.

3. Indeed, as my Duke University colleague, W.H. Poteat pointed out to me, such a mind would not even possess the means if imputing the knowledge it is presumed to possess to the nature of any existing world. In fact, the conditions for the existence of such a discarnate mind are such that, were they satisfied, no actual grounds for the propagation of what it was thought to know could be conceived to exist.

4. Michael Polanyi, *Personal Knowledge* (New York: Harper Torchbooks, 1964), p. 141.

5. "Norm" seems undoubtedly to have etymological affiliations with the Latin *forma*, "form, mould, shape"; cf. Eric Partridge, *Origins* (New York: Macmillan Co., 1958).

6. Norwood Hanson, *Patterns of Discovery* (Cambridge: Cambridge University Press, 1958), p. 19.

7. Thomas Kuhn, *Structure of Scientific Revolutions* (Chicago: Phoenix Books, 1962), p. 125; cf. esp. chap. 10.

8. Marx W. Wartofsky, *Conceptual Foundations of Scientific Thought* (New York: Macmillan Co., 1968), p. 283.

9. Polanyi, p. 296.

10. Cf. Rudolph Arnheim, *Visual Thinking* (Berkeley and Los Angeles: University of California Press, 1969).

11. Hanson, p. 13.

12. Claiming, as a political scientist, no special competence in this area, I am relying for this example upon the interpretation of a distinguished

physical chemist. The following account is essentially a paraphrase of his interpretation. Cf. Polanyi, pp. 43-48.

13. Ibid., p. 45.

14. Ibid., p. 45.

15. Ibid., p. 360: "Physiology is a system of rules of rightness. . . ."

16. Robert Dahl, "The Concept of Power," in Sidney Ulmer, ed., *Introductory Readings in Political Behavior* (Chicago: Rand McNally Co., 1961), p. 125.

17. Talcott Parsons, *Essays in Sociological Theory* (New York: The Free Press, 1949), p. 391.

18. This, as I interpret it, is the logical structure of William Connolly's argument in *Political Science and Ideology* (New York: Atherton Press, 1967). After an examination of the problems underlying the competing theoretical models of several important contemporary theorists of power, Connolly is prompted to reexamine the model of total detachment and objectivity in political inquiry. His chap. 2, "The Ideological Context of Power Analysis," should be consulted as a supplement to the argument of the above few paragraphs on the conceptual status of power.

19. This example grows from an actual debate between two esteemed political scientists which I once witnessed during my undergraduate career. One of the principals was vehemently attacked by the other for structuring a talk on the regulatory commissions in terms of appraisal. The gist of the criticism was that the presentation had been "severely miscast in its analysis" because it was not "objective." The speaker's reply, essentially, was that he felt that he was being perfectly objective in perceiving an element of "failure" in the performance of the regulatory commissions.

20. Gabriel Almond, "Political Development," *Comparative Politicial Studies*, I (1969), p. 461.

21. Ibid., p. 461.

7 Objectivity and Commitment

In the previous chapter, we documented the increased sophistication in recent years about the cognitive foundations of science. This new sophistication is grounded largely, we argued, upon the recognition of the complexity of scientific perception. An essential part of any perception, it is now recognized, are the patterns of organization which structure, identify, and give coherence and meaning to the data. Since norms are patterns and standards of order, they often perform a descriptive function in the capacity of an organizing framework. This descriptive role of norms has been obscured in the past, we contended, because of the widespread implicit acceptance of the Laplacean view of description as a rendering of the results of passive observation. The new understanding of perception as theory-laden from the outset reveals the bankruptcy of the Laplacean model and of the Baconian view of theory formation which accompanied it. In its place, there is the model of the descriptive paradigm, whose often tacit functions are essential to all description and to all theory.

The implications of this abandonment of the Laplacean descriptive ideal and the correlative recognition of the descriptive role of norms extend all the way down to the basic epistemological model operative in the West since the seventeenth century. Together with the deflation of the verifiability theory of meaning, the collapse of the Laplacean model suggests that this traditional epistemological paradigm is, in Kuhn's phrase, "somehow askew." Basically, what is called into radical question is the whole Cartesian program of critical doubt. Descartes's epistemological program, which has been the basis for the traditional paradigm, was composed of a dialectic between total doubt and equally total certainty. Beginning with the former, one could advance critically to the latter. In fact, however, our new understanding of cognition reveals that both poles of this dialectic are illusory. One can never dissolve all of one's preconceptions to become an untutored, hence unbiased, intelligence. Nor can one ever reach a state of absolute certainty guaranteed on impersonal grounds.

Another way of stating the implications of the new understanding of cognition is to say that the traditional notion of objectivity is based upon illusory premises. For the concept of objectivity in conventional parlance stands for the epistemological ideal-state suggested by Cartesian and Laplacean assumptions. This ideal has spawned various attitudes toward our intellectual capacities. It has engendered a pattern of intellectual pride on the one hand, stemming from the contemplated capacity to produce certain knowledge, complemented by intellectual despair, which arises from the repeated failures to attain the allegedly attainable end. In recent years, the increase of persuasive evidence of the impossibility of reaching the ideal of absolute, impersonal truth has led in some quarters to an abandonment of the notion of truth altogether. This abandonment is reflected in the recourse to such characterizations of scientific theories as useful fictions which are convenient and simple, but not true. As Abraham Kaplan has noted, however, this latter view is almost self-contradictory: fictions would not be useful.[1]

If we are to avoid both the pattern of oscillation between pride and despair and the recourse to such epicyclical notions as useful fiction, a more massive revision of our epistemological postulates seems necessary. In short, the Cartesian program of doubt and the model of autonomous critical reason that goes with it must be replaced by a model which more accurately portrays and accounts for both the genuine powers and the genuine limitations of human knowledge. The chimeras of Descartes and Laplace which have divided and debilitated political theory need to be put to rest in favor of a more realistic assessment of our cognitive capacities.

This fundamental epistemological reassessment implicitly involves the development of a more adequate ontology than the one offered by objectivism, for although epistemology often claims to be autonomous, it is always rooted in a substantive cosmological vision which gives it meaning. Karl Mannheim recognized this relationship:

138

The theory of knowledge claims to be a strictly self-contained rational system; in the light of a structural analysis it can be shown, however, that the axioms from which any epistemological system takes its departure are mainly derived from metaphysical-ontological presuppositions. Although epistemology claims to furnish a standard in terms of which the truth of metaphysical systems can be judged, it turns out itself to have its basis in definite metaphysical positions.[2]

The presence of this relationship is especially obscured by positivist philosophy, with its explicitly antimetaphysical bias. However, it could hardly be otherwise, for epistemology is itself an ontological enterprise in a sense; as an account of the structure of knowledge, it is at least in part an account of the capacities of a living being to be conscious of, and to participate in, the world of which he is a part.

Accordingly, the epistemological failures of the objectivist tradition, as we have tried to indicate throughout, are rooted in the inadequacy of the same tradition's cosmology. It should hardly be expected that an ontology which is incapable of finding a place within its empty spatiality for a human being should be capable of providing a coherent account of the act of knowing. If it cannot account for the agent, it cannot account for the act. The objective purity of the Cartesian world of *res extensa* was reached by extricating the knowing subject from it, and this necessity made it rather difficult to conceive of the means of the minimal acquaintance between knower and known that would make knowledge possible.

This intrinsic relationship between epistemology and ontology also stands as the basic reason that the epistemological dilemma of contemporary theory cannot be resolved by a straightforward return to the classical tradition represented by Aristotle. Whatever the virtues of Aristotelian epistemology, it was predicated ultimately upon ontological assumptions which we can no longer reasonably accredit. Aristotle's model of cognition was, in short, fashioned to be peculiarly operable in a finite world in which the basic patterns of order were unchanging and, as a whole, complete and coherent. Both perception and *noesis* were, for Aristotle, "the unerring core of a stable physical-metaphysical situation."[3] Several interrelated characteristics of this cognitive model help to illustrate the basic contention. First, Aristotle's account of reasoning is the picture of a closed process, a process that is thoroughly self-contained. This self-containment is immediately obvious in the case of his deductive logic, the demonstration of undoubted particulars from undoubted universals; but it is descriptive of Aristotelian induction as well. In the words of Marjorie Grene, "Aristotelian induction consists in drawing out the universal that is already clear in the particular. . . . [It] moves securely and permanently from a sense-perceived particular to an intellectually apprehended universal and remains there."[4]

The fact that Aristotelian induction "remains there" when it reaches a universal reflects another aspect of the closed cognitive model of which it is a part: knowledge, once attained, has for Aristotle a radical certainty and finality to it. Once one has apprehended the *ousia* of anything, he may feel confident that his understanding will retain its validity forever, because the lines of substance, the species of being, are assumed to be eternal. There is here no inescapable indeterminacy, no heuristic groping toward patterns of order which may prove impermanent. Aristotelian knowledge has a kind of untroubled complacency about it, the serenity of knowing that its goal can be irreversibly attained by sorting out what is potentially known already. The stability of a finite world guarantees that an accurate perception will never be outgrown by reality. Similarly, the central instrumentality of human thought, speech, also possesses this finality and radical determinacy for Aristotle. Proper definitions were so all important in Aristotle's philosophical methodology, because they embodied the impenetrable and immutable boundaries of the substances they represented. The involvement of this linguistic paradigm with the deeper ontology which sustained it is reflected explicitly in the word used for the process: de-finit-ion. It was conceivable to Aristotle that the entire cosmos could be exhaustively represented by a complete set of univocal definitions.

The entire Aristotelian process of knowing, then, is tailored to be peculiarly, if not exclusively, effective within the stable, finite Greek cosmos. Any attempt to apply Greek epistemology to a world for which it is not suited will inevitably run into severe difficulties. Therefore, a return to classical epistemology would necessarily entail a return to classical ontology as well. And this Western man could not do without renouncing several of his distinctive intellectual achievements.

Three very important concepts in Western intellectual history have made the Greek model of the finite cosmos obsolete. First is the concept of inertia, discussed in an earlier chapter. It would be possible, certainly, to refrain from Hobbes's precedent of extending this paradigm throughout the entire plentitude of reality and instead quarantine it as a special exception to the otherwise teleological coherence of the world. The biological realm, too, can no longer be compressed into the finite categories of Aristotelian thought unless we are willing to renounce the discovery of evolution. The profusion of biological species can no more be conceived within finite continuum of actuality-potentiality than can inertial motion. Moving into the area of human and social phenomena, the model of classical finitude seems equally incapable of expressing the pervasive historicity of the Western world. Whether conceived of in the manner of existentialism or in the manner of Christianity, Western man exists in the indeterminacy of nonfinitude no less than do biological species. If man is to find order in his life, he cannot do so in the modern world by conforming to any immutable coherence of his world. Nature has become historical and can no longer perform the function of uniting essence and existence.[5]

Given the inadequacies of positivist epistemology on the one hand and the limitations of classical epistemology on the other hand, it becomes apparent that a satisfactory cognitive model for a post-critical political theory must transcend both. And the critical task requisite to this feat is surmounting a deeply entrenched presupposition which both Aristotelian and objectivist epistemology hold in common. Just as Hobbes's cosmology was a substantive reversal but a formal continuation of classical cosmology, so objectivism retains some of the ultimate epistemological notions of classical epistemology at the same time that it completely transforms the substantive context in which it must operate. Despite their radically different views as to what the content of knowledge will be, then, both epistemologies presume that genuine knowledge must be impersonal, precise, fully specifiable, universal, and predictable in a univocal language.[6]

In both instances, this epistemological ideal received sustenance from the ontology within which it was set. Predication could be univocal and final in the Greek cosmos because the substances were seen as univocal and final; a similar finality and complete specifiability of knowledge could seem plausible in a Laplacean universe of abstract, unambiguous points in motion. But an adequate contemporary political theory can inhabit neither of these unambiguous cosmologies and cannot, therefore, retain the parallel epistemological assumptions which they permitted. We are not Greeks; we have irrevocably suffered the dissolution of the natural bonds of essense and existence. Nor are we locationless Archimedean points; we cannot secede from history for the sake of perfect knowledge. We must therefore reappraise our cognitive powers with an eye to doing the one thing which neither former epistemology did—namely, to grant genuinely cognitive worth to the inescapably contingent and groping historical phenomenon of human thought, recognizing both its positive accomplishments and its inherent limitations.

This reappraisal of our cognitive powers has been carried out piecemeal in many quarters by implication rather than explicitly. Some of these sources have been relied upon in the course of the argument already.[7] However, the one preeminent attempt to provide a fundamental alternative to the older models of knowledge is to be found in the work of Michael Polanyi.[8] Therefore, we shall invoke and rely upon some of his central insights here, for it is only through a creative alternative to objectivism that the cognitive standing of political theory can properly be assessed.

The proper origin for a reassessment of our cognitive capacities is a careful examination of the actual structure of the process of inquiry as it is practiced by acknowledged scientists. Such an examination must recognize at the outset that, to cite Abraham Kaplan, "Descartes' 'methodological skepticism' is hopelessly at variance with logic-in-use." He continues, "Nowhere in science do we start from scratch. There is only one place from which we ever can start, Peirce said, and that is from where we are."[9] This seeming truism, moreover, is not simply a peripheral amendment to Cartesian methodology; it concerns the essential structure of inquiry.

> This proposition is not a matter of "mere" psychological fact; it is essential to the logic of inquiry. . . . Where all is problematic, nothing is left with which a problem can even be formulated, let alone be solved. Science is no miraculous creation out of nothing, no spontaneous generation of knowledge from ignorance. When presuppositions are denied logical status, we remain mired in skepticism. . . . Methodology does not rob us of our footing; it enjoins us, rather, to look to it.[10]

The recognition that all perception, scientific or otherwise, is theory-laden from the start is a suggestive result of heeding Kaplan's admonition to "look to our footing." Knowledge in practice always begins with an original act of faith, the decision to accredit certain concepts which permit us to "see" at all, at least for the time being. This act of accreditation is, of course, usually implicit and more subconscious than our own explicit reconstruction of the logic of inquiry, for we all begin with assumptions, preconceptions, and beliefs, taken by osmosis from our cultural background, which give us a basis for further inquiry, however much we may modify our original commitments later on.

The needed reassessment of our cognitive powers must begin, to put the matter in a slightly different way, with the recognition that doubt is actually a particular instance of the more general category belief, rather than its opposite. The Cartesian assumption of the autonomy of doubt—seen as the suspension of all belief—is in fact both a logical and a practical misconception. As Polanyi observes, doubt of any proposition must take one of two forms: "contradictory" doubt or "agnostic" doubt.[11] Contradictory doubt is clearly logically equivalent to belief; "I doubt p" (where p is a proposition) here is simply another way of saying "I believe not p." In agnostic doubt, "I doubt p" means "I believe that p is either not proven or not provable." To say this, however, implies the acceptance of a framework within which the concepts of not proven or not provable are meaningful. The difficulty which positivism had in finding a cognitive status for the verifiability principle (which was admitted to be itself unverifiable) illustrated this logical situation quite neatly. A prior act of commitment, then, underlies the possibility of meaning anything—including giving meaning to doubting.

This view of the irreducible "fiduciary rootedness" of all knowledge both implies, and in turn is sustained by, the inescapable tacit component of knowledge. Whenever we consciously know something, bring it to the focus of our attention, we can do so only by relying upon subsidiary components of our knowing act, which for the moment remain unconscious. The structure of all knowledge involves a from-to pattern. We attend *from* particular subsidiary existential-intellectual structures of order, which we implicitly accredit by imaginatively inhabiting them for the purpose of attending *to* a more comprehensive focus which makes sense of the subsidiary components by integrating them into a larger unity. In part, the recognition of this structure of knowing is a recognition that all knowing proceeds from a certain historical locale. Knowledge cannot proceed from nowhere; to recall Kaplan's admonition, "epistemic bootstraps" are no better than any other kind. But this historical rootedness of knowledge was obscured by the objectivist ideal, which, by depicting ideal knowledge as wholly explicit and impersonal, made knowledge wholly focused upon the object to which it is directed without having anywhere from which to proceed.

This reestablishment of knowledge within its historical and personal setting by recognizing its tacit component is a theme which the French phenomenologist Maurice Merleau-Ponty also emphasizes. In his exploration of the structure of attention and perception, he argues that the world must be "put back into its cradle of consciousness." And consciousness, he continues, "must be faced with its own unreflective life in things and awakened to its own history which it was forgetting."[12] The whole process of thought, he suggests, is a continual indwelling of changing patterns of order, which are integrated on the basis of its tacit, or indeterminate, components. "This passage from the indeterminate to the determinate, this recasting at every moment of its own history in the unity of a new meaning, is thought itself."[13]

By examining pathological cases of failure in the achievement of tacit integration, Merleau-Ponty arrives at the conclusion that attention merges with intention in the structure of human knowing. Attending from tacit assumptions to something which is desired to be known is an act of human intentionality—a teleological feat that has an irreducible temporal component. The pathological subject who cannot project himself into the future suffers an eclipse of his cognitive faculties.[14] Knowledge is given its historical footing once more, then, not only in the sense that it requires a knower with a tacit grounding within the historical time-flow but in the sense that the structure of the knowing act itself involves a temporal component. Reaching out from tacit particulars towards an explicit object of knowledge which will integrate the particulars into a comprehensive entity is a futuristically oriented quest.[15]

It is quite impossible ever to eliminate this tacit dimension of knowledge. We always "know more than we can say." Since no knowledge can be entirely focal, no knowledge can be wholly explicit; the goal of fully specifiable knowledge is a chimera. The goal of fully specifiable knowledge is not only systematically elusive, but can also be destructive in practice. Several examples serve to illustrate this threat, which follows from the fact that attending to tacit particulars dissolves the comprehensive entity of which they are a part. First, take the case of a skilled bodily performance, which is one kind of knowing. If a tennis player focuses upon his racket instead of the ball, he will fail to make the shot, however formally perfect his swing; if a carpenter focuses on his hammer instead of the nail, he is likely to hit his finger; if a basketball player focuses on the ball instead of the basket while shooting, his shot will go awry. In fact, it is even misleading to speak of a tennis stroke or a basketball shot apart from the constituting *telos* which structures them; the particulars of the stroke or shot will gradually fall apart when not integrated by this *telos*, for they are essentially subsidiary and cannot be made focal except destructively. Similarly, in using a word and recognizing a face, one can perform successfully by relying upon the subsidiary particulars of letters or sounds (depending upon whether the word is spoken or written) and of individual features rather than by attending to them. Repeat the word "roof" over and over again and you are no longer speaking of anything but are instead making a noise which sounds rather like a poor imitation of a dog. Attend carefully to the nose or eyebrows or lips of a friend and you soon dissolve his face.[16]

This logical structure extends to the making of assertions as well, where the tacit component is always, in part at least, the personal affirmation of the speaker. Every confident assertion, every statement to which one is willing to commit oneself, has tacitly appended to it the prefix "I believe" or "I affirm." In Polanyi's words, "an articulate assertion is composed of two parts: a sentence conveying the content of what is asserted and a tacit act by which this sentence is asserted."[17] This tacit component of any assertion, the commitment which lies behind it and makes it an assertion rather than a mere collocation of words, cannot be rendered fully explicit itself. In effect, the linguistic form "p is true" (when p is a proposition) is an attempt to do precisely this. But this type of statement leads to apparently irresolvable self-contradictions and dilemmas, foremost among them the "paradox of the liar" and the fact that such a statement is subject of an infinite regress. By properly recognizing that "p is true" is a mistaken attempt (fostered by the objectivist ideal of total explicitness) to render explicit an act of commitment which, because it is an act and not an impersonal proposition, must remain tacit, these difficulties can be avoided. Further, "p is true" is not a sentence, but "stands for an a-critical act of acceptance which is not something one can either assert or know."[18]

Recognition that every act of knowing involves a personal, tacit coefficient and acknowledgement that this coefficient is not a corruption of knowing but a necessary and vital contribution leads to a broadened and renewed appreciation for the Augustinian admonition that one must "believe in order to understand." Far from being an injunction to blind faith, it represents in its broader setting awareness that since one cannot begin thinking from no premises, he must accept certain "givens," which he may explore and come to terms with through raising them. If these givens do not produce intellectually satisfying results in their heuristic deployment, then they can be revised in light of their lack of fruition; but they can be neither dispensed with nor critically scrutinized before their original tacit acceptance. The process of inquiry, then, emerges as a dialectic between the object of knowledge and the premises employed in exploring the topic; each is examined in light of the other.

To heirs of the Western epistemological tradition, and we all fall into this category, this seems a peculiar form of intellectual liberation indeed. At first sight it would seem to deliver knowledge over to the anarchy of complete subjectivism, flying in the face of long-standing encomiums to relentless objectivity in thought. Yes, as Polanyi emphasizes, his is no counsel to subjectivity, which is a concept derived from the assumed disjunction of subject and object posited so poignantly, and ultimately inescapably, by Descartes. Grounding knowledge in commitment does not equate it with subjective opining. The interpretation offered by Polanyi transcends the assumptions which make "subjective" and "objective" dichotomous terms. Recognizing that all knowledge is fiduciary simply affirms that it cannot escape being grounded in the commitment of a knower, that knowledge cannot escape contingency; it does not mean that the knower is not bound by an obligation to a reality which lies beyond him. Personal knowledge is indelibly responsible knowledge: "The freedom of the subjective person to do as he pleases is overruled by the freedom of the responsible person to act as he must."[19]

A knowing act, then, is a dialectic between a personal agent and an external reality upon which the person is contingent. Each pole of the dialectic is equally essential, so while the transcendent reality is conceived of as existing beyond the knower, it is not seen as existing wholly apart from him. The condition of knowing something is not a simple correspondence between subjective impressions and a wholly impersonal and objective reality but rather a felicitous indwelling of the knower in the world. In this respect, Polanyi's notion of truth bears real affinity to the tradition of pragmatism, purged however of its biologic and subjectivist connotations. The interplay of the knowing person and a reality which lies beyond him, of compulsion and freedom, of responsibility and belief are reflected in this summary of the basic structure of epistemological commitment:

> The enquiring scientist's intimations of a hidden reality are personal. They are his own beliefs, which—owing to his originality—as yet he alone holds. Yet they are not a subjective state of mind, but convictions held with universal intent, and heavy with arduous projects. It was he who decided what to believe, yet there is no arbitrariness in his decision. For he arrived at his conclusions by the utmost exercises of responsibility. He has reached responsible beliefs, born of necessity, and not changeable at will. In a heuristic commitment, affirmation, surrender and legislation are fused into a single thought, bearing on a hidden reality.[20]

Although Polanyi is a philosophical realist, in a manner of speaking, his realism is not the closed intellectual realism of Aristotle because it is not predicated upon a closed and finite world. Polanyi takes the process of inquiry, discovery, learning, in contrast with demonstration, as paradigmatic of knowledge in its fullest structure. Knowledge is essentially heuristic, then, instead of hypotheticodeductive. The full implications of an act of discovery can never be wholly apprehended at its outset, because it is revelatory of an open, evolutionary reality and will therefore have indefinite and indeterminable ramifications in the future. Knowing reflects the world's capacity for originality.[21]

Because the reality toward which the knowing person moves is indeterminate and because he himself, as a creature of this reality, partakes of its indeterminacy, there is no indubitable foundation to render his knowledge final and complete. Knowledge radiates outward in all directions from its contingent, nonabsolute center of personal intellectual desire to a reality which is open and indeterminate in all directions. Because there are no immutable lines of substance (in the Aristotelian sense) to give coherence to the thought which is the interplay between person and reality, this coherence must be supplied by an intentional circularity of thought. Each concept of a comprehensive world view or scientific paradigm dovetails with its fellows, producing a coherent whole; any objection to one concept can be met by reference to some complementary concepts which, operating within the same basic framework, serve to absorb the anomalies of the original concept.[22] It is true that circularity can provide dangerous reinforcement to fundamentally mistaken ideas, but this is simply a fact of intellectual life. The belief of a madman that he is Napoleon or the belief of naturalists of a previous era in phlogiston may be sustained by a highly stable circle of mutually reinforcing notions. It simply reinforces our basic contention to observe that no purely formal and specifiable means can suffice to break a logical circle which we judge to be "vicious." Such a vicious circle can persist indefinitely until it is dissolved, usually as a whole, by the knower's relinquishing of his fiduciary commitment.[23]

The contention that full-scale conceptual systems are ultimately circular receives confirmation in the situation in which two paradigms are competing for acceptance in a scientific field. The positivist belief that such a competition can be adjudicated objectively is dependent upon the now largely discredited belief in the existence of pure, neutral observation languages. In reality, however, "the competition between paradigms is not the sort of battle that can be resolved by proofs."[24] The circularity of each paradigm prevents the assumptions of the other from gaining a foothold. The comprehensiveness of the paradigm makes its individual components incommensurable with the components of the competing paradigm. "Just because it is a transition between incommensurables, the transition between competing paradigms cannot be made a step at a time, forced by logic and neutral experience. Like the gestalt switch, it must occur all at once (though not necessarily in an instant) or not at all."[25]

Acceptance of the task of knowing anything when knowledge is admitted to have no indubitable foundation is admittedly a hazardous undertaking. But these hazards are inherent in the fallibility of the human intellectual enterprise and are only intensified rather than ameliorated by the persistence of a belief in an objectively given intellectual *axis mundi*. There is therefore, nothing obscurantist about an insistence upon the personal element in all knowledge and upon the circularity of our knowledge. Such a position is obscurantist in the sense that it casts an irreducible shadow upon the bright luminosity of the ideal of wholly objective explicit knowledge. But, in the deeper sense of the word, the true obscurantist is the one who would perpetuate an illusion which, however appealing, ultimately dissolves into self-contradiction. The failure of the verifiability criterion to sustain its own claim to meaningfulness reveals that the ultimate basis of all comprehensive intellectual systems is the responsible belief of its adherent. The best we can do, then, in elaborating an epistemology is to admit this fact into the system itself. The system becomes thereby ultimately circular, but it achieves the virtue of self-consistency, which can be attained in no other way. The final choice is between self-consistent paradox and self-contradictory pseudocertainty; there is no third option.[26]

Although ultimate circularity is an unavoidable feature of human thought which is made less dangerous by its acknowledgement, acceptance of this circularity by no means implies that the content of the formal circle may therefore be arbitrary. A check upon the content of the conceptual circles we affirm is their capacity to mediate effectively between our intellectual passions and the reality which these passions are seeking to comprehend. Just as intellectual commitment is kept from disintegrating into mere subjectivity by the responsibility of universal intent, so the ultimately circular nature of all our beliefs is kept from arbitrariness by the capacity of reality to reveal itself to us and by our corresponding capacity to discern order in reality. Remaining consistent with the fiduciary program, of course, we must confess our faith in this complementary rationality of known reality and knowing person to be finally just that—a faith. Our experience would seem to make it a not unreasonable faith, however.[27]

Moreover, the ultimate circularity of comprehensive conceptual systems and the impossibility of finding neutral grounds for adjudicating between competing systems do not imply that no warrants whatever exist for choosing between competing systems. As Kuhn has replied to those who made this charge against him, nothing about this thesis

> implies either that there are no good reasons for being persuaded or that those good reasons are not ultimately decisive for the group. Nor does it even imply that the reasons for choice are different from those usually listed by philosophers of science: accuracy, simplicity, fruitfulness, and the like.[28]

What his, and our, argument does insist, however, is that the various warrants for holding a particular theory cannot be impersonally, neutrally, and finally applied. Instead, the use of these warrants involves an uneliminable act of intellectual judgment on the part of a responsible knower. That knower, therefore, may later turn out to be mistaken, and he may differ with others who are equally as scientific in their use of these warrants as he.

> If two men disagree, for example, about the relative fruitfulness of their theories, or if they agree about that but disagree about the relative importance of fruitfulness and, say, scope in reaching a choice, neither can be convicted of a mistake. Nor is either being unscientific. There is no neutral algorithm for theory-choice, no systematic decision procedure which, properly applied, must lead each individual in the group to the same decision.[29]

A quick recapitulation of the basic tenets of Polanyi's epistemology reveals that he has transformed some of the central tenets of both objectivism and classical realism. The ideal of strict impersonality in knowing is rejected as a misconstruction of the only objectivity possible for a contingent knower—the objectivity of a responsible personal commitment. The irreducible tacit coefficient in all knowledge renders the ideal of total specifiability and precision obsolete.[30] And the concepts of heuristics and belief make indubitability and finality of knowledge false standards of truth. In short, the model of knowledge which emerges is neither the static and closed Aristotelian reason nor the wholly impersonal, objective and autonomous critical reason. Postcritical reason is the dialectic of genuine cognitive power and equally genuine limitations of a contingent person, striving responsibly to fulfill his obligation to understand a reality which transcends him. Such an understanding of human reason helps to solve some of the irresolvable dilemmas of objectivism and classical realism, doing so at the price of confessing the inescapable contingency of all the products of the human mind.

In the context of political theory, such a model offers the basis for bridging the artificial gap between empirical and normative theory, enabling the former to solve its dilemmas by permitting the conscious and responsible use of norms and delivering the latter from the absurd program of justifying preferences which had been set for it. All political theory, like all knowledge, is embedded in historicity and sustained by personal appraisals of patterns of order, yet it is not arbitrary or subjective just because it may be controversial and not indubitable. Most of what has been termed empirical theory involves a high ratio of relatively unambiguous "facticity" to conceptual judgment, especially at the lower levels. At the opposite end of the empirical-theoretical continuum (Kaplan's phrase) this ratio becomes reversed, but the component of personal judgment and appraisal cannot be severed from facticity. Empirical and normative theories differ in degree, not in kind; they are complementary, not antagonistic. All political theorizing responsibly and knowledgeably undertaken, whatever the proportion of data to norm, has a genuine claim to cognitive status, although no political theorizing can claim either indubitability or finality.

Understanding and adopting Polanyi's model of postcritical reason would have the great virtue of allowing social theorists seriously to come to grips with the problems raised by the sociology of knowledge. Recently, a theorist of comparative politics acknowledged that Karl Mannheim's insights into the inescapable influence of the theorist's social setting upon the basic ordering concepts and criteria of relevance he employs have been largely ignored by political analysts:

> The underlying theme of my argument here is that we have not, in fact, resolved the Mannheim Paradox and that perhaps the future of social science will be better served if we acknowledge this fact and face up to its intellectual and theoretical implications. [31]

The basic epistemological problem raised by the sociology of knowledge is this: What are the implications for epistemology of the discovery that the structure of any social theory is inescapably rooted in a particular, contingent historical situation? This problem is justly associated with Mannheim, for he first gave it full articulation as a problem and strove responsibly to lay the basis for an answer to the problem. Because his treatment of the question was somewhat sporadic and even at times inconsistent, his formulations have never been fully understood, accepted, or incorporated into the epistemological self-understanding of political theory. However, if Mannheim's basic outlook is integrated into the context of Polanyi's more comprehensive epistemological model, with which it is basically compatible, it receives a more systematic foundation, which helps to resolve some of the objections raised against it. [32]

150

According to Mannheim, the epistemological problem posed by the sociology of knowledge receives its decisive modern impetus from the Marxian notion of false consciousness. With this concept the particular conception of ideology merges into what Mannheim calls the total conception of ideology. The former conception accuses its adversary of conscious or unconscious falsification deriving from his own sociopolitical interest; this critique proceeds against the psychological and personal bias of the adversary. The total conception of ideology is more radical. Viewing the adversary's ideas as irreducible functions of his social situation, the total conception of ideology discredits the entire structure of the adversary's consciousness, and he is considered "no longer capable of thinking correctly."[33] This theoretical insight was obviously a very potent political weapon, which was used for the purpose of unmasking the opponent's pretentions to, and capacity for, objectivity.

The original advantage obtained by the Marxist through his insight into the situational components of social thought was short-lived, however. The sword of unmasking, as the opponents of Marxism soon realized, could cut both ways. As Mannheim says, "nothing was to prevent the opponents of Marxism from availing themselves of the weapon and applying it to Marxism itself."[34] Once unmasking is transformed from the special property of a particular mode of thought to a general tool of all social thought, the entire status of social theory is itself transposed onto a new plane.

> It is interesting to observe that, as a result of the expansion of the ideological concept, a new mode of understanding has gradually come into existence. . . . For as soon as all parties are able to analyze the ideas of their opponents in ideological terms, all elements of meaning are qualitatively changed and the word ideology acquires a totally new meaning. . . . This point of view ultimately forces us to recognize that our axioms, our ontology, and our epistemology have been profoundly transformed.[35]

Once the discovery is made that no social theory grows out of a sociological vacuum but is partly an expression of a form of life grounded in a particular biological and historical matrix, the next question concerns the bearing which this discovery has upon epistemology. There are, says Mannheim, three basic alternatives at this juncture. One might conclude that this discovery vitiates all truth claims in social and political theory. In this view, the partiality of perspective revealed as a characteristic of all thought completely contaminates it and dissolves the very basis for speaking of the validity of an idea. The failure of reason to attain complete autonomy is seen as a total failure, leading to complete intellectual relativism. On the other hand, one possible response is to deny that the empirical discoveries of the sociology of knowledge have any relevance whatever to the question of validity. The standard of a valid proposition as wholly pristine in its impartial objectivity and finality is maintained, and it is denied that the origin of an idea has any bearing on its validity. This latter position may take a scientific or a philosophical form, since both positivism and political theorists who insist upon a final and absolute solution to the basic problems of political theory implicitly take such a stance.

In effect, these positions represent opposing inferences based upon a vital common assumption: namely, that the validity of knowledge is dependent upon its total autonomy. Both positions agree that genuine knowledge must not be implicated in the corruptibility of historicity. In this respect, both positions rely upon epistemological implications of nonhistorical ontologies, and they can take either positivist or classical philosophical form because both the finite Greek cosmos and the infinite spatial universe of the seventeenth century were nonhistorical ontologies. Mannheim, always aware of the ontological grounding of epistemological tenets, recognizes this relationship in the present context, although by focusing upon philosophical dualism rather than nonhistoricity, he perhaps does not strike at the real heart of the problem.

> The ideal of a realm of truth as such (which, so to speak, pre-exists independently of the historical-psychological act of thought, and in which every concrete act of knowing merely participates) is the last offshoot of the dualistic world-view which, alongside of our world of concrete immediate events, created a second world by adding another dimension of being.
>
> The positing of a sphere of truth which is valid in itself (an offshoot of the doctrine of ideas) is intended to do the same for the act of knowing as the notion of the beyond or the transcendental did for dualistic metaphysics in the realm of ontology, namely to postulate a sphere of perfection which does not bear the scars of its origins, and, measured by which, all events and processes are shown to be finite and incomplete.[36]

In contrast to both of these positions, Mannheim articulates a rather tentative and exploratory epistemological model, which he terms relationism. This model bears real affinity to Polanyi's epistemological reflections; it is basically assimilable with them, as assimilation which would be substantially broadened and deepened thereby. Specifically, Mannheim's picture of political knowledge parallels Polanyi's account of the dialectic between fiduciary rootedness and universal intent. Just as Polanyi insists that knowledge contains an irreducible element of personal involvement and commitment, Mannheim insists that knowledge has an irreducible sociological and historical component. And just as Polanyi insists that the personal coefficient is "no mere imperfection but a vital component of knowledge,"[37] Mannheim insists that "we cannot emphasize too much that the social equation does not always constitute a source of error but more frequently than not brings into view certain interrelations which would not otherwise be apparent."[38] Pursuing the same theme, he argues that

> human thought arises, and operates, not in a social vacuum but in a definite social milieu.
> We need not regard it as a source of error that all thought is so rooted. Just as the individual who participates in a complex of vital social relations with other men thereby enjoys a chance of obtaining a more precise and penetrating insight into his fellows, so a given point of view and a given set of concepts, because they are bound up with and grow out of a certain social reality, offer, through intimate contact with this reality, a greater chance of revealing their meaning.[39]

Inescapably rooted in a personal and social matrix, the process of knowing involves nevertheless the necessity to strive to transcend this partiality of vision through "universal intent," to use Polanyi's language. Although the knowing subject cannot step completely out of his social and historical setting, he can indwell other social and historical perspectives, if only imaginatively, in order to balance and correct the limitations of his original vision.[40] In this way, political theory reaches what might be termed a relative transcendence of its origins; it can move beyond its partiality to a more comprehensive vision, but it can never escape from its grounding in the contingency of historicity. If theory fails to move beyond its origins, then it falls back into being a mere reflection of social interest; while if it claims to have wholly freed itself from its finite grounding, it becomes an epistemological form of idolatry, arrogating unto itself a form of transcendence which no human activity can attain.

Paradoxically, perhaps, these two errors—the failure to reach a position of relative transcendence and the claim to have reached the total transcendence implied by a claim to complete objectivity— often go hand in hand, for the sine qua non of relative epistemological transcendence is the critical recognition of one's own presuppositions and their relationship to one's own historical contingency. The attempt to claim that one has escaped such a fiduciary rootedness altogether simply leads to the hypostatization of one's uncritically accepted presuppositions, which must be repressed in order to make the claim plausible. In this case, the claim of attaining an impossible goal of full epistemological transcendence (complete objectivity) leads to a failure even to reach the relative transcendence which the human mind may attain. He who tries to get more than is possible ends by getting less.[41]

The systematic epistemological reflections of Michael Polanyi, then, perform at least two services for Mannheim's sociology of knowledge. First, and most important, Polanyi provides a much more full-scale and profound philosophical framework for Mannheim's central observations than Mannheim himself ever provided. It is no indictment of the German sociologist to observe that he never went too far along these lines, since he had other legitimate concerns. However, as William Connolly observes, "It is fair to say that while Mannheim repeatedly asserts that the sociology of knowledge possesses important implications for epistemology, he nowhere carefully develops just what those implications are."[42] Polanyi's more sustained reflections, then, provide a context in which these epistemological implications become more visible and are, moreover, related to similar patterns in other sciences and to the larger philosophical setting of Western science in general. Mannheim's penetrating observations are revealed to be not intimations of scandalous and unique defects in social science but rather intimations of the situation of knowledge in general—a situation, moreover, that is a scandal only by reference to long accepted, but quite implausible, standards.

Because Polanyi's thought does provide this crucial setting for Mannheim's ideas, it also helps to suggest the appropriate responses to the criticisms which are most often lodged against Mannheim. The two principles of these criticisms are, first, that Mannheim's views are circular and, second, that he provides no fully specifiable criteria for truth. The implication of Polanyi's ideas is that the answer to each of these criticisms is formally similar—namely, the observations are correct, but they gain the status of criticism only by reference to assumptions which are in fact false.

This contention warrants a bit of elaboration. The "classic reproach [against Mannheim is] that of the circle," in the words of Jacques Maquet, "The arguments by which he proves relativism belong themselves to mental productions tainted with relativism, and consequently his affirmations on the nature of activistic knowledge do not, themselves, have any theoretical value."[43] The same basic criticism is levied by Fred Frohock in a more recent work:

The sociology of knowledge is presented as a universally valid

154

proposition, but the substance of the thesis is that there are no propositions which totally escape the relativity of circumstances. If this paradox seems familiar, we shouldn't be surprised. Once more we have the inappropriate marriage of a closed claim (*all* knowledge) with an assertion of contingency (is culturally *relative*). No amount of maneuvering can evade his paradox.[44]

The basic response to this critique is quite simple, although it will be unacceptable to those who continue the quest for epistemological indubitability: namely, this paradox is not to be evaded, but must be quite forthrightly affirmed. There is nothing improper in this paradox, for it is a reflection of the inescapable ultimate circularity of all human thought—a circularity which can be repressed only by confining inquiry to proximate questions and denying the dependence of these proximate questions upon irreducible presuppositions. A clear-sighted recognition of the irreducibility of ultimate presuppositions and a recognition of one's own contingency, admittedly from a perspective which is itself contingent, leads to the necessity of accepting the ultimately paradoxical structure of our knowledge, including our knowledge of our knowledge. Because epistemology is inherently reflexive—that is, it is thought about thought, to the point of infinite regress—it can finally rest only upon self-confessed circularity which will be "paradoxical" or upon an affirmation of certainty which will be dogmatic. There are no other alternatives. The choice between these two ultimate paradigms must itself be a matter of personal judgment. The former alternative, self-confessed paradox, would seem preferable because it incorporates and accepts its own contingency. As Robert Merton has suggested, this justification of knowledge resembles Munchhausen's feat of extricating himself from a swamp by pulling on his own whiskers.[45] But the alternative resembles standing on thin air, a tenuous basis for laughing at Munchhausen's efforts. The hard fact is that the rejection of the chimerical Archimedean-point model for a knower's location leads to the recognition that there is no absolute footing upon which an aspirant to knowledge may stand.

Confronted by this dilemma, it may seem logical to lapse into complete and utter skepticism. On the other hand, disdaining the apparent hopelessness of the task, we may choose to go on "pulling on our whiskers," sustained by our conviction that while our past efforts of this sort have not been a total success, neither have they been a total failure. Distinguishing clearly between the grounds and the intent of an affirmation, we shall continue making statements with universal intent on the basis of contingent grounds. To aim for less would be irresponsible, even though the goal is admittedly unattainable in any final sense. Human thought must emulate the bumblebee, who, apparently aerodynamically incapable of flight, continues to buzz around somehow nevertheless. We must "lose ourselves in the performance of an obligation which we accept, in spite of its appearing on reflection impossible of achievement. We undertake the task of attaining the universal in spite of our admitted infirmity, which should render the task hopeless, because we hope to be visited by powers for which we cannot account in terms of our specifiable capacities."[46] Acceptance of this paradox replaces the modern epistemological cycle of pride and despair with a complementary relationship of humility and hope. Such a scheme is not perfect, but neither are we; it is the best we can do.

The second common criticism of Mannheim's suggestions about the epistemological relevance of his sociology of knowledge runs as follows: Mannheim rejects the notion of truth-as-such, but does not offer a criterion of truth to replace the rejected ideal. The view from an Archimedean point would be a true view of things. Once this model is rejected as chimerical, what serves as the replacement model of a true view? Mannheim's reflections on this problem led him to a position that is rather like pragmatism in a sociological-historical setting. That view is true, or at least relatively truer, which is most capable of considering and synthesizing other perspectives.

> It is natural that here we must ask which of the various points of view is the best. And for this too there is a criterion. As in the case of visual perspective, where certain positions have the advantage of revealing the decisive features of the object, so here pre-eminence is given to that perspective which gives evidence of the greatest comprehensiveness and the greatest fruitfulness in dealing with empirical materials.[47]

The similarity of this formulation to the emphasis on heuristic value by contemporary logicians of science should be apparent here.

Supplementary to the criteria of comprehensiveness and fruitfulness, Mannheim suggests that consensus, or agreement, among those involved in inquiry are important. As Hans Speier noted when reviewing *Ideology and Utopia*, however, these standards are neither final nor unambiguous. In the first place, the very recognition of the inferior truth value of a particular perspective and the choice of the most relevant elements for attaining a synthesis presuppose criteria which cannot themselves be derived from these perspectives. And the test of agreement does not wholly satisfy this need either.[48]

The implicit substratum of Mannheim's conception of truth is actually his modified Hegelian view of history, As Mannheim admits at one point, "The metaphysical assumption that is involved here . . .

is that the global process within which the various intellectual standpoints emerge is a meaningful one. Standpoints and contents do not succeed each other in a completely haphazard way, since they are parts of a meaningful overall process."[49] With this assumption in mind, Mannheim can say that a theory is "wrong if in a given practical situation it uses concepts and categories which, if taken seriously, would prevent man from adjusting himself at that historical stage."[50] The problem remains, however, without a final resolution, for one could easily ask, first, what are the criteria of adjustment, and, second, on what basis does Mannheim arrive at this theory of history?

Obviously, then, Mannheim does not provide any final, unambiguous criterion for deciding what is true. This inability, however, cannot legitimately be construed as a failure on Mannheim's part, for the presupposition which lies behind the designation of this inability as a failure is faulty. That is, the request for final and unambiguous truth-criteria is itself based upon a misconception—the belief that it is possible to find wholly impersonal and unequivocal standards by which to adjudicate the truth or falsity of an idea. As our consideration of the verifiability criterion demonstrated earlier, while such standards may be provided on a proximate level, the hope for locating such standards for adjudication between ideas that differ at an ultimate level is a chimerical residue of faith in the Cartesian method of universal doubt. Mannheim therefore cannot be criticized for not achieving such a feat, for it is inherently impossible.

He does suggest clues, indicators of the truth, or warrants for belief, such as comprehensiveness and fruitfulness, and he suggests that intersubjective transmissibility is a helpful indicator of truth, as well. Ultimately, however, in order to avoid an infinite regress, he must agree that no one can escape the necessity of accepting personal responsibility for what he is willing to accredit as true. As Polanyi has made clear, this fiduciary grounding of knowledge is both a logical and a practical necessity. We all understand "truth" to mean accuracy and fruitfulness in the intellectual apprehension of reality, but none of us possesses a neutral tool to measure truth impersonally. Mannheim, therefore, should not be faulted for not escaping the universal intellectual predicament of man. He is unique not in his failure but in his candid appreciation of man's epistemological situation, even though he did not possess the philosophical resources to articulate it clearly. It is this latter failing which Polanyi overcomes, along with the help of other recent philosophers of science such as Kuhn and Hanson.

In summary, Polanyi's model of postcritical reason has much to recommend it in the context of political theory. Even though Polanyi's principal attention has been devoted to the epistemology of the natural sciences, his conclusions are highly relevant and useful for the study of politics as well. In the first place, his philosophy of knowledge allows political theory to confront Mannheim's trenchant observations on the sociological grounding of social theory without flinching. Mannheim's insistence that all knowing proceeds from a personal, historical location was an embarrassment under the Cartesian dispensation, which required knowledge to be unsullied by time, place, or personality; the same insistence is no longer an embarrassment after Polanyi's demonstration that "into every act of knowing there enters a passionate contribution of the person knowing what is being known, and that this coefficient is no mere imperfection but a vital component of his knowledge."[51]

Second, the model of postcritical reason does not suffer from the severe limitation of objectivist reason which Hobbes clearly recognized as logically inescapable: namely, the incapacity to perceive order in reality and thereby to identify the particular entities with whose relationship science is concerned. As Hobbes put it, "Reason serves only to convince the truth not of fact, but of consequence."[52] The legacy of this incapacity is the conception of empirical theory as the investigation of causal interrelationships of variables, without any apparent resources for identifying and characterizing the variables themselves. This glaring deficiency has been systematically ignored, principally because of an implicit acceptance of that other chimera of objectivism—the belief that data are neutral and hence perceptible unproblematically. Since this belief has clearly been shown to be untenable, the problem of identifying variables must soon be confronted; once again Polanyi's epistemology can make good the bankruptcy of the objectivist tradition.

Finally, as we have suggested all along, the recent attempt to keep the theoretical enterprise in politics severed into two hermetically sealed divisions has been both destructive and unrealistic. The conceptual dilemmas that begin to arise on both sides of the hiatus indicate that the underlying premises of the divorce are unsound. Polanyi's inquiry into the incapacities of objectivist dicta in science helps to clarify the nature and sources of these unsound premises. And by providing an alternative model of knowledge, he gives us the foundation upon which the necessary reconciliation between the alienated components of political theory begin.

Notes

1. Abraham Kaplan, *The Conduct of Inquiry,* (San Francisco: Chandler Publishing Company, 1963), p. 47.

2. Karl Mannheim, "Historicism," in *Essays on the Sociology of Knowledge,* Paul Kecskemeti, ed. (New York: Oxford University Press, 1952), p. 112.

3. Marjorie Grene, *The Knower and the Known* (New York: Basic Books, 1966), p. 57. The following few paragraphs are largely inspired by the formulations of Dr. Grene, both in *The Knower and the Known* and in her *Portrait of Aristotle* (London: Faber and Faber, 1963), and by conversations with Dr. William H. Poteat.

4. Grene, *The Knower and the Known,* p. 43-44.

5. Grene, *Portrait of Aristotle,* p. 249: "The bonds of finitude were broken and essence and existence fell apart. In Aristotelian metaphysics, as both Gilson and Owens have emphasized, there was no such separation, no such problem." Cf. the concluding section of R.G. Collingwood, *The Idea of Nature* (New York: Oxford University Press, 1960).

6. The suggestion that objectivism was in these respects not simply a departure from certain classical assumptions is implicit in the inquiries of Grene, *Knower and the Known,* esp. pp. 36-63; and *Portrait of Aristotle,* pp. 234-240.

7. E.g. the work of Kuhn, Grene, Hanson, Collingwood, and Whitehead. The schools of existentialism and phenomenology have made contributions as well, represented preeminently in the present context by Maurice Merleau-Ponty, *Phenomenology of Perception,* Colin Smith, trans. (London: Routledge & Kegan Paul, 1962). Arthur Koestler explores some important aspects of the problem in *The Act of Creation* (New York: Macmillan Co., 1964). Karl Mannheim made some important suggestions in the field of sociological theory, as we shall argue shortly, particularly in *Ideology and Utopia,* Louis Wirth and Edward Shils, trans. (New York: Harcourt Brace, 1936) and *Essays on the Sociology of Knowledge,* Paul Kecskemeti, ed. (New York: Oxford University Press, 1952).

8. Polanyi's principal book-length contributions are: *Personal Knowledge* (New York: Harper Torchbooks, 1958), *The Tacit Dimension* (London: Routledge & Kegan Paul, 1967), *The Logic of Liberty* (London: Routledge & Kegan Paul, 1951), and *The Study of Man* (London: Routledge & Kegan Paul, 1959), and *Science, Faith, and Society* (Chicago: University of Chicago Press, 1946). His numerous articles are scattered throughout scientific and philosophical journals.

9. Kaplan, *The Conduct of Inquiry,* p. 86.

10. Ibid., pp. 86-87.

11. Polanyi, *Personal Knowledge,* pp. 272-274.

12. Merleau-Ponty, *Phenomenology of Perception,* p. 31.

13. Ibid.

14. Merleau-Ponty, *Phenomenology of Perception,* p. 121: "As soon as there is consciousness, and in order that there may be consciousness, there must be something to be conscious of, an intentional object, and consciousness can move towards this object only to the extent that it 'derealizes'

itself and throws itself into it. . . . If a being is consciousness, he must be nothing but a network of intentions."

15. Grene, *The Knower and the Known*: "Knowing . . . is essentially learning; and learning is a telic phenomenon, in which the end in sight, even only guessed at, draws us toward a solution. . ." (p. 244)."Whitehead's 'fallacy of simple location' must be applied to time as well as space" (p. 246).

16. It is the failure of his powers of tacit integration which lies behind the pitiable failures of Schneider (Merleau-Ponty's case study in pathology of intentionality) in both sexual expression and intellectual comprehension. Although his biological sexuality is not impaired, Schneider cannot perform competently in the erotic arena because he has lost the intentional, projective structure of his activity. Therefore, while the subsidiary particulars of the sexual act are apprehended by him, they are not effectual precisely because they are explicitly apprehended and not tacitly integrated by a transcending purpose; cf. *Phenomenology of Perception*, pp. 154-158. Similarly, his powers of intellectual comprehension are pathologically inhibited precisely because of his need to be excessively explicit. "What impairs thought in Schneider's case is not that he is incapable of perceiving concrete data as specimens of a unique eidos, or of subsuming them under some category, but on the contrary, that he can relate them only by a quite explicit subsumption" (ibid., p. 128). Consistent pursuit of the unattainable goal of wholly explicit knowledge ultimately turns the pursuer into an intellectual Schneider, cognitively impotent, who like Nietzche's "last man" has forgotten why he ever began.

17. *Personal Knowledge*, p. 254.

18. Ibid., p. 305.

19. Ibid., p. 309.

20. Ibid., p. 311.

21. Polanyi, *Personal Knowledge*, p. 124: "We have seen already that whenever we make (or believe we have made) contact with reality, we anticipate an indeterminate range of unexpected future confirmations of our knowledge derived from this contact. The interpretive framework of the educated mind is ever ready to meet somewhat novel experiences, and to deal with them in a somewhat novel manner. In this sense all life is endowed with originality and originality of a higher order is but a magnified form of a universal biological adaptivity."

22. The de facto existence of this circularity can be easily seen in various aspects of cognitive life. Any word of a language may be "defined" by other words of the same language, each of which is in turn defined by a complex of words which eventually includes the original word. Ptolemaic astronomers devised a theory of epicycles to keep their system intact under strain. The Freudian concept of repression helps to absorb difficulties arising in other parts of the Freudian conceptual circle. Threats to one magical notion in a primitive tribe may be countered by reference to other magical notions.

23. The analogy used by Arthur Koestler in *The God that Failed*, Richard Crossman, ed. (New York: Harper Brothers, 1950), is suggestive. Koestler likens the dissolution of his commitment to the conceptual circle of Marxism to the "snapping of an elastic rope."

24. Kuhn, *Structure of Scientific Revolutions*, p. 147.

25. Ibid., p. 149.

26. Polanyi calls this the "paradox of self-set standards." Cf. *Personal Knowledge*, p. 256: "If the criteria of reasonableness, to which I subject my own beliefs, are ultimately upheld by my confidence in them, the whole process of justifying such beliefs may appear but a futile authorization of my own authority.

Yet so be it. Only this manner of adopting the fiduciary mode is consonant with itself: the decision to do so must be admitted to be itself in the nature of a fiduciary act."

27. The capacity for discerning rationality in nature is a tacit feature of all verification, which is why verification is only a proximate phenomenon. Cf. Ibid., pp. 13-14: "Any critical verification of a scientific statement requires the same powers for recognizing rationality in nature as does the process of scientific discovery, even though it exercises these at a lower level. When philosophers analyze the verification of scientific laws, they invariably choose as specimens such laws as are not in doubt, and thus inevitably overlook the intervention of these powers. They are describing the practical demonstration of scientific law, and not its critical verification. As a result we are given an account of the scientific method which, having left out the process of discovery on the grounds that it follows no definite method, overlooks the process of verification as well, by referring only to examples where no real verification takes place."

The personal coefficient of verification is not equally substantial in all scientific perceptions; it is relatively small, for example, in observations of impersonal and unambiguous data. But it is present, although generally unproblematic, even here. Ibid., p. 321: "As we pass from verification to validation and rely increasingly on internal rather than external evidence, the structure of commitment remains unchanged but its depth becomes greater."

28. Thomas S. Kuhn, "Postscript" to 2nd ed. of *The Structure of Scientific Revolutions* (Chicago: University of Chicago Press, 1970), p. 199.

29. Ibid., pp. 199-200.

30. Ibid., p. 252: "The indefinite and futile regress on which we enter when asking whether the application of the term 'precise' is itself precise, suggests that such a question should be avoided by denying the word 'precise' the character of a descriptive term. When we say that a word is precise (or apt, or fitting, or clear, or expressive), we approve of an act of our own which we have found satisfying while carrying it out."

31. Joseph La Palombara, "Decline of Ideology: A Dissent and an Interpretation," *American Political Science Review*, LX (1966), p. 6. The phrase "the Mannheim Paradox" seems to have a dual usage. La Palombara uses it to mean Mannheim's perception that social theory is always partial because of the theorist's sociological and historical location. Others use the term to refer to the paradox of Mannheim's own assertions about the partiality of theories being themselves claims to universal validity. The former usage refers to a critique by Mannheim; the latter embodies a critique of Mannheim. This latter critique will be examined below.

32. Mannheim was a very wide-ranging thinker, who never gave his various ideas a full systematic coherence, if indeed this was a possibility.

Therefore, while I find it impossible to share some of his Hegelian notions that lie just beneath the surface of some of his formulations or to share his belief in and hope for a form of social engineering, acceptance of these aspects of his thought is not necessary for an appreciation of his exploration of the epistemological significance of the sociology of knowledge.

33. Mannheim, *Ideology and Utopia*, p. 69.

34. Ibid., p. 75.

35. Ibid., p. 76.

36. Ibid., p. 297. The notion of the transcendent to which Mannheim refers is not necessarily the notion in its generic form, but specifically in the form it received within the cosmologies of Plato and Aristotle. Other images of the transcendent, for example the Christian interpretation, need not be incompatible with the attribution of genuine ontological status to history and hence with the attribution of genuine epistemological status to the historical phenomenon of human thought.

37. Polanyi, *Personal Knowledge*, p. xiv.

38. Mannheim, *Ideology and Utopia*, p. 172.

39. Ibid., p. 80.

40. This sort of self-correction and deepening of one's outlook corresponds closely to the account which George Herbert Mead gives of self-knowledge through "taking the role of the other" (cf. *Mind, Self, and Society*, Charles W. Morris, ed. [Chicago: University of Chicago Press, 1934], esp. pp. 138ff.) and to the account which R.G. Collingwood gives of historical knowledge as a "re-thinking-of past thoughts" (*Idea of History* [New York: Oxford University Press, 1956], esp. Part 5).

41. Such, essentially, is the meaning of C.S. Peirce's observation: "Find a scientific man who proposes to get along without any metaphysics . . . and you have found one whose doctrines are thoroughly vitiated by the crude and uncriticized metaphysics with which they are packed" (*The Collected works of C.S. Peirce*, Charles Hartshorne and Paul Weiss, (Cambridge, Mass.: Harvard University Press, 1931), I, 129.

42. *Political Science and Ideology*, p. 74.

43. Jacques Maquet, *The Sociology of Knowledge: Its Structure and Its Relationship to the Philosophy of Knowledge*, J.F. Locke, trans. (Boston: Beacon Press, 1951), p. 84.

44. Fred M. Frohock, *The Nature of Political Inquiry* (Homewood, Ill.: Dorsey Press, 1967), p. 31.

45. Robert Merton, *Social Theory and Social Structure* (Glencoe, Ill.: The Free Press, 1957), p. 507.

46. Polanyi, *Personal Knowledge*, p. 324.

47. Mannheim, *Ideology and Utopia*, p. 301.

48. Cf. Hans Speier, "Review of Ideology and Utopia," *American Journal of Sociology*, XLIII (1937), 155-156, 165.

49. Mannheim, *Essays on the Sociology of Knowledge*, p. 177.

50. Mannheim, *Ideology and Utopia*, p. 95.

51. Polanyi, *Personal Knowledge*, p. xiv.

52. Hobbes, *Leviathan*, Everyman ed. (New York: E.P. Dutton Co., 1950), p. 328.

8   Conclusion

The logic of exposition does not always coincide with the logic of
inquiry. In the case of this essay, the starting point for inquiry was
the conviction that political science has rapidly been developing
some conceptual dilemmas in its theoretical enterprise that were not
really soluble within the confines of the conventional wisdom about
the basic structure and status of political theory as a form of
knowledge. In Kuhn's terminology, this origin point of inquiry
would be termed the perception of anomalies growing from an
established paradigm. Some of these anomalies were discussed in
Chapter 5.

The perception of anomalies then leads logically to an
examination of the paradigm which has produced them. In the
instant case, the direct source of the conceptual strain and distortion
seemed to lie in the presumed necessity of maintaining an absolute
distinction between empirical and normative theory, allegedly on
epistemological grounds. Further examination then suggested that
this axiom for structuring political inquiry was one clearly derivative
manifestation of the dominant epistemological model of the West
since the intellectual watershed of the seventeenth century. Pushing
the inquiry outward in scope, it then became apparent that a similar
pattern of conceptual difficulties was manifest in various intellectual
disciplines, from the natural sciences and on through the social
sciences into linguistics and philosophy. This recurrence of a basic

163

pattern across various fields, it was argued, was not purely fortuitous but instead grew out of a common grounding in some faulty epistemological presuppositions.

It was then suggested that some highly provocative reconsiderations about the nature of scientific inquiry are underway which offer the possibility of escaping the conceptual binds which traditional assumptions seemed inevitably to produce. Foremost among these reconsiderations, which cut very deeply into some of the most venerable tenets of traditional Western thought since Descartes, are the reflections of Thomas Kuhn on the role of the paradigm in scientific knowledge. Complementary to these is the more full-scale reassessment of the cognitive status of science carried out by Michael Polanyi. The implications of these highly significant inquiries for our understanding of political science have hardly begun to be appreciated, even though several distinguished members of the profession have indicated an appreciation of the utility of Kuhn's insights.

This essay has made no claim to deal exhaustively with these implications for political science of the recent transformations in our understanding of scientific cognition. A few of the more important ones, however, have been indicated. In the first place, we shall clearly have to concede that the quest for a final, closed, indubitable grand theory of politics is an intrinsically impossible dream. The demise of the belief in pure and neutral sense-data, the collapse of the search for a perfect language, and the abandonment of the verifiability principle in its original form combine to point unarguably to that conclusion. Political science suffers from no peculiar incapacity here; it is simply that no science is of this nature. Our tendency to believe otherwise is not a product of the careful examination of science but rather a product of the delusive, a priori definitions of science propagated by objectivist philosophy.

The quixotic pursuit of impossible dreams, of course, often has some positive results. In the context of political science, these benefits have included a vast refinement and sophistication of technical tools of inquiry, a broadened intellectual scope, and the development of some highly productive conceptual formats. The faulty premises of quixotic enterprises, however, eventually lead to debacle because of their unreality. The productivity of the original intense aspiration reaches a point of diminishing returns, and the counterproductivity of misconceptions begins to increase. If the assessment of the situation underlying this essay is sound, political science is rapidly approaching that turning point, if indeed it has not already reached it.

If the new understanding of scientific cognition involves forsaking some very appealing, however delusive, dreams, it does offer some significant opportunities and challenges for political science. The most immediate advantage, of course, is simply that it enables us to grasp the reasons for some of our most pressing conceptual problems. The most far-reaching value of the new model of scientific knowledge, however, is the opportunity which it offers for the reconciliation and reintegration of empirical and normative theory. Recognition of the descriptive functions of norms explains why it has seemed impossible wholly to cleanse purely descriptive studies of normative implications, however strenuous the intention to accomplish that feat whenever any theoretical depths were approached. Furthermore, the frank avowal of the ordering functions of norms upon data should permit them to be handled openly, critically, and more competently. Theoretical conception, unlike some other forms of conception, cannot be satisfactorily accomplished in the dark.

One important and understandable objection will be raised against those who accept the necessity of interplay between norms and empirical data in all forms of theory. Such a program raises the specter of political science, in its broader theoretical endeavors, becoming indistinguishable from ideology. Obviously, this result would carry with it some potentially dangerous implications. The inference that political science would become dissolved into ideology is not a necessary one, however. It is correct to infer that the classic simplicity of the objectivist distinction would be no longer tenable. That is, one can no longer meet any inquiry with the response that scientific theory is objective and ideology subjective. Since all science must be seen to involve a fiduciary component of personal judgment, the grounds for this kind of clear contrast between science and ideology cannot be maintained.

No science, including political science, is possible apart from commitment, then. The scientific status of the political scientist cannot be grounded on the striking of a noncommital posture. Several important grounds of distinction between political science and ideology nevertheless remain. In the first place, the fiduciary component of science, however intense and personal it may be, is a form of intellectual commitment, not commitment to a program of political action. The old disjunction between thought and action may have been overdrawn at times, but it remains true that a commitment to a theoretical paradigm in the service of truth is not the same as a commitment to a partisan program in the service of particular political goals. Political science obviously has bearing upon political action. Men act upon the basis of what they believe reality to be. However, no finite political act can legitimately claim the sanction of political science, first, because of the ineluctable element of contingency within scientific knowledge itself and, second, because of the equally inescapable slippage between the judgment that such-and-such is true and the judgment that thus-and-so should be done, even where the normative component of truth is recognized.

This latter distinction between a truth judgment and prescription for action is not a return to the old dichotomy of "is" and "ought." It refers rather to the fact that political actions must be made as choices between competing goods and competing obligations and between options that are advantageous to some and options advantageous to others. The prudential choices and compromises that must be made in this characteristic political situation simply cannot be the product of scientific authority. Furthermore, political action seems inevitably to take place in a context of intrinsically insufficient information, where not even the most refined science could be of genuine practical assistance either because of the inaccessibility of necessary data, because of insufficient time, or because of the impossible scope and delicacy of relevant predictions.

The first basis for distinguishing political science and ideology, then, once the old objective-subjective dichotomy is recognized as based upon an untenable epistemology, is essentially the distinction between intellectual and political commitment, between thought and action. Other grounds of distinction, partly interrelated, are also available and significant. Central among the grounds for distinguishing political science and ideology is their different locations within the context of human purposes. Ideological constructions are intellectual products, but they are contingent products in their functions. An ideology tends to be the rationale for a program of political action; it performs in the service of the program's goals and therefore is usually shaped by the content of these goals. What data are considered relevant, the interpretative bias, and so on are significantly influenced, if not determined, by the practical outcomes which the ideologue desires. There is nothing absolutely illicit about such intellectual constructions which perform in the service of political programs. In fact, political action is likely to be more productive and coherent when it has a rationale than if it is a series of purely ad hoc responses or a pure pursuit of self-interest, wholly unencumbered by any of the strictures of reason whatever. It is simply that the ideologue is not a political scientist, by virtue of the fact that his intellectual operations are subordinate to finite political purposes.

In contrast to the contingency of ideology upon finite political ends, political science is distinguished, or at least should be distinguished, by its autonomy fro... such limited political ends, however noble and pressing these ends might be. Perhaps no political inquiry can ever be absolutely and totally free from its practical political context, and consequently, this autonomous nature of political science may be a matter of degree rather than an absolute distinction of kind. However, whether a distinction of degree or kind, the distinction is important. The responsibility of the political scientist is to find and to tell the truth, whatever its nature and whatever its consequences. Conversely, this overriding responsibility to the truth alone carries with it a corresponding freedom from subordination to any particular set of practical political purposes. The obligation and the freedom of the political theorist, then, form a different pattern from the obligations and the freedom of the ideologue, even where the theorist must cope with questions of political norms and standards of political performance.

Finally, because it must strive relentlessly for ever greater comprehensiveness of vision, political science is distinguished from ideology by an inherent tension in its intellectual quest. The tension of the ideologue is political rather than intellectual; his striving is to give historical embodiment to his vision. Preoccupied by the practical aspiration to fulfill the ideals of his ideology, the ideologue is likely to be complacent, if not frozen, in his intellectual stance. Such complacency and rigidity is wholly out of place in the context of any science, the science of politics included. The obligation of the political scientist includes the obligation to pursue continually the goal of a broader and deeper vision, whatever the consequences. Unlike the ideologue, the political scientist should always carry to this quest a ready eye for what Weber termed the inconvenient fact for any partisan position, including those facts which are inconvenient for his own theories and which may therefore serve as the impetus toward a better theory. As Karl Mannheim appreciated so well, the recognition of the illusoriness of the Cartesian ideal need not lead to the dissolution of political inquiry into ideology, for the true scientist is always seeking to enlarge his perspective to gain greater catholicity and accuracy in his perception of reality. The replacement of "the false ideal of a detached, impersonal point of view" is neither skepticism nor the prostitution of science to ideology, but instead is "the ideal of an essentially human point of view which is within the limits of a human perspective, *constantly striving to enlarge itself.*"[1]

The abandonment of the old Cartesian-based grounds of distinction between political science and ideology—is unavoidable if we are to take seriously the view of science emerging from the work of contemporary authorities. It does not follow, we have argued, that no grounds for distinction remain. The commitment of the scientist is intellectual, his inquiries autonomous, his attitude questing; the commitment of the ideologue is political, his formulations contingent on his practical goals, his intellectual stance complacent. These distinctions may not satisfy those who can accept nothing less than the view that political science and ideology are as contained and distinctive as the impenetrable essences of Aristotle. They are, nonetheless, very real and important differences.

Whether it is dreaded as a sullying of the alleged epistemological purity of science or welcomed as a liberation from a crippling intellectual asceticism, the reconciliation of the empirical and normative strands of inquiry in political theory is fast becoming a necessity. If the argument of this essay has any merit, it is also a genuine possibility within the province of science. This reconciliation will entail, of course, some revision in our image of science, but this revision is long overdue anyway and has already been largely accomplished within the philosophy of science.

This reintegration of the theoretical enterprise in political science is a necessity because politics is the intersection of order and power. The latter cannot be wholly abstracted from the former, however diligent the effort, and the former cannot be described apart from patterns and standards which are perceptual, interpretative norms. The achievements of the behavioral revolution in political science have been vast. However, it is rapidly becoming obvious that one thing this revolution has not achieved is the inherently impossible conversion of the intellectual task of theorizing into a purely technical, impersonal function. It is therefore altogether likely that we are on the verge of entering a postbehavioral era in political science, a time when the many advances of the behavioral era will be consolidated and refined and when the theoretical problems suggested by our new data and techniques will be faced squarely.[2] If this essay has contributed anything to the understanding of the nature and reasons for the tasks which now face us or to the resolution of some of the conceptual problems presented, then it will have performed its intended service.

Notes

1. Karl Mannheim, *Ideology and Utopia*, Louis Wirth and Edward Shils, trans. (New York: Harcourt Brace, 1936), p. 297 (emphasis added).

2. Cf. David Easton, "The New Revolution in Political Science," *American Political Science Review*, LXIII (1969), 1051-1061.

Bibliography

Almond, Gabriel, and G. Bingham Powell, Jr. *Comparative Politics: A Developmental Approach*. Boston: Little, Brown, 1966.

———. "Political Development," *Comparative Political Studies*, 1, (1969).

———. "Political Theory and Political Science," *American Political Science Review*, LX (1966).

———, and James Coleman. *Politics of the Developing Areas*. Princeton, N. J.: Princeton University Press, 1960.

Apter, David. *The Politics of Modernization*. Chicago: University of Chicago Press, 1965.

Aristotle. *Metaphysics*.

———. *Physics*.

Arnheim, Rudolph. *Visual Thinking*. Berkeley: University of California Press, 1969.

Ayer, A. J. *Language, Truth and Logic*. 2d ed. New York: Dover Publications, 1946.

———. "On the Analysis of Moral Judgments," *Philosophical Essays*. London: MacMillan, 1954.

Bachrach, Peter, and Morton Baratz. "Two Faces of Power," *American Political Science Review*, 56 (1962).

Barber, Bernard. "Resistance by Scientists to Scientific Discovery," *Science*, CXXXIV (1961).

Bay, Christian. "Politics and Pseudo-Politics," *American Political Science Review*, 59 (1965).

Becker, Carl. *The Heavenly City of the Eighteenth-Century Philosophers*. New Haven, Conn.: Yale University Press, 1932.

Berger, Peter, and Thomas Luckmann. *The Social Construction of Reality: A Treatise in the Sociology of Knowledge*. Garden City, N. Y.: Doubleday, 1966.

Black, Max, ed. *The Importance of Language*. Englewood Cliffs, N. J.: Prentice-Hall, 1962.

Bluhm, William T. *Theories of the Political System*. Englewood Cliffs, N. J.: Prentice-Hall, 1965.

Boorstin, Daniel. *The Genius of American Politics*. Chicago: University of Chicago Press, 1953.

Brecht, Arnold. *Political Theory*. Princeton, N. J.: Princeton University Press, 1959.

Burtt, Edwin A. *The Metaphysical Foundations of Modern Physical Science*. 2d ed. London: Routledge and Kegan Paul, 1959.

Butterfield, Herbert. *The Origins of Modern Science*. Rev. ed. New York: Collier Books, 1962.

Capek, Milio. *The Philosophical Impact of Contemporary Physics*. Princeton, N. J.: Van Nostrand, 1961.

Cassirer, Ernst. *The Philosophy of the Enlightenment*. Translated by

Fritz C. A. Koelln and James P. Pettegrove. Boston: Beacon Press, 1955.

Charlesworth, James C., ed. *A Design for Political Science: Scope, Objectives, and Methods.* Philadelphia: American Academy of Political and Social Science, 1966.

——————, ed. *The Limits of Behavioralism in Political Science.* Philadelphia: American Academy of Political and Social Science, 1962.

Collingwood, R. G. *Idea of History.* New York: Oxford University Press, 1956.

——————. *The Idea of Nature.* New York: Oxford University Press, 1960.

Connolly, William, ed. *The Bias of Pluralism.* New York: Atherton Press, 1969.

——————, ed. *Political Science and Ideology.* New York: Atherton Press, 1967.

Crick, Bernard. *The American Science of Politics.* Berkeley: University of California Press, 1959.

Dahl, Robert. "The Behavioral Approach in Political Science: Epitaph for a Monument to a Successful Protest," *American Political Science Review,* 55 (December, 1961).

——————. "The Concept of Power," in Sidney Ulmer, ed. *Introductory Readings in Political Behavior.* Chicago: Rand McNally, 1961.

——————. "Further Reflections on 'The Elitist Theory of Democracy,'" *American Political Science Review,* 60 (1966).

——————. *Modern Political Analysis.* Englewood Cliffs, N. J.: Prentice-Hall, 1963.

——————. *A Preface to Democratic Theory.* Chicago: University of Chicago Press, 1956.

Davis, Lane. "The Cost of Realism: Contemporary Restatements of Democracy," *Western Political Quarterly,* 17 (1964).

Descartes, René. *Discourse on Method.* Translated by E. S. Haldane and G. R. T. Ross. Great Books Series, Vol. 31; Chicago: University of Chicago Press, 1952.

——————. *Meditations.* Translated by E. S. Haldane and G. R. T. Ross. Great Books Series, Vol. 31; Chicago: University of Chicago Press, 1952.

——————. *Rules for the Direction of the Mind.* Translated by E. S. Haldane and G. R. T. Ross. Great Books Series, Vol. 31; Chicago: University of Chicago Press, 1952.

Deutsch, Karl. *Nerves of Government.* New York: Free Press, 1966.

——————. "Social Mobilization and Political Development," *American Political Science Review,* 60 (1961).

Dowse, Robert. "A Functionalist's Logic," *World Politics,* 18 (1966).

Duncan, Graeme, and Steven Lukes. "The New Democracy," *Political Studies,* 11 (1963).

Easton, David. *A Framework for Political Analysis.* Englewood Cliffs, N. J.: Prentice-Hall, 1965.

——————. *The Political System.* New York: Alfred Knopf, 1953.

——————. *A Systems Analysis of Political Life.* New York: Wiley, 1965.

Eulau, Heinz. *The Behavioral Persuasion in Politics.* New York: Random House, 1963.

Feigl, Herbert, and May Brodbeck, eds. *Readings in the Philosophy of Science.* New York: Appleton-Century-Crofts, 1953.

Frohock, Fred M. *The Nature of Political Inquiry.* Homewood, Illinois: Dorsey Press, 1967.

Fulbright, J. William. *The Arrogance of Power.* New York: Vintage, 1966.

Gerth, Hans and C. Wright Mills, eds. *From Max Weber.* New York: Oxford University Press, 1958.

Gibson, Quentin. *The Logic of Social Inquiry.* London: Routledge and Kegan Paul, 1960.

Greer, Scott. *The Logic of Social Inquiry.* Chicago: Aldine, 1969.

Gregor, A. James, "Political Science and Functional Analysis," *American Political Science Review,* 62 (1968).

Grene, Marjorie. *The Knower and the Known.* New York: Basic Books, 1966.

——————. *Approaches to a Philosophical Biology.* New York: Basic Books, 1968.

——————. *Portrait of Aristotle.* London: Faber and Faber, 1963.

Haas, Michael, and Henry Kariel, eds. *Approaches to the Study of Political Science.* Scranton, Pa.: Chandler Publishing Company, 1970.

Hallowell, John H. *Decline of Liberalism as an Ideology.* Berkeley: University of California Press, 1943.

Hampshire, Stuart. *Thought and Action.* New York: Viking, 1959.

Hanson. *Patterns of Discovery.* Cambridge: Cambridge University Press, 1958.

Hare, R. M. *The Language of Morals.* New York: Oxford University Press, 1964.

Hartz, Louis. *The Liberal Tradition in America.* New York: Harcourt, Brace and World, 1955.

Hempel, Carl G. *Fundamentals of Concept Formation in Empirical Science.* Chicago: University of Chicago Press, 1952.

173

_____ . "Problems and Changes in the Empiricist Criterion of Meaning," *Revue Internationale de Philosophie,* 40 (1950).

Hobbes, Thomas. *English Works,* ed. by William Molesworth. London: John Bohn, 1839.

_____ . *Leviathan.* Everyman's Library Edition; New York: E. P. Dutton Company, 1950.

Holton, Gerald. *Science and the Modern Mind.* Boston: Beacon Press, 1958.

Horowitz, Irving L., ed. *The Rise and Fall of Project Camelot.* Cambridge, Mass.: M.I.T. Press, 1967.

Hull, Clark. *Principles of Behavior.* New York: Appleton-Century-Crofts, 1943.

Huntington, Samuel. "Political Development and Political Decay," *World Politics,* 17 (1965).

Hyneman, Charles S. *The Study of Politics: The Present State of American Political Science.* Urbana: University of Illinois Press, 1959.

Kalleberg, Arthur L. "Concept Formation in Normative and Empirical Studies: Toward Reconciliation in Political Theory," *American Political Science Review,* 63 (1969).

_____ . "The Logic of Comparison: A Methodological Note on the Comparative Study of Political Systems," *World Politics,* 19 (1966).

Kaplan, Abraham. *The Conduct of Inquiry.* San Francisco: Chandler Publishing Company, 1964.

Kaplan, Morton. *On Historical and Political Knowing.* Chicago: University of Chicago Press, 1971.

Kariel, Henry. *Open Systems.* Itasca, Ill.: Peacock Publishers, 1969.

_____ , ed. *Frontiers of Democratic Theory.* New York: Random House, 1970.

Knight, Isabel. *The Geometric Spirit: The Abbé de Condillac and the French Enlightenment.* New Haven, Conn.: Yale University Press, 1968.

Koestler, Arthur. *The Act of Creation.* New York: MacMillan, 1964.

Koyré, Alexandre. *From the Closed World to the Infinite Universe.* New York: Harper Torchbooks, 1958.

Kress, Paul. "Self, Systems, and Significance: Reflections on Professor Easton's Political Science," *Ethics,* 77 (1966).

Kuhn, Thomas. *The Structure of Scientific Revolutions.* Chicago: Phoenix Books, 1964.

Lakatos, Imre and Alan Musgrave, eds. *Criticism and the Growth of Knowledge.* Cambridge: Cambridge University Press, 1970.

Landau, Martin. *Political Theory and Political Science*. New York: MacMillan, 1972.

La Palombara, Joseph. "Decline of Ideology: A Dissent and an Interpretation," *American Political Science Review*, 60 (1966).

Lasswell, Harold. "The Policy Sciences of Development," *World Politics*, 17 (1965).

———. *Politics: Who Gets What, When, How*. 2d ed. New York: Peter Smith, 1950.

———, and Abraham Kaplan. *Power and Society*. New Haven: Yale University Press, 1950.

Lerner, Daniel. "Social Science: Whence and Whither," *The Human Meaning of the Social Sciences*. New York: Meridian Books, 1959.

Lowenstein, Karl. "Report on the Research Panel on Comparative Government," *American Political Science Review*, 38 (1944).

Mannheim, Karl. *Essays in the Sociology of Knowledge*, ed. by Paul Kecskemeti. New York: Oxford University Press, 1952.

———. *Ideology and Utopia*. Translated by Wirth and Shils. New York: Harvest Books, 1936.

Maquet, Jacques. *The Sociology of Knowledge: Its Structure and Its Relationship to the Philosophy of Knowledge*. Translated by J. F. Locke. Boston: Beacon Press, 1951.

McCoy, Charles and John Playford, eds. *Apolitical Politics*. New York: Thomas Crowell, 1967.

Mead, George Herbert. *Mind, Self, and Society*, ed. by Charles W. Morris. Chicago: University of Chicago Press, 1934.

Meehan, Eugene J. *The Foundations of Political Analysis: Empirical and Normative*. Homewood, Ill.: Dorsey Press, 1971.

———. *Value Judgment and Social Science*. Homewood, Ill.: Dorsey Press, 1969.

Merleau-Ponty, Maurice. *Phenomenology of Perception*. Translated by Colin Smith. London: Routledge and Kegan Paul, 1962.

———. *The Structure of Behavior*. Translated by Alden L. Fisher. Boston: Beacon Press, 1963.

Merton, Robert. *Social Theory and Social Structure*. New York: Free Press, 1957.

Myrdal, Gunnar. *Objectivity in Social Research*. New York: Pantheon Books, 1969.

———. *Value in Social Theory*, ed. by Paul Streeten. London: Routledge and Kegan Paul, 1958.

Nagel, Ernest. *The Structure of Science*. New York: Harcourt, Brace and World, 1961.

Natanson, Maurice, ed. *Philosophy of the Social Sciences*. New York: Random House, 1963.

175

Nye, J. S. "Corruption and Political Development," *American Political Science Review,* 61 (1967).

Owens, Joseph. *The Doctrine of Being in the Aristotelian Metaphysics.* 2d ed. Toronto: The Pontifical Institute of Medieval Studies, 1963.

Parsons, Talcott. *Essays in Sociological Theory.* New York: Free Press, 1949.

——————. *The Structure of Social Action.* 2d ed. New York: Free Press, 1966.

Pennock, J. Roland. "Political Development, Political Systems, and Political Goods," *World Politics,* 18 (1960).

Petras, James. "Ideology and United States Political Scientists," *Science and Society,* 29 (1965).

Polanyi, Michael. *Beyond Nihilism.* London: Cambridge University Press, 1960.

——————. *Logic of Liberty.* London: Routledge and Kegan Paul, 1951.

——————. *Personal Knowledge.* New York: Harper Torchbooks, 1964.

——————. *Science, Faith, and Society.* Chicago: University of Chicago Press, 1946.

——————. *The Study of Man.* London: Routledge and Kegan Paul, 1959.

——————. *The Tacit Dimension.* London: Routledge and Kegan Paul, 1967.

Pool, Ithiel de Sola, ed. *Contemporary Political Science: Toward Empirical Theory.* New York: McGraw-Hill, 1967.

Popper, Karl. *Conjectures and Refutations.* New York: Basic Books, 1962.

——————. *The Logic of Scientific Discovery.* New York: Basic Books, 1959.

Pye, Lucian. *Aspects of Political Development.* Boston: Little, Brown, 1966.

——————. *Communications and Political Development.* Princeton, N.J.: Princeton University Press, 1963.

Ranney, Austin, ed. *Essays on the Behavioral Study of Politics.* Urbana: University of Illinois Press, 1962.

Russett, Cynthia. *The Concept of Equilibrium in American Social Thought.* New Haven, Conn.: Yale University Press, 1966.

Scheffler, Israel. *Science and Subjectivity.* Indianapolis, Ind.: Bobbs-Merrill, 1967.

Schütz, Alfred. *The Phenomenology of the Social World.* Translated by George Walsh and Frederick Lahnert. Evanston, Ill.: Northwestern University Press, 1967.

Skinner, B. F. *Science and Human Behavior*. New York: Mac-Millan, 1953.

——————. *Walden Two*. New York: MacMillan, 1948.

Somit, Alfred, and Joseph Tanenhaus. *The Development of American Political Science: From Burgess to Behavioralism*. Boston: Allyn and Bacon, 1967.

Stevenson, C. L. "Persuasive Definitions," *Mind,* 47 (1938).

Storing, Herbert J., ed. *Essays on the Scientific Study of Politics*. New York: Holt, Rinehart, and Winston, 1962.

Strauss, Leo. *Natural Right and History*. Chicago: Phoenix Books, 1965.

——————. *The Political Philosophy of Hobbes*. Chicago: Phoenix Books, 1963.

Taylor, Charles. "Neutrality in Political Science," in *Philosophy, Politics, and Society*. 3d series. Edited by Laslett and Runciman. New York: Barnes and Noble, 1967.

Toulmin, Stephen E., and June Goodfield. *The Architecture of Matter*. New York: Harper and Row, 1962.

——————. *The Discovery of Time*. New York: Harper and Row, 1965.

——————. *The Fabric of the Heavens*. London: Hutchinson, 1961.

Truman, David. "The Impact on Political Science of the Revolution in the Behavioral Sciences," *Research Frontiers in Politics and Government*. Washington, D.C.: Brookings Institution, 1955.

Urmson, J. O. *The Emotive Theory of Ethics*. New York: Oxford University Press, 1969.

Van Dyke, Vernon. *Political Science: A Philosophical Analysis*. Stanford, Cal.: Stanford University Press, 1960.

Voegelin, Eric. *The New Science of Politics*. Chicago: Phoenix Books, 1966.

Walker, Jack. "A Critique of the Elitist Theory of Democracy," *American Political Science Review,* 60 (1966).

Wartofsky, Marx W. *Conceptual Foundations of Scientific Thought*. New York: MacMillan, 1968.

Watson, John B. *The Ways of Behaviorism*. New York: Harper Brothers, 1928.

Weber, Max. "The Meaning of Ethical Neutrality in Sociology and Economics," *The Methodology of the Social Sciences*. Translated and edited by Edward Shils and Henry Finch. New York: Free Press, 1949.

—————. "Objectivity in Social Science and Social Policy," *The Methodology of the Social Sciences*. Translated and edited by Edward Shils and Henry Finch. New York: Free Press, 1949.

Whitehead, Alfred N. *Science and the Modern World*. New York: Mentor Books, 1948.

Willey, Basil. *The Seventeenth Century Background*. Garden City, N.Y.: Doubleday, 1953.

Winch, Peter. *The Idea of a Social Science*. London: Routledge and Kegan Paul, 1958.

Wisdom, John. "The Metamorphosis of Metaphysics," in his *Paradox and Discovery*. Oxford: Blackwell, 1965.

—————. "Metaphysics and Verification," *Mind*, 47 (1938).

Wittgenstein, Ludwig. *The Philosophical Investigations*. Translated by G. E. M. Anscombe. Oxford: Blackwell's, 1953.

Wolin, Sheldon. "Paradigms and Political Theories," in *Politics and Experience*. Edited by Preston King and B. C. Parekh. London: Cambridge University Press, 1968.

—————. "Political Theory as a Vocation," *American Political Science Review*, 63 (1969).

—————. *Politics and Vision*. Boston: Little, Brown, 1960.

Index

179

180